Dianna's Way

JOHN CATENACCI

Dianna's Way

JOHN CATENACCI

Life as a Spiritual Journey
Best done with Dogs & Dear Friends

Having Cancer is Optional

SPIRIT DOG TALKING PUBLICATIONS

Spirit Dog Talking Publications
7773 Wexford Court
Onsted, Michigan 49265
517-467-8152
www.spiritdogtalking.com

In collaboration with

Hillcrest Media Group
212 3rd Avenue North, Suite 290
Minneapolis, MN 55401
612.455.2294
www.hillcrestmedia.com

ISBN: 978-0-985247-90-4
LCCN: 2012948106

Portraits by Jon Catenacci
Photos courtesy of Giovanni Sanitate
www.diannasway.com

Book Design by Mary Nelson

Printed in the United States of America

For Marty

live long, live well

John Yi

and Dianna too

:)

Charcoal drawing of Dianna, by Jon Catenacci, 2011

For Dianna

I know these words are not enough, sweetheart,
but it is the best I know how to do.
Thank you for choosing me.

Contents

Part IV   Keep on Smiling

Prologue

"You shouldn't call wolf, honey. People won't believe you when you really mean it," she says, staring ahead at the traffic building in front of us on US-12, a trip we have made—and will make—too many times to count. I smile as I glance over at her. She is sitting up straight in her seat as she always does, as if she has to be ready for something. I like to lean way back, using the driver's seat like a La-Z-Boy.

"*Cry* wolf, honey," I say.

She turns her head toward me and looks me in the eye. One eyebrow goes up just a little. "Well, that's what I said."

She turns back to the road, always driving for me. I study her in profile. She looks to be completely at peace with the world.

"Not exactly," I say casually. "The saying is *cry* wolf, not *call* wolf. I look back to the road, gauging the traffic…and the weather…looks like rain. There are dark rolling clouds gathering ahead of us as we head east.

She is quiet for probably a minute, maybe even two minutes, still staring straight ahead—and enough time passes so I have already mentally moved on to other things.

"Well…whatever," she says lightly, picking at some lint on her sweater, then adjusting the seat belt across her still-tender, saline-filled breasts. "You know what I mean." Her words sail off into space like a dove letting go of a branch and lifting into flight.

"Yes, I do," I say, reaching over and taking her hand into mine. I squeeze, a little. She squeezes back, a little.

"I love you so much, sweetheart," I say with an overwhelming surge of feeling that almost brings tears to my eyes.

She stares at me intently for a long moment before turning back to the road again.

"I know you do," she says, staring straight ahead, a look of complete serenity on her face.

The traffic is coalescing into the weather in front of us. Neither of us could know what the road ahead would bring. Doesn't matter. It is the road we are on.

Part I
When the World Was New
1985-1990

1

Dianna at First Sight

Wet snow swirling. Clumps of translucent ice slide silently down the cold side of the windows in wide erratic furrows. In the warm, loud voices jumble together in a packed room, people talking all at once.

I first see her on the far side of the room surrounded by other people, talking and laughing. She is in Technicolor and everyone else is in black and white.

It will always be this way for me.

2

The Party

I am at a business-sponsored Christmas party in December 1985, hosted by a good friend, Janet Parkes, a talented designer who has done projects for me at the Dow Chemical Company in Midland, Michigan, where I work.

Wonder who she is? I'm thinking as I study a tall blonde, hair barely falling to her shoulders, framing her face just the way hair should. She works the crowd, laughing, chit-chatting, perfectly at ease with everyone, and seemingly gaining energy as the night wears on. Still, there's something faraway about her, too—a fashion runway model you can look at but cannot have kind of distance.

"Who is *that?*" I ask Janet as she hurries by.

"Oh, her name is Dianna Spence. She is a good friend," Janet replies as she rushes past me with someone else to handle some party detail.

I sit quietly, watching Dianna, while comfortably ensconced in a corner with several female friends, totally at ease with them and totally ill at ease with everyone else, none of whom I know. Large parties don't work for me. Just not adept at talking about nothing. Never learned how to do it—never *wanted* to learn how to do it.

Clearly, Dianna *loves* it.

All I know for sure is, the rest of the room is out of focus, and she fills it up.

Janet will later tell me she noticed Dianna was not at the party, called her, urging her to come. Dianna tried to beg off, tired after a long day at work. And looking at the prospect of getting dressed, doing makeup, and driving the twenty-five miles to Midland from Mount Pleasant seemed like just too much effort. Besides, it was cold out, and how about the roads? And she would probably have to get gas, and…

"Come on, Dianna, you might meet someone. There are lots of people here."

And so, however reluctantly, Dianna gave in to her friend's wishes and just…*showed up.*

She negotiates the room with a couple of guys circling around her like gnats. I can't take my eyes off her. She will challenge me on it later; but, no, it is not her breasts.

Many years later, I question one of my close friends, Marji, who was with me at the party, about what Dianna was wearing that night. She is able to report—easily, I might as well add—Dianna wore a heavy, gray wool sweater with a cream-colored (or *possibly* white, Marji muses pensively) elephant stitched into the front of it, and a gray wool skirt. I am stunned she remembers this.

As far as I'm concerned, Dianna is so deftly covered up with a heavy suit kind of outfit (so I was wrong about the suit part, and I don't even remember the elephant), I barely notice her anatomy. If you would have asked *me* later, I would have had nothing to say other than she is neither fat nor skinny; she is tall and blonde, …and alive and *present*.

Most of all, she feels like a mystery. Well, that, and, admittedly, she is definitely not hard to look at, either. She is, indeed, very attractive.

I don't even attempt to approach her that night. I know I can get her phone number from Janet and ask her to run a little interference for me. She knows I am not a convicted rapist.

3

Falling in Love with Spirit

I am blunt when she answers the phone.

"Look, you do not know me, but I saw you at Janet's party the other night and felt attracted to you. Would you be interested in getting together sometime for lunch or dinner, or whatever works for you? I will tell you up front, I'm divorced with three sons, and older than you are."

Boom. That was all of it.

"Divorced? Like, how old?" she asks, after a moment, sounding open and friendly.

"I'm forty-seven. My guess is you're about twenty?" I know she is not twenty.

She laughs. "Well, I was twenty once. I am twenty-eight, though."

"So, is that a stopper?"

"Well…, no. Not really. It's just, hmmm…dinner…well, you're paying, right?" She laughs again.

I love the changing lilt to her voice. Sometimes more earthy, sometimes like feathers floating in the air, not quite ready to land just yet.

"Only if I have to," I say, laughing with her. My heart leaps. She has a sense of humor. What a relief.

"You do have to," she says, still laughing.

She is quiet for a moment.

"What do you do…, I mean, what kind of work do you do?"

Her female mind moving into calculations and measurements mode, I'm thinking, but okay with me.

"I'm a chemical engineer by training…with Dow Chemical, here in town. These days, though, I'm doing less technical work and more team-building stuff, with operators and maintenance people, those guys. It's fun. In fact, I'm having more fun than I've ever had in my life. What about you?" I ask.

"I love what I do, too. I'm a cosmetologist, mostly hair, at a beauty salon on campus. Lots of my customers are young people, so I have to be up on the latest styles. It's so creative. I love that."

"On campus? Meaning Central Michigan University?"

"Yes. Our salon is right on campus. In fact, it's called the Campus Salon."

So, this explains why she looked like she just came out of a beauty salon. She *is* always just coming out of a beauty salon!

I, on the other hand, couldn't care less about fashion, as anyone who takes one look at me knows. If I had my way, I would happily rotate three T-shirts with some sweats, jeans, or shorts, depending on the season; and three-year-old tennis shoes—for work and everything else. Okay, I do shave once in awhile...though there have been periods in my life when I didn't do that, either.

She could be in for a shock, I'm thinking. I catch myself smiling. She's not even sure who I am or what I look like.

Does she know I have flirted with hippydom, and beatnikdom before that, stumbling along the edge, in one form or another, all my life? Do I know she is the straightest arrow in any quiver?

No and no.

Not one to let the fire go out, I suggest getting together Wednesday night, just a few days away.

"Well, would love to, but I can't. I'm busy that night."

"Oh. Have a date, if I am not being too nosy?"

"Well, sort of...I guess you could say that. Actually, I'm busy every Wednesday night. So, Wednesdays are definitely out."

"Hmmmm. Am I interfering with something you already have going on? I don't want to horn in."

She laughs. "No. Nothing like that."

There is a short silence at the other end of the phone.

"Every Wednesday night after work, I visit Ester. She is an older Russian lady who lives alone. I wash and do her hair and spend the evening talking with her. She's such an interesting person, with so many stories to tell. She likes to talk about her husband, who died not long ago, and about her adventures when she was younger, and..., lots of different things. She has no one now."

"How old is she?" I'm curious now.

"Well, I can't say exactly. Maybe in her eighties? She used to come to the salon, but is pretty much housebound these days, so I go to her."

"Extra money, then?"

"Oh, no. I would never accept money from her. She tries, but that's not why I go."

She is quiet for a moment.

"Once in awhile, she gives me little figurines or other things from her treasure chest. She gives these things from her heart, so I say yes, then."

The back of my neck tingles. My antennae are standing straight up on alert.

"So, why do you go, then?" I ask, but I have already taken in the answer somewhere.

"I go because I want to go. We give each other hugs. That's the main thing." She pauses, then adds, "She's a gift in my life."

I am quiet and my throat tightens. Finally, I recapture my voice. "And I'm sure you are in hers as well."

"Hmmmm, I'm sure that's true. I guess we're good for each other," she says. "Hope you're not upset, but I won't rearrange my schedule to see anyone else. She likes our routine; and I suppose she would be fine if I changed it, but she could be disappointed, too. So, I'm not going to change it."

"Perfectly fine with me, Dianna." And it is. "Actually, I completely agree with you. And, anyway, sometimes there are six other days in the week."

We both laugh.

After more dancing around, she agrees to dinner but, to my surprise, suggests meeting me at my house. We can have dinner in Midland, she says. "Why don't you pick the place."

I quickly calculate that doing it this way means I won't have a fix on where she lives, and she will get to see how and where I live. *Bold strategy,* I think to myself, but I like it.

4

Dianna Meets Breaker...and Me, Too

"Hi! I'm Dianna!" she explodes the instant I open the door, her brilliant smile matching her rising ebullient voice. "You're John?"

Still smiling, she stares straight into my eyes. I feel surrounded, like there is no one else in the world she would rather be with, in this exact moment. I am in the center of her universe.

I'm bent over, holding onto my golden retriever as he strains to push through the half-open storm door.

"Ooooh. What a pretty dog! Let me see her," she says.

"Him," I say, still hanging onto his collar.

It is a bitter cold winter day and, already, the metallic-gray January light is fading fast. I quickly open the door all the way while still holding the dog; and she slides through, her soft brown wrap catching momentarily on the door handle. I notice she is dressed more for late fall or early spring than the dead of winter. Women. Always too cold, and always wondering why.

"Oops," she says, laughing, as she unhooks it, then drops to her knees.

When she looks up at me, our eyes meet again. The back of my neck and shoulders are tingling. Something I can't quite get to...*what?*

She looks away, focused now on my dog who is feverishly vying for her attention.

...blinding white sheets flashing...waiting...her eyes closed, in another world. I take her hand, she squeezes...sun exploding, shadows sharp, intense....

"What's his name?" she asks.

I feel disoriented, then stumble back into the sense of her question.

"Breaker," I say finally, after a too-long pause. She doesn't seem to notice anything...different.

What was *that?*

I loosen up on Breaker's collar so he can meet her nose to nose. He slathers her hand with saliva and proceeds to sniff around her body

9

feverishly. She doesn't recoil at all, taking it all in. This is very, very, very good.

"Oh, my God, he's so soft and silky." She puts her hands on each side of his head and he nuzzles into her gentle touching. They both ignore me completely as I stand over them, reveling in this connection, the three of us.

"I absolutely love dogs."

"Me, too. This guy is two years old, and a lover. Can't hunt worth a damn, but what's to be done about it? He's my best friend anyway." So, we both love dogs. Huge plus. For too many reasons to count, and for reasons that cannot be counted.

"What an interesting name. How'd you think of that?"

"Well, as a matter of fact, I struggled with his name for a couple of months. Just kept calling him 'dog.' People were giving me 'Well, for God's sake, get on with it' kinds of looks."

She laughs.

"Then, his name came to me in a dream. I woke up knowing it was Daybreaker. So, that's his 'legal' name, but I'm not going to run down the street, yelling, 'Here, Daybreaker; here, boy,' so I shortened it for reasons having to do with maintaining my manhood, such as it is."

"It *is* a great name," she says while still on her knees, now scratching his neck.

"Well, *that's* the right thing to say."

She stands up finally, and I can see she is only a couple inches shorter than me, and a big-boned woman. She glances around the room, taking it all in without comment. After I suggest we head out to dinner, she suggests taking my car.

So, we hop into my 1981 Ford Escort, a real chick magnet, black and gray, and only four years old. Needless to say, we fill up the space. It's not a big car.

As we turn the corner onto M-20 and head east into Midland, she notices the huge gray tree lichen, probably eight inches across, perched on my dashboard.

"What *is* that?" she asks, pointing.

"A tree lichen, of course," I say, laughing. "Found it while grouse hunting last fall, and liked it too much not to turn it into a totem. Do you like it?" I'm teasing her now.

"Well, have never seen one before… interesting place to put it, though," she says without missing a beat.

I start laughing; and, then, she does, too.

We get to Captain Nemo's where, over steaks, rice, and a nice dry red wine, in a secluded booth, she in half light, half shadow, our conversation bathed in low lighting and the quiet murmuring of other patrons made even softer by the dark plush carpeting, she proceeds to give me a no-nonsense lecture—in a light and breezy way—about sex. She isn't handing out any. And if that's what I have in mind, she is not the girl for me. And I might as well know this about her straightaway, in which case we can just have a nice dinner together and be on our way—all this sprinkled in amongst many laughs and not too much wine.

She alludes to her long, dreary experience dating men interested in little more than sex with a young, attractive, buxom blonde with a good figure, as she describes herself without any self-consciousness whatsoever, as if she were talking about someone else wearing her particular body.

"You have to kiss a lot of frogs before you find your prince," she tosses my way, smiling.

By this time in my life, with three grown sons, and a divorce under my belt, I actually do not have sex front and center on my mind; so I enjoy her little lecture with a certain magnanimity and amusement. Doesn't hurt my opinion of her, either. I wait until she finishes her speech.

"Well, I don't remember suggesting anything about sex; and, anyway, I don't really believe in it."

She pauses for a moment, staring at me blankly, then laughs.

We don't have sex this day, or for a long time thereafter. At the end of the night, we give each other a perfunctory hug and agree to get together soon.

5

Dianna Goes Mining

"So, tell me about yourself," she says as we alternate taking sips of a decent Cabernet before dinner. We are in a local Mount Pleasant restaurant called The Embers. It's Thursday night with a few scattered patrons here and there. Pretty quiet.

"What would you like to know?"

"Everything." She smiles. I love the way she smiles. Her whole face, and especially her eyes, lights up. She leans back into her chair to listen.

I tell her about being born the oldest son in a traditional Italian family, as close to royalty as anyone can be without the title, along with a heavy obligation not to disappoint, but one I accepted unconsciously, without resentment. I always felt lucky to be in this family. I tell her how my dad immigrated from Italy via France when he was seventeen, married my mother when he was twenty-nine and she, only seventeen; that he owned a cement construction company so I had a built-in job from the time I was thirteen years old.

"He was the best possible father I could've asked for—kind, gentle, forgiving, and devoted."

"Sounds like a wonderful man, John."

"He was. I can't remember him ever saying, 'I love you.' And there was never a moment I didn't know it."

"Was?"

"He died on July 5, 1966, on a hot summer night. I was living in Midland by then, while my parents lived in East Detroit. I was visiting at the time. He had been ill and was sleeping. When I went into his room to check on him, he had just died."

"Oh, that must've been awful," she says, twisting in her chair, then leaning forward, reaching across the table and putting her hand over mine.

"You have no idea."

That night will always be etched in my memory, walking down the dark narrow hall to his bedroom, already *knowing*—his normally labored breathing replaced with a heartbreaking silence I will never forget. Later that night I had to tell my mother he was gone. She had begged me earlier in the evening to bring her home. *Now,* she said. *Now,* she demanded in a pleading voice through the phone. She had just talked with him, so she knew what I did not know. But she was in a hospital being treated for depression—how could I bring her home? I told her everything would be fine, not to worry. Just how wrong can a person be? Our footsteps echoed in the wide dimly lit hospital hallway as I approached her, my friend Steve Kridelbaugh at my side. I didn't have to say a word. I will never forget her crumpling face when she saw me, collapsing to the floor between two aides, her screams careening off the walls and knifing into my heart.

I decide not to go into all this with Dianna. Some other day.

"What was your mom like?" Dianna asks quietly, studying me. I take a long breath.

"My mom is an amazing woman. She lives for her kids. I guess she is a mixture of wannabe artist, fun-loving firecracker, and a fierce defender of all she loves. My friends used to love coming to our house—the child in her was alive and well in those days, and no one could cook Italian the way she did."

"You talk about your mom and dad with great respect."

"Well, that's true…, but I picked them, so I give myself full credit for that," I say, laughing.

"That's an odd way to look at it. What do you mean?"

"I believe that while still in spirit we make agreements about what we have come here to do and with whom. I also don't believe there are any accidents in life, not even the events we call accidents."

One of her eyebrows goes up as I say this. "So you believe everything is fated?"

"I don't think anything is fated. All along the way we are presented with choices, and each choice has consequences—we are creating our lives, choice by choice. So, we create, learn, and grow—or not—and, then, we get to do it again if we want."

"So, you believe in reincarnation, that we live many lives?"

"I do."

"Interesting." She seems to be thinking this over when the waiter appears for our order. We wave him off.

"What about the rest of your family?"

"I have a younger sister and brother—I picked them, too, so naturally they are the best."

She laughs but says nothing, still staring straight into my eyes.

I tell her a story about my sister Elena, about how I accidentally knocked her down the basement stairs when we were kids—how I can still see her tumbling head over heels down those wooden steps until she hit the bottom and, all in one motion, popped up screaming at me, furious, defiant.

"Over the years, she hasn't really changed all that much, either," I add, laughing. "But she has always been there for me when I needed her most."

"My family is like that, too. I can really count on them," Dianna says.

"We are both blessed then. And what made you pick them, Dianna?"

She looks at me, her eyes wide. She is wearing a soft, light-blue sweater that makes her blonde hair more blonde.

"I…I never thought of it like that. I don't know…, Actually, they sort of look at me as an outsider, I think. I feel a bit that way, anyway."

"You don't feel loved?" I ask.

"Oh no. Nothing like that. I feel completely loved. And I love them all dearly. I just feel…, I'm just…different, I guess."

"What about your brother?" Dianna asks, shifting the conversation back to me, while reaching into the bread basket on the table between us. I push the butter tray toward her. I have already figured out, she loves butter. About one stick of butter a year works for me.

"Hmmmm. The easiest way to summarize Ed—sometimes he likes to be called Onorio, his real name, our dad's name—would be to say he has incorporated all of our dad's best qualities in a way I never would be able to do if I lived another hundred years. He is kind, gentle, forgiving, and an amazing family man. I admire him in the same way I admire my father—for most of the same reasons, and some different ones, too."

"So, you've lived a charmed life," Dianna says, leaning back in her chair and munching on a heavily buttered slice of bread. It's white bread, too.

"I guess it would look that way from the outside. But like all snapshots, that's all they are," I say, thinking that one over. She remains quiet, listening.

"But I guess I do feel that way on the inside, too," I say, after thinking about how my life has gone.

Outside, the day is closing down and the light is yellower, making it feel darker inside, too. The place is beginning to slowly fill up and become slightly louder.

"How did you end up here, in Midland?"

I give her a short summary of my career. How I knew, in my eleventh grade chemistry class, what my career was going to be about, refined it to chemical engineering fifteen minutes into my first college math class, and never looked back. No career drama for me. How I managed to father my oldest son, Jon, with my high school sweetheart, Shirley (now Elizabeth, I tell Dianna), when I was seventeen—then our second son, Stephan, during my sophomore year in college. How hard Shirley and I worked during those years with my parents helping in any way they could—they were so honored to have their children graduate from college, for them, an unmitigated dream come true.

"You seem pretty sure about your life. Are you happy with it?" Dianna asks, shifting the conversation to another level.

"Happy? …I guess, mostly. But, ah, I'm a seeker. Do you know what I mean by that?"

"No. Not really."

"It means I'm never satisfied," I say, laughing.

"*Never?*"

"*Never.*"

"So, are you never happy then?"

"Not about being happy. I'm not focused on being happy. Ever notice sometimes we're happy and sometimes we're not? Happiness comes and goes, like the weather. No, I mean, I always want to know more, do more, and most of all, be more."

"More…what?"

"I guess more conscious about the spiritual aspects of life, who we are, why we are here, what happens when we die, how to relate to God, is there a personal God or just Energy…like that. What interests me most, I guess."

"My mom always claimed I was born old," I add, laughing.

"Hmmmm." She looks me in the eye, and in this light her eyes look darker—sometimes they go green, when the light is bright; but now, in this weak light, they look hazel, maybe.

I go on to tell her about being a fervent Catholic until I hit the University of Detroit, a Jesuit school where, thanks to all those philosophy and theology classes, my Catholic faith was eviscerated. The more I learned, the less sense it made to me. I didn't know what the truth was, but I knew *that* wasn't it. God was okay, but Catholicism was not going to be my pathway to God. So I set out on a path of my own, through Zen Buddhism—then into what is still unnamed—and I have loved wandering and wondering ever since. How I ran across the *est* Training, providing me with powerful tools to explore life and gain consciousness, helping me see what I had done to my family, and how to heal myself.

Dianna listens intently through all this, leaning forward over the table.

I know she's taking notes, and that's fine with me. I am who I am; take it or leave it.

The waiter comes, and we have to wave him off again. So, we start studying the menu.

"I know what I want," she says after a moment, laying down her menu and turning back to me. "So, did you start at Dow out of school?"

"Not quite."

I tell her how straight out of college, I went into the Air Force. My thinking was: if I was going to reserve the right to criticize my country, I should be willing to serve it. So, I showed up in my brand-new, heavyweight, blue wool uniform in August in the California Mojave Desert, sweating bullets. And how I loved doing engineering research at the Rocket Propulsion Laboratory there in the desert, working on the Apollo 11 Project. How I won awards, almost got court-martialed for insubordination, was offered the rank of captain to stay, then left when my three-year term was done. "Nobody ever leaves California once they come," everyone said. But I never doubted I would go home.

"California! That must have been exciting. I've only been there once, but I loved it," she says, lighting up.

"I did like it there for many reasons. But there is more than one California, you know. The Mojave Desert is not San Francisco or LA. Actually, when I think about it, it's infinitely better."

I tell her my youngest son, Eric, was born there in the desert. Not long after, we came home to Michigan. "I accepted a job with Dow in Midland partly so our children would be near our families."

Dianna shifts in her chair and leans back again. It's dark outside now and the ceiling lights are bathing her in a soft yellow glow. She's looking better and better to me—in every light.

"Well, must've been a nice adventure, anyway," she says.

"It was that. No regrets."

"What about your marriage? Do you want to talk about that?" she asks.

"Sure. But that's a long story. Let me just say, the marriage ended because our work together was done. We had raised our sons and that was our job, and we did it—me, not as well as I could have."

"What do you mean?"

"I was just a kid myself when we married, not ready for the responsibilities of it all—and I was completely focused on college. I told Shirley when we married, my first priority was school; everything else was secondary. A chemical engineering curriculum entails endless homework—it consumes your life. It consumed mine. So, my sons and wife got very little of my time, attention, or energy."

"That must've been tough on everybody."

"Well, even that might have been semi-okay, but I was also a dictatorial, controlling father—and husband. So, I did a lot of damage." I look off toward the windows, but there is nothing to see in their shiny blackness other than a reflection of myself. "Maybe, it would have been better if I had been around even less," I say, running my hand through my hair. This is a new thought for me.

"You're pretty hard on yourself," she says, leaning toward me.

"No. I was pretty hard on *them*."

"Look, I have forgiven myself, so I'm not wallowing in guilt. No regrets either…finally. I realize I did the best I could, given who I was. But this doesn't undo what's been done, either."

"Well, I don't think you…," she says, but I cut in before she can toss me any sympathy.

"You know, there are certain unavoidable facts of life. Kids don't care how busy you are, what your priorities are, what your weaknesses are. And they need to know you love them. Simple fact is, I did not give them the same certainty my parents gave me. They need you when *they* need you, not when you get around to growing up—or showing up. Their needs can't be scheduled. And, they model what they experience. So, I did not fully meet my parental—or partner, for that matter—responsibilities."

She is quiet, taking it all in.

"Simple as that," I add.

The waiter shows up and takes our order.

"Would you do it any differently if you could do it over again?"

I start laughing.

"Are all women alike? Shirley asked me that exact question once. I'll tell you what I told her. The answer is no. She got really angry when I said that."

"Well, what *do* you mean by that?" Her brow furrows a bit.

"Look, simple logic tells you if I had a 'do over,' given who I am *now*, of course I would do it better. If I had a 'do over,' given who I was at the time, of course, I wouldn't do it better—I would've have made the exact same choices. It's just a pointless question."

Dianna looks at me, expressionless.

"I think she was asking you if you were sorry. You did not sound sorry, so she got upset. Like, you hadn't learned anything," she says, her voice as soft as a summer rain.

"Well, I don't get *that* at all."

I squirm in my chair. Wish I could just stand up and walk around. And we haven't even had dinner yet.

Dianna smiles and changes the subject. "Are you a controlling person now?"

"I don't know. I live alone, so I don't have anyone to control," I say, laughing.

She lifts one eyebrow a little and is about to say something when our waiter arrives with our meals. We both suddenly realize we are past hungry.

While we are eating, she starts quizzing me again. "So, what else do I need to know about you?"

I laugh. She starts laughing, too. It's so easy to be with her. I feel comfortable, relaxed, even while I know I'm being grilled.

"Well, you might as well know I'm a bit of a rebel in some ways, maybe bent in some ways most people aren't."

"Really? Like the tree lichen in your car..., and rolling your own cigarettes...*in public no less...,* and which, by the way, are not good for you, you know."

"Yep. Like that," I say, ignoring her comment about smoking.

"What else do I have to watch out for with you?"

"Let's see. I meditate twice a day, do astrology, believe in reincarnation, walk or ride a bicycle to work most days, write controversial letters to the editor—some people in town know me only by my letters—I don't walk my dog on a leash—I drive too fast—I...."

"I noticed *that,*" she says, interrupting. "That can be very dangerous, you know."

"True."

I start eating again and stop talking.

"How far is it to work?" she asks.

"Oh, maybe five miles, depending on which route I take and where I have to go once I'm in the plant. It's a huge facility, you know—probably three miles across and two miles wide—there are probably eighty separate chemical plants in there."

"Wow. I didn't know that."

"So, what's it like to work for Dow?"

I think that one over, wondering how to summarize another long story.

"Well, after twenty years of technical problem solving, it all started looking too familiar. Challenge was gone...for me, anyway...and I began to get interested in the 'we–them' problem I see all around me."

"The 'we–them' problem? What's that?"

"The divide between managers in their offices and workers on the floor. So, this got me interested in team building, in breaking down the walls. One thing just led to another. That's what I'm really doing now."

"That sounds fun."

"It is."

We finish dinner and have coffee. The waiter brings the check and I pay him.

"So, is the inquisition over? And, I have to pay to be interrogated, too. Something is definitely wrong with this picture," I say, laughing, and she starts laughing with me as we get up to leave.

"A girl needs to know what she is getting herself into. Anyway, I just wanted to know more about you. All kidding aside, is it okay with you?"

"It's absolutely okay," I say.

We head out into the cold, dark February night. Dianna shivers, complaining, but the air feels great to me. I'm dressed for it.

Good to be outside.

6

The Campus Salon

We are on our third date and Dianna begins telling me about her life. We are at the Tease, another section of The Embers we were in the week before. It is cold and dark outside, but too warm in here.

"I would have loved to go into medicine. I've always been interested in it. Just didn't think I could stand the blood-and-guts part."

"So, you wouldn't care much for gutting a deer, then?"

She makes a face. "When hell freezes over."

I laugh while she goes on.

"I would love to see the world—Mount Pleasant *is* a pretty small place, you know. Went back and forth about becoming a stewardess or satisfying my artistic side with cosmetology." She pauses. "Had to think hard about which would be best for me."

"Well, I'm glad you picked cosmetology, or you wouldn't be here," I say gallantly. "What made you choose?"

She ignores the first part, focused on her story now.

"Flying would be exciting, but it would also take me away from my family. They mean a lot to me." She shifts in her chair as she picks at her salad, thinking. I notice she seems to move her body, even her hands, with a natural grace, a lightness to every motion.

She looks up at me and continues, "So in high school, I started my training; and as soon as I graduated—I was only seventeen—I was hired by Mary Lou, who owns the Campus Salon. Been there ever since. We're good friends and I love the clientele. Mostly I do young people who want the latest fashions, so I go to conferences and trainings. I want to be up on the latest—doing it well is an art…but, John, I just love the older ladies, too. I usually don't get them in my chair—Bonnie takes most of them—but we all talk in the salon. I love listening to their stories."

Maybe that's what she likes about me. I am nineteen years older than she is, after all. Do I tell good stories, I wonder? I smile inwardly. Probably not.

"The other thing I like about this career is I can go to women's shelters and show them how to do makeup, hair, even help choose clothes flattering to them."

"That's a really nice thing to do, Dianna."

"It is," She says without a hint of arrogance. Just a simple acknowledgment of what's so. I love this about her.

"For women, especially, how we look on the outside affects how we feel on the inside. If we look good, we feel better about ourselves. Pumps us up a bit, you know. This is something abused women really, really need."

I have my own inner commentary going on. I feel best when I'm comfortable, and that means being unshaven, wearing old sweats and a familiar T-shirt...and, on the second and third day, they become really comfortable. I know. Pathetic.

"My work has opened so many doors for me, John. My dear friend, Kathy, is a special ed teacher in a poor rural area. Some of her kids have one pair of shoes, no boots for winter. So occasionally she invites me over to her school. I bring scissors, cape, curling iron, dryer, hair spray, all that stuff—and I cut their hair. They love the attention, and I love doing it."

I sit there, letting it all in.

Suddenly, Dianna leans over the table toward me, excited. I love the way the light is hitting only one side of her face, looking like an abstract painting.

"But, John, what I *didn't* expect is for the whole world to be sitting down in my chair *every day*!"

"What do you mean?"

"Well, professors and students come from all over the world to CMU, and they come to our salon. So, while I do their hair, they tell me about faraway places, how they live. I learn a lot about different cultures!"

"I didn't think of that. That *is* amazing. So, you didn't have to become a stewardess to see the world, after all...the world came to you."

We both laugh.

"Not only that." She drops her eyes a little. "The only two serious boyfriends I've had in my life, I met in the salon—one from Iran and, later, the other from Saudi Arabia."

Dinner comes and we begin eating.

"Tell me more about them, Dianna, if you don't mind."

"Not at all."

I can see she really doesn't mind.

"I met the young man from Iran, and we became close. It was all such an adventure, being with all his friends, male and female, learning to speak a bit of Farsi, learning their way of cooking—I love to cook, by the way, and I'm good at it—and such fun getting together at their parties. They're such wonderful people."

"So, what happened?"

"Well, we were considering getting married when he decided to return to Iran for a visit in 1979. While he was there, the Iranian revolution happened. He couldn't get back out again. I waited a long time, but eventually I could see it was never going to work out."

"So, what happened to him?"

"I wish I knew. After awhile, we began arguing during our phone calls… the calls dwindled, and then the war with Iraq began in 1980. I honestly don't even know if he's still alive."

"That's sad."

"It is sad."

We both fall silent while eating our food.

"And what about the guy from Saudi Arabia?" I ask finally.

"Oh, he was very sweet, and I loved him very much; but we knew from the beginning our relationship couldn't go anywhere."

"Why?"

"His culture, his life, his family. There was no room in any of that for me. He was honest about it from the beginning though, and I never felt mistreated or used. We had great times together; and then…eventually, he went home and that was that."

"So, no regrets?"

She is quiet for a moment. Then, she says, speaking very deliberately and slowly, "No, no regrets."

"Actually, a lot of good came out of it all. I have some very wonderful friends because of him. So, no, I'm glad I had that experience."

"But it hurt when he left," I say.

"Oh, sure. No denying that. But, John, life is what it is. I take it as it comes, and make the best of it. I'll always respect the person he is, and I am happy for him in his new life. And I'm moving on. I look forward to everything life has to offer."

"So, you are a free woman?"

"Absolutely."

"So, really, you went to school on people, while doing hair at the salon."

"I guess that's true. You learn a lot about women, especially—and men, too—doing hair. Women come in to get their hair done, but they also come in to share their stories, their latest dramas, especially if someone listens without judgment...and with compassion. They come in to 'let their hair down,' as they say."

She laughs, then abruptly excuses herself to go to the restroom. I am left there, sipping my wine, which is a quite dry Valpolicella, one of my favorites. She likes it, too, which surprises me.

I feel completely at ease with her. I'm guessing she makes other people feel this way, too, that her customers feel safe to be themselves with her. Having a vibrant, but kind, edgeless sense of humor couldn't hurt, either.

It is fun being with this chatty, sunny, optimistic, eager person.

Nice.

Is this enough?

7

Confusion

"Marji, I'm just not sure I'm going to continue seeing this woman."

We are sitting in my dark living room with dark paneling on the walls, dark, even though it is midday. Since my divorce, the entire 1,400-square-foot modest ranch nestled into a modest middle-class neighborhood at the western edge of Midland has been turned into "my space"—a cave complete with meditation room, guest room, and—since I'm living alone—who needs a living room? So I proclaimed it my office, and put a desk in there—mainly because it has a nice picture window with a view down a long street, and why not?

Marji, a longtime friend and confidant, is perched on a couch across the room, drinking coffee, her legs tucked underneath her. "I'm surprised. I thought you liked her."

She looks around the room. "I wish you would do something about *this*." She is an interior designer and decorator with exquisite taste. I know all this, but I don't share her vision or her priorities right now. So, I ignore her comment, which I have heard many times before anyway.

"I do like her. Really like her. She is such a good person, and we get along so well, too. But we have been out half a dozen times now, and all I get is a kind of surface talk. Very cheery, bright—she is certainly quite intelligent. But can't seem to get in *there*, you know what I mean?"

"You're saying she's not very open?"

"Well, maybe. She's not willing to share her feelings underneath all that shining light, I guess. She has told me about a couple of previous boyfriends; but, somehow, it feels to me like all along the surface. Interesting though—one boyfriend from Iran, one from Saudi Arabia, and I have the impression she loved each one a lot."

"Well, John, then she is just being cautious. She has been hurt before and not anxious to be hurt again. Give her time."

"I'll give her one more date. After that, if things stay the same, I'm done."

"Sometimes, you can be way too intense." She smiles, sipping her coffee. "Life does not *always* have to be serious and *meaningful*." She puts a big stress on "always" and an even bigger one on "meaningful."

"Well, life *is* too short to make it anything else…for me anyway."

"So, could this be about sex?"

"Marji, sex happens or it doesn't. I'm not worried about that. I do feel there is chemistry there, and that's enough for me right now. My last marriage taught me that sex can be very expensive in a million ways. No need to hurry."

Marji laughs.

"Sure, go ahead and laugh. But I'm just saying I'm not anxious to engage in it at this particular moment in time with all the entanglements, expectations, and brooding implications that come along with it."

"Then, what are you stressing about?"

I lean back in my office chair and put my feet up on the desk. "Fair question."

I take a swig of coffee and sigh out loud. "I don't know. Intimacy, I guess. Which is about trust, isn't it? Hard to love someone who is not open with me, doesn't trust me."

"Well, have you been open with her?"

I feel like Marji is boring a hole through me now. Suddenly I'm feeling less certain. I put my feet back down on the floor and sit up straight.

"I don't know. I guess. I think so."

We become silent. A car zips by outside, and Marji gets up to leave.

"One way or another, I'm going to give it one more date. Something's gotta change."

Marji smiles. We give each other a hug, then she's out the door and gone.

Now, I'm confused.

8

Kara's Gift

We're sitting in the Brass Saloon, a gathering place for professionals, mostly lawyers, in Mount Pleasant, and where she hangs out with her friends some Friday nights.

"I pop in here occasionally with Kathy, my very dear friend," Dianna almost yells over the din of other people talking and laughing. "Do you like this place?"

Not really, I think to myself. Noisy, smells like beer, and maybe I see it as more her world than mine.

"Okay," I say. "How do you know Kathy?"

"I met her at the salon…around 1976, I think. She came in with her daughter, Alissa. Kathy told me she had seen a little girl in a grocery line who had a winsome Dorothy Hamill haircut, as she called it. She just loved it. So Kathy asked the mother who had done the little girl's hair. Well, that was *me!*"

Dianna smiles, sitting up a bit straighter.

"The rest is history. I gave all of her three children, Alissa, Jason, and Kara, their very first haircuts. We became close friends along the way. I just love those kids."

As Dianna says this in her usual airy way, without warning her bright shiny mood falls off a cliff, and she bursts into tears. "Kara was *only four years old* and, John, she was the most beautiful little girl," she blurts out. "And…she had a terrible, terrible accident. Just last May…May 1…, and… John, she *died.* I still…I just can't believe it." Dianna crumples up small into her chair and covers her face with her hands.

I'm stunned.

I lean across the table, pushing a napkin at her, saying nothing. I don't *know* what to say. The music is too loud; people are talking too loud, laughing too much. Leaning forward, I mutter something. I might as well be pissing in the wind. Nothing's going to fix this.

I learn Kara had been trapped by a faulty garage door coming down on

26

her, lost oxygen to her brain for too long, and was brain-dead by the time the ambulance arrived.

"Oh, John, when they finally decided to unplug her from life support, my heart was just breaking…." She squeezes my hand in her hands, staring straight into my eyes, her mascara running, which is fine with me.

She is quiet for a long moment, gathering herself, then takes a deep breath. "Kathy gave me the *honor* of dressing Kara and doing her hair for the funeral." Dianna pauses, then says oh so quietly, but so clearly, "I did her hair for the first time and I did her hair for the last time."

Tears are streaming down her cheeks.

"Meant so much to me," she says, her voice soft as wind through tall summer grass. She slumps back into her chair and falls into a deep silence.

I feel tears sliding down my own cheeks. Just like that, I know my life will never be the same. We have crossed our own Rubicon.

9

The Big Shift

Relationships either progress or they die. When ours becomes sexual, Dianna begins staying at my house in Midland and commuting to the salon. Some of her clothes are at my house and some in Mount Pleasant.

"I could have sex every day. I love having sex with the one I love," she tells me one day. She is bright and perky when she says this, like she's talking about a new aerobics class. Maybe sex is like exercise for her. When I tell her this, she laughs.

"Well, I could have sex every day, too, if I didn't have anything else to do," I say, laughing with her.

She leans over and smacks me with a kiss.

So it all works out.

We do not have sex every day.

10

Watermelons and Seagulls

During the summer of 1986 we are visiting my aunt and uncle, Rosemary and Ed Corradi, in Charlevoix, Michigan, an upscale town on the western shore of Lake Michigan, one bead in a necklace of communities that starts in the south around Frankfort and runs up the Lake Michigan coast through Traverse City, Petoskey, Harbor Springs, and to the Straits of Mackinaw at Mackinaw City. This whole necklace is locally referred to as the Gold Coast.

I know of a secluded beach where dogs are supposed to be leashed, but no one cares—I can run Breaker into the breakers washing up against the mixed sandy, rocky shore without being hassled.

"Get dressed, honey, and let's go," I say.

She comes out of the bedroom with an outfit that stops me in my tracks.

She is wearing quintessential Dianna, a loose-fitting top with shorts almost reaching her knees. The top consists of wide horizontal bands of bright yellow, blue, and green sprinkled with a variety of simple childlike drawings of kiwi, cherries, grapes, and tomatoes, centered by a chest-high slice of watermelon. "SUMMER" is splashed across the bottom hem in huge white block letters.

"Wow, I really like that. Turn around," I say, laughing, as she spins around, throwing her arms out in a la-de-dah.

The back is used up by an enormous bright-red strawberry against a blue background and an equally large "=FRUIT" is printed along the bottom hem. Every fruit is labeled in script, of course, just in case. The short sleeves are made up of alternating bands of bright red-and-white stripes, which somehow looks right, playing off the reds in the various fruits maybe.

The shorts are matching and almost equally startling. From the front, one leg is red, the other green; and from the back, one leg is yellow, the other blue. Why not?

"I really like it, Dianna. No one is going to miss you in that one," I say, smiling.

"Well, it says summer, doesn't it?" she says, slipping on her sandals.

"In just about a million ways…and it says, Dianna, too."

"I know. It does, doesn't it?" she says without a trace of self-aggrandizement.

This explosion of color will come to be known as "the watermelon outfit" amongst insiders.

We jump into the car, get Breaker settled into his rear seat, and head out on a perfect Michigan summer day. It is a short drive to Lake Michigan and, within minutes, we are walking along the beach, Dianna looking for Petoskey stones while I toss sticks out past the surf to give Breaker exercise.

As the sun drops down toward the western horizon, Dianna spies some white dots circling up high in the distance. "Oh, honey! Seagulls! I'm going back to the car—we have a loaf of bread there, I think."

"So?" I yell over the roar of the waves piling into the rocks in front of us.

She is already disappearing behind a row of cedars while I wonder what she could be thinking. I walk down the beach, shooing Breaker away from a few rotting fish, then eventually circle back to see how she is doing.

Dianna is standing with her feet close together, her sandals half buried in sand, legs connected to the beach like two straight sticks. Her top and shorts are fluttering as a steady on-shore breeze lifts her hair off her shoulders, glints of silky yellow dancing in the sunlight.

She is holding a slice of bread high over her head, waving it back and forth slowly, trying to attract the attention of these nearly unidentifiable specks in a clear blue sky.

I just shake my head and go back down to the water's edge to enjoy the wind and water and light. But I can't help it. I finally start laughing so hard I can hardly breathe.

She is standing, on her tiptoes now, and calling, "Here, seagulls! Come here! I'm over here."

The seagulls must be a quarter-mile away and lazily riding currents of air we cannot see. They might as well be on Mars.

"Honey, even if they see you, they are *never, ever* going to come here and pick a slice of bread out of your hand."

She glances over at me, makes a face, but does not miss a beat as she slowly waves her arm back and forth above her head, switching hands now.

I go on down the beach with Breaker who is completely drenched, completely happy, and completely absorbed in sniffing dead fish, and finally cannot resist rolling on one, twisting back and forth on his side, then over on his back. Nothing to be done about it now. I toss more sticks into the surf for him to chase, hoping he will wash off the scent, knowing this is not going to happen. When I return twenty minutes later, her routine is unchanged.

"Honey, give it up. They aren't coming. Not in your lifetime," I yell over to her.

"Why not? They've come to me before," she yells back.

"Really. When? Where?" I ask, as I get closer to her.

"I was in Florida once, and we sat at an outdoor table at a restaurant, and those seagulls would not leave us alone. We fed them all through dinner."

"Dianna, do you see any restaurants around here?"

She ignores my question.

"They will come. You'll see," she says, looking at me triumphantly, a smirk on her face. She changes hands again and keeps on waving.

"Here I am! Come over here!" she yells, but not nearly loud enough, her voice merging with the waves and the wind.

I stretch out on the warm sand with my hands behind my head. Feels like a pre-warmed futon. The sun slowly drops into the west while the sky is coloring up into a million shades of pastel yellows, oranges, and tinges of red. Breaker comes over to me, flops down, pushing up tight up against me, then quickly sinks into a dog kind of stupor, eyes half-closed, completely spent now, but ears and nose still twitching, not missing anything. He smells exactly like dead fish.

All is right with the world as the light turns gold against the poplars and cedars backing up the beach. The air is cooler now and cooling fast. The colors on the horizon are deepening by the minute.

"Honey, *these* guys don't know *those* guys," I yell over to her a few minutes later without looking her way. "Those birds were trained by lots of humans. These birds are wild. They avoid humans. They don't go to the same conferences. I'm telling ya, it ain't happening."

I roll over on my side so I can watch her. I don't know if she hears me or not. She doesn't act like it.

She continues on for another ten minutes, the same slice of bread still high over her head, waving slowly back and forth, first in one hand, then the other.

I can tell she is not angry, not frustrated, not even discouraged. Still optimistic about her chances—and completely unwilling to give up.

The cedars, and the deep fir forest behind them, begin losing their green, deepening before my eyes. I just watch her, smiling, silent now. Yeah, it's dumb, but for some reason, I admire her for it anyway. This is the Dianna I know and have grown to love. I feel proud of her for absolutely no logical reason.

"Let's go, honey. We're going to be late for dinner," I say finally. I know she is probably starting to get chilly and she gets cranky when she suddenly discovers she's hungry. It seems to come over her all at once. Now she isn't, now she is—sort of like a digital switch.

Another couple of minutes go by, and I say nothing more.

Finally, she turns to me and says, without ceremony, "Okay, let's go. I'm getting cold…, and I'm hungry."

She flips the bread off into the grass without even looking at it. I walk up to her and she smacks me with a spontaneous kiss.

"You smell kind of funny."

"So does Breaker," I say without explaining it.

I put my arm around her waist as we trudge through the loose sand. We pass through a mixture of junipers and hemlocks, nearly silhouettes now. And when I glance back, I see the color is nearly drained from the sky, leaving nothing behind but a faint purple glow over the lake.

"Don't you think we need to wash him?" she asks.

"What do you mean 'we'? Anyway, dogs love being like this. Let him be happy for a while."

"I don't see how he could be happy," she says.

"If you were a dog, you would. They're predators. Whatever disguises their own scent makes 'em happy."

She is quiet as we walk the beach toward the car. I take a last look at the lake. The waves have almost collapsed now as the lake stills down. Peace has descended upon the land, water, and sky.

"So, you'll wash him?" she asks.

"I'll wash him."

We walk in silence for a few more minutes and are almost back to the road. The wind has completely died now. All we can hear is the quiet.

"You could take a shower yourself, honey." She doesn't look at me when she says this, and her voice is light, like the air around us.

"Could," I say. I don't look at her, either.

We finally reach the car, and I'm fishing for the keys.

"Maybe they just couldn't see me."

"Maybe," I say, but she can't see me smiling in this light.

The Famous Head Tilt

It takes me awhile to recognize it as a form of communication, and even longer to bring it to a level of consciousness where I do not require even more communication—like, actual words—to "get it."

When she tilts her head to one side, she is saying a lot. Something like, "Oh, honey, enough of this now; I've got things to do, places to go, a life to live; and I don't have time for any more of this…, so we need to get on with it. Life is short."

I would learn eventually that there is even a deeper, underlying communication happening. Something like, "Let it go, honey. Once we have learned what we can learn from the past, let it go emotionally, mentally, and move on. Don't drag around the past and let it shape your future."

But this entire communication is almost always done with a radiant smile. This is what throws me off for so long. The smile is there because she is, with a whole heart, going along with it (whatever *it* is at the moment), out of a sort of kindness. But nevertheless, "it" has run its course as far as she is concerned.

There is also the rare head tilt with *no* smile. Then, it is *definitely* time to move things along, and figure out where and when I went off the tracks.

It takes me even longer to understand that Dianna communicates an immense amount of information by not saying anything at all.

Seems like an anomaly—so supremely talented at small talk, yet so comfortable with silent spaces in conversation, and often content with *choosing* not to have the last word. Letting *that* be her final communication on the matter.

I come to experience her silences as little kindnesses, like scattered flower pedals floating on the still surface of a forest pond.

In late June of 1988 we are standing in front of our house in Midland, and she is already out the door, on her way to meet some friends. She looks so beautiful, the day, so perfect; and the climbing red roses hugging the wrought iron ladders holding up our porch are exploding into full bloom.

I stop her. "Honey, wait up a minute. Let me grab my camera. I want to take a couple of pictures."

She pauses. She's in a hurry, but she also loves the idea. She knows when she looks good.

I have her stand in front of the roses and snap shot after shot.

Finally, she does her now famous (to me) head tilt.

"Just one more, sweetheart," I say, pleading.

She stands there, head still tilted, her smile more radiant than the sun in the sky that day. I snap the shutter. Neither she nor I could know it then, but she has given me the image for the back cover of this book.

11

Being Both a Man and a Fool is Easy

We have some sort of disagreement, whatever it is, and I decide my feelings are hurt and decide to pout about it. So I take off in my little Escort with Breaker for some alone time. I drive a couple of miles down Pomranky, a gravel road near home, then turn off onto a barely visible two-track that cuts into a huge field of tall grass along the Tittabawassee River. After about a quarter mile, I park and take Breaker for a walk through scattered aspen and maple saplings. He noses around while I stay busy feeling sorry for myself. After about an hour, we return to the car and I am standing there, watching the sun sink over the river, smoking a cigarette.

Pouting is one of my most highly developed skills.

I hear a car behind me out on the main road and, suddenly, I see this little white car bobbing up and down, sometimes visible above the tall grass, slowly making its way toward me. It's Dianna.

She parks a few feet away and slowly opens the door and steps out, a huge smile on her face. "Honey, I was getting worried about you."

Like nothing happened.

"How did you know where I was?" I'm sure my voice is incredulous. I *am* incredulous. I know she has never been here before.

"Magic," she says, walking up to me. She puts her arms around me and gives me a solid hug. I reluctantly give her a tepid hug back.

"I can't believe you found me here."

"Well, I do have my ways," she says pertly, stepping back and looking at me, her hands on her hips. "Can we go home now?" She is still smiling, her head tilted to one side now. I suppose she ought to be, but I don't think she's gloating.

"Okay," I say, finally, after a long pause and a shrug.

I drop my cigarette and step on it, then throw in a weak half-smile at the end. What else can I do? What any idiot has to do. Follow instructions. I feel really foolish.

So we get in our cars.

All the way home, I'm wondering how she could possibly find me. I never do figure it out.

But then, she invariably manages to find her way to places she has not been for years—*or has never been before*—without knowing street names or, often, even without having directions—"turn here, I think"—and, anyway, she might as well look at maps upside down for all the good they do her.

"I can read a map, dammit. It's just with *you*, I get flustered."

I doubt this.

Anyway, what difference does it make? I'm the one who needs them.

12

More Surprises

The summer of 1986 slips away and, as usual, fall is here and gone in a flash. Tonight, snow is coming down so hard, we can hardly see past the sidewalk in front of our Midland home. It is shooting almost sideways through the light from the lamp across the street. Intoxicating.

"Dianna, let's take Breaker for a walk in this—will be fun."

We dress up for it and head out. I'm a little in front with Breaker as we walk around the block. He noses into the snow, then rolls over on his back, making a snow angel, doggy version. Dianna pitches a snowball at me when I'm not looking—missing, of course, and so it starts.

It ends when I attack her, pushing her into a snow bank, then giving her a light face-wash. While she clambers out of the snow, I dash back into the house, laughing. I peel off my coat, done for the night, and settle down to watch TV. That was fun.

A few quiet minutes later, without warning, Dianna suddenly appears in the doorway of the TV room with her arms cradling a ton of snowballs and starts pitching them at me, one after another, in rapid succession, me ducking, sometimes successfully, but not always.

We are both laughing with each throw, and I do notice there may be just a hint of retribution smeared across her face mixed in there. She doesn't like losing.

Didn't know she had it in her.

Good for her.

13

Well?

"So, honey, I love being with you, but my clock is ticking. I would like to know what your intentions are with me, with us."

This feels like a bullet aimed straight between my eyes.

It is toward evening in January of 1987, and we are sitting in the living room. Dianna is walking around the room, flipping on several of her accent lights, the ones serving no useful purpose whatsoever—can't see much with 'em and can't read by 'em, either. But it makes the room look the way she wants it to look.

Right now, she's not paying any attention to the lights. "Well?" she asks, bringing me out of my thoughts.

"I *do* want to marry you. I have no doubt about that. But I'd like to wait another year."

She is quiet for a few moments, studying me from across the room. I can't really tell what's going on in there. Those damned lights. Useless.

"Wait for what? To see if you've changed your mind? What does waiting do for us? For you?" she asks, her voice completely calm and even.

We are both quiet for a while. It's now completely dark outside. I'm not sure what I want to say, so I say nothing.

Finally, she stands up.

"I think I should move back to Mount Pleasant and give you some time to think it through for yourself. If you don't want to marry me, I'll be disappointed, but I'll be okay. I'll just get on with my life. I'm going to be thirty soon. I want a child before I'm too old to have one."

"I understand that."

She goes off into the kitchen, leaving me with the accent lights. It doesn't take me long to see she is right about all of it. I have known I want to marry her for a long time. It's not about her. It's about the promise I made to her about having one child—our compromise between zero and who knows how many.

I am fifty years old. Do I really want to start that all over again? The honest answer is no. But I do not want to lose her, either.

I ask her to stay awhile longer while I think things through.

The next day, my mind drifts back to a summer evening two years ago, not long after my divorce. Sitting alone in my living room/office, I come to a surprising realization: I *love* living alone. I love the texture of the quiet, the peace of it, a feeling of knowing how to do this, that maybe I've lived other lives just this way. Being alone, yet *never* feeling lonely, was, in every sense, incredibly, satisfyingly, familiar for me.

At that same time, this seductive ease also felt vaguely frightening, like I was on the verge of making a huge blunder. I did not come here to live like this again. I came here to experience something…, something I can only experience in marriage…, something missed in my last marriage. The street light blinks on, instantly piercing the accumulating darkness outside my window. Staring out into this new arrangement of light and shadow, I see it all so clearly. I must and I will marry again.

Six months later, Dianna showed up.

So why am I hesitating now, with opportunity staring me in the face?

I have no doubt she will leave. I can either choose to experience Dianna's request as pressure, or as the simple request that it is—to choose what I want in my own life. She has a right—even an obligation to herself, if she loves and honors herself—to ask. She deserves an answer.

This is not any different than the choice I faced with my first wife—only that was a choice I made without owning it, a huge distinction I eventually came to understand way too late to make a difference.

Not going to make that mistake again.

As to the timing of her request, well, she is right about that, too. Nothing will be gained by waiting.

A few days later, we go out to dinner at Binz's Apple Mountain not far from Midland.

I propose. She accepts.

Well, she accepts, but not before spending a round of appetizers, all of dinner, dessert, then finishing off our bottle of wine, grilling me in different ways about whether I'm really sure this is what I want.

It is what I want.

So the train is still on the tracks.

14

Blue Skies...and Rain...and Blue Skies

I choose our wedding date. I know it has to be June 21, in this year of 1987, the Summer Solstice, the longest day of the year. I want the most Light.

I write our invitation salutation for us, "On this day, I married my best friend, the one I laugh with, dream with, love."

I am, of course, excluding Breaker, concerning the best friend part; but, hey, we are all allowed some poetic license. Dianna laughs when I tell her this. She thinks I'm kidding.

Not entirely, but mostly.

We are completely on the same page and happy. There are no clouds in the unbroken blue skies of our relationship...or in the actual skies overhead, either. And in Michigan, this is always an experience worth savoring.

As the weeks hurry by toward our wedding, we get nothing but blue skies, until finally, it's clear we are going through a full-blown drought. It has rained not a single drop for over a month, and local farmers are forlorn and past complaining. We are getting married outside in the Dow Gardens, the most beautiful place in Midland, right next to the almost equally beautiful Midland Center for the Arts.

So, of course, on the morning of the wedding, it is absolutely pouring rain.

I hear later that Dianna woke up to the rain, cried her heart out, let it go, then dove into helping her helpers turn her into the most spectacular bride on the planet.

And of course, she *shows up*. On time, laughing, she dashes into the Art Center under an umbrella, surrounded by an entourage of female attendants. One of them is trailing behind her, holding up her simple, long-sleeved, full-length, cream-colored, V-neck silk dress.

Suddenly she is standing before me, a vision in cream, a pencil-thin ribbon of burgundy streaming from her hair. Slightly wider, long, shining, burgundy ribbons slide down off each shoulder, and a wide burgundy sash bunches in at the waist (I can say this with utter certainty because, as I write this, I'm staring right at her dress hanging on the door). Dianna and her mom, Pat, collaborated in creating it—Dianna's elegant, yet understated vision, combined with Pat's skill in making it. One of the few things Dianna is not good at is sewing. Her mom is a whiz.

Dianna's hair is up in a deceptively casual yet elegant style with a burgundy rose mixed in with several tiny red roses off to one side, and a halo of baby's breath sprinkled throughout her hair. She holds a bouquet of burgundy roses mixed with white carnations, strands of burgundy ribbons tumble down out of the bouquet.

She is a dream I have not dreamed before.

Outside, it is raining hard.

So we improvise on the spot and have the ceremony in the lobby of the Art Center, standing on a beautiful variegated red stone floor, against a backdrop of gracefully curved muted red-brick walls that form the lobby area. It is perfect.

The low-key reception happens immediately after the ceremony in the adjoining Garden Room where floor-to-ceiling windows face the gardens. It feels good to be with friends and family, laughter sprinkled into the steady murmur of many conversations, the tinkling of glasses, and the soft music of a lone guitar player. I stand by the windows, sipping wine, watching this much-needed rain trace crooked rivulets down the windows, turning the trees and grass outside into richer tones of green and green and green...all is right with the world.

After the wedding, we return to our Midland home with our closest friends and family. It is still raining.

Some of the ladies are standing around our dining room table, beautifully decorated with, among other things, crocheted white place mats, a much valued Spence family heirloom created many years ago by Dianna's great grandmother. One of the ladies accidently spills coffee on one of them. In tears, she confesses to Dianna.

Dianna consoles her, smiling, then immediately puts the place mat into cold water. When she realizes the stain isn't going to come out, she lifts it out of the water and begins examining it more closely.

"Hmmm. You know, this is a nice sort of an antique color." She turns it around a couple of times. "Actually, I like it," she says, almost to herself.

She quickly removes all the place mats from the table, makes a coffee bath in the sink and soaks them all, right then and there, while still in her wedding dress.

"Aren't these beautiful?" she says a few minutes later, pulling them out of the bath, speaking to everyone, but most pointedly to the forlorn-looking lady who "dyed" the first one. She holds up one of them, still dripping, to the light.

"Thank you," she says to her, beaming, then gives her a big hug. The woman is visually relieved. *Dianna knows exactly what she is doing,* I think to myself.

Not much later, we drive west out of town for our little honeymoon.

We spend a nice weekend at a B&B in Saugatuck, listening to jazz late into the night, then on to Grand Rapids the next day. I am laying in the weeds for her.

"Honey, what do you have up your sleeve? You said you have a surprise for me. I can't wait," she says. She is thrilled by surprises, only one of the many reasons she loves Christmas…opening Christmas presents or watching others open theirs.

We are sitting in a little restaurant in downtown Grand Rapids that, based on my research, has the best seafood in town. Our seafood dishes, a mixture of scallops and shrimp, her favorites, show up before I can answer.

"I'm soooo hungry." She dives in.

"Well, you know this town is called Grand Rapids for a reason, right?" I say, studying her face to see what happens next.

"Well, never thought about it." She continues eating.

She so naturally entrains into whatever is present in the moment and she looks so happy in this exact moment, I have second thoughts about torturing her.

Oh, what the hell.

"Most people don't. Actually, it's because *right here* are the only class III whitewater rapids in the state." I thought it might be a stretch to claim Class IV or V. Even she might know this part of Michigan is way too flat for class anything rapids.

"So?"

"Honey, I have set us up with a rubber raft trip through the Grand Rapids! Isn't that exciting?"

Dianna pauses, her fork frozen midway to her mouth. She slowly lays down her fork and looks at me. She can't swim from one side of a bathtub to the other and has always been afraid of water. She loves the water—but not without a solid sense of bottom underfoot. Actual swimming is out of the question.

"Oh, I don't know, John. Do you think this is a good idea?' Her brow is furrowed. "We could drown."

"Honey, very little chance of that. I have hired a guide who knows these rapids really well. No problem. Besides, we will be wearing life preservers, in case the raft flips." I squeeze any hint of a smile out of my face. It's hard.

"Do people ever die doing this?" She is studying me very intently now, searching for reassurance.

"Knew you'd want to know that, so I researched this very carefully. Turns out very few people actually die."

"Very few? ...like, how many?" She is barely picking at her food now, and her brow is even more furrowed.

"Let's see, if I remember correctly, ...the average is, *at most*, two to three each year. That's it. The percentage is incredibly small." I smile now reassuringly. "No sweat, sweetheart."

"Ohhhhh, I just don't know about this, John." She pushes a scallop around on her plate. "How big are these rapids, anyway?"

"Well, they *are* called the *Grand* Rapids, after all, so...I guess you could say they are...grand?" I don't have the slightest idea how big they are or even if they exist—or ever existed—could have been wiped out by a dam for all I know.

"I'm not sure this would be safe to do, John."

"Honey. You can trust me. I would never put you in danger. Tell you what, after dinner, we're going over to this park that's right on the river. We'll meet our guide there. You can take a look at the river and decide then. But I would never try to force you to do something you don't want to do...."

She stares at me.

"Well, sweetheart, if you don't *want* an adventure, we can just forget it then." This keeps her in the game. She sits quietly for a moment, then straightens up, weighing her options.

Finally, she sighs and puts down her fork. "Okay. I'll try it. I hope I don't live to regret this...well, that's the wrong thing to say, isn't it?" She laughs at her own joke, and so do I.

"Finish your dinner, honey, or we will be late. Have to meet our guide in thirty minutes."

"I'm not hungry anymore."

I feel a little twinge. She loves seafood, and she *was* hungry. She takes one more bite, finishes her glass of wine in one gulp, brushes back her hair from her face, and we are out the door.

We cross the open area of the park where a man, maybe in his forties, with a shock of dark hair, is setting up a hot air balloon. There are about thirty onlookers standing around, watching. It is already partially inflated and, every minute or two, a short deep roar fills our ears as the heated air is blown up into the rapidly filling balloon.

We walk up and I introduce us.

"Dianna, this is our river guide, Frank." I have already filled him in about my plan during our phone calls.

"Wait for me here," Frank says, then pointing toward a line of trees. "The river is right there through the trees; and as soon as I get this balloon ready for these folks and get them on their way, we will head for the river. I have a pretty good raft ready to go." He pauses. "Kind of old, but should get us through okay." A small smile flashes across his face.

Nice touch. I look sideways over to Dianna. She is stone-faced and standing flatfooted, back stiff, on alert.

"Are there any rules for doing this sort of thing?" she shouts over the roar of the gas burner. Dianna likes rules, and she especially likes rules that work.

"Only the ones we make up as we go," he answers, smiling broadly. He glances over toward me. He is *good*.

"Hey, Dianna," he says, "Could you climb up those little steps and jump into the basket there, so we have a bit of ballast? This balloon needs a little weight while I fill it the rest of the way."

Dianna looks at me, then back to him, then slowly climbs in. He helps her over the basket sidewall, which is surprisingly low—maybe waist high.

She relishes being the center of attention, so this is a more-fun situation. She relaxes as she looks out over the crowd of people who are standing in a semicircle around us, about forty feet away.

The man walks over to me as the burner roars again and whispers for me to jump in as soon as he does, then loudly gives me a bogus instruction to hang onto the tether. "Don't touch the tether though," he whispers.

Less than five minutes later, the balloon looks to be fully inflated, towering above us in all its spectacular red-and-white vertically striped glory. The basket is barely touching the ground, and the tether tightens.

Frank jumps in, telling Dianna to stay put for a minute. Then, I quickly climb the little stairs and jump into the basket. Frank releases the tether and, as the gas burner roars, the balloon shoots off the ground with lightening speed. Within seconds, we are gliding past the treetops into a clear blue sky.

Dianna's mouth and eyes are just big O's, and she is hanging on to me with one hand and the basket rim with the other.

Soon, we are high above the city. The streets look like ribbons and the houses like toys. The sudden silence is deafening.

Dianna scooches over and gives me a big hug.

"No rapids?"

"No rapids. I would never do that to you, sweetheart."

"Oh, honey, this is just the *best. Just...The...Best.*"

Frank is beaming. He drops us down lower, just above the trees so we can kibitz with onlookers below. We can hear their voices clearly as they shout greetings, and we answer them back. Such fun. A few minutes later, Frank produces a bottle of champagne, two plastic glasses, pops the cork, and pours us each a full glass. Then, with a few short bursts from the gas burner, he takes us up a lot higher and we drift west toward the "big lake." We sip champagne, arm in arm, silently taking in the spectacular, sprawling ragged Lake Michigan coastline below. We don't have to talk. There is nothing to say. The world drifts by beneath us in sacred silence only occasionally interrupted by another whoosh from the gas burner.

As we slowly head back to earth on our long descent, laughing, we toast everything...the premature demise of our rafting trip through the Grand Rapids, the cloudless clear sky blue surrounding us, to life, and most of all, to our adventure ahead.

We are flying high.

The Rules

Part I

Dianna was two years old in 1959, and her brother Julian was four when they were visiting relatives with their father, Bernie. It is Julian's earliest memory of his sister.

> Dad tells us we can have a soda from the basement refrigerator, so I go down to retrieve two sodas while Dianna can only watch from the top of the stairs—she is too small to go down herself.
>
> I can still remember looking up at her. She is standing there, silently watching me from the top of the stairs. I feel like she is checking on me, intent on making sure I did exactly what I am supposed to do.
>
> Dad then told us that, each hour, we could take one piece of candy from the candy bowl in the living room while the adults are busy playing cards. So I immediately walk over to the bowl and take two pieces. Dianna, (who I would learn later to my frequent dismay, misses nothing) catches me doing it. So, she immediately toddles over to our father and complains about this transgression. Too engrossed in the card game to care, he brushes her off.
>
> So she goes back to the candy bowl and puts her piece of candy back into the bowl to make up for the two I had taken.
>
> Julian still shakes his head and laughs as he tells this story about his sister—the gate-keeper.

Part II

Julian again.

John, I was sitting here looking out over the river tonight, thinking about Dianna, how much I miss her; and I suddenly realized something I want to share with you.

As you probably know (or have heard the stories over and over again) while the four of us kids were growing up—it seemed like the three of us were always cautious or guarded around Dianna. Not because we didn't like (or love) her, but because Dianna was always committed to playing by all of the rules our parents designed for us, and including a few of her own. Not that she was bossy or thought she was better than the rest of us. Deep down inside we all knew she was just trying to make our lives work better—and that meant perhaps there just needed to be a few more rules we could abide by that Mom and Dad had somehow missed over the years.

I remember when thinking about something I wanted to do, I would automatically consider the following criteria (in order of likely punishment):

1. Did it go against Mom and Dad's Rules? Y/N
2. Did it go against Grandma Rhal's Rules? Y/N (Pat's mom, the tough one)
3. Did it go against Dianna's Rules? Y/N
4. Did it go against Grandma Rose's Rules? Y/N (Bernie's mom, the gentle one)

Then the next set of criteria was:

1. Would Mom and Dad ever find out? Y/N
2. Would Dianna find out? Y/N
3. Would Dianna tell if she found out? (The answer to that was always a yes)

So looking back, I have to credit Dianna with keeping the rest of us on the straight and narrow—and having much to do with our learning to make the right choices very early in our childhood. While Mom and Dad were busy working, I realize now, Dianna was both our local resident guardian as well as our ethical yardstick in those days.

It's not much of a story, I suppose—but I do think it

says so much about what a strong influence she had on all of us growing up on Baseline Road. At the time, we surely did not appreciate it...and it took having children of our own before we would realize the strength she brought to our lives back then.

I think all of us (Trish, Dave, and I) owe much of whoever we are today, to whatever extent we are loving, forgiving, patient, romantic..., to the guidance she provided.

15

Doing it Differently

Married now and living in our Midland home, Dianna is commuting the twenty-five miles to work at the Campus Salon while I continue working at Dow in Midland.

"Dianna, don't you think it's time to sell your house?"

I am sitting at the dining room table, watching her get dinner together. I grew up on Italian food, and she is used to regular American stuff—not bad, just *not* Italian. But she is a talented cook, able to make anything taste good.

"I will," she says quietly, whisking some eggs into a bowl of flour. That's all. She continues whisking, maybe even faster now.

"You've been saying that for months. What's going on?"

She continues whisking away. Then stops, staring down into the bowl. "I don't know. It was my home for so long. I put my heart and soul into it. I guess it's hard for me to say goodbye. It feels like I'm leaving all my memories behind."

"Feel like moving back?"

She turns to me with a blank look. Then, as my words sink in, she smiles brightly. "Honey, of course not. It's not *that*."

She has some flour on her cheek, but I like it there and say nothing.

"Then what do we have to do about it?"

My wheels are turning fast now, trying to sort out what is really going on. We are talking about the only home of her own she has ever known. She launched herself into the wide world from there as a seventeen-year-old girl, supported herself, dyed her hair blonde, tooled around town in a red Camaro, met people from all over the world, and fell in love with some of them. She had recreated her life there.

"I can understand why it means so much to you, honey. But you don't live there anymore."

"I know that, John," she says finally with a sigh, starting to whisk again, faster. "I'll figure it out."

Whatever is in that bowl must be pretty well mixed by now.

I study her profile in the fading light. She has strong features, large hands. Her fingers are fatter than mine, which I like to tease her about now and then. And yet, she moves with such a natural grace. She feels like the wind in my arms on the dance floor, and she feels the same to me in life.

I drift back to the point of all this and wonder what it's going to take to break this logjam. We don't need a mobile home twenty-five miles away that no one is living in—and she absolutely refuses to rent it.

"Is there anything I can do to help?"

"No, it's okay. This will be ready soon."

"I mean with the house."

"Oh…no, I don't see anything you can do right now."

I fall back into my own thoughts while staring out the window into the backyard. Breaker comes in through the open door and nuzzles my drooping hand. I pet him absentmindedly.

While Dianna and I were dating, her brother David often regaled us with hilarious stories about Dianna.

They grew up in a ranch home tucked into a scattering of trees on a wind-swept tabletop populated with fields of corn, hay, and soybeans, edged with narrow tree-lines and brushy low spots a few miles outside of Mount Pleasant, just about in the middle of Michigan's lower peninsula. The nearest neighbors were more than a stone's throw away. Kids rode the school bus and biked down gravel roads to play with other kids.

Country people.

"She was always different," David says. "The rest of us wondered if she had been dropped into the wrong family by mistake." Everyone laughs, including Dianna. "Or maybe she was adopted!" he goes on, sweeping his arms wide, like a conductor directing his orchestra, his voice getting louder when everyone laughs louder. "Are Mom and Dad keeping secrets?" he whispers in a conspiratorial tone, leaning down close to his mother's ear. Pat has her arms folded across her massive chest, smiling.

"Me and Julian and Tricia would play ball—or be down at the creek— you know, doing all the stuff *normal* kids do. What was *Dianna* doing? No guessing there. She would be redecorating her room…*again*…until she got tired of that and *forced* us—that's right, *forced* us—to help her move a truckload—yes, a *truckload*—of heavy furniture up into the hayloft in the barn. Why? So she could create *her own place*. Dave is running on all cylinders now with arms waving, voice rising and falling on all the right notes. "Then, she would spend *hours* hiding away up there, decorating it first *this* way, and then *that* way."

Dianna takes it in all in without saying a word, sipping a Coke, beaming. She loves the attention and knows it for what it is—love. There never seemed to be any lack of that in her family.

So, I'm beginning to understand.

When I first visited Dianna's own home while we were dating, I was amazed.

The outside looked like any other white mobile home plunked down in any other average mobile home park. Inside, though, her place was nothing short of elegant. Certainly, it was decorated with infinitely more thought than my own house. She had a keen sense of style and some of the things she did were edgy, like the thirty-inch-high wicker elephant standing prominently in her living room.

As my mind flashes through all this history, it finally coalesces for me while I am looking at her standing straight, still whisking away. Okay, so men are painfully slow.

"Honey, I think I'm beginning to see the problem."

My guess is she's feeling like an alien here, in what had once been another woman's home, surging with desire to put her own stamp on it, but with a lack of money she has earned herself—and still a bit unsure of our situation, too proud to complain about it, much less ask for the license and financial help to do it.

Having been married and living here only a few months, we had not worked out any of this yet. I just never thought about it before.

"You do?" She looks surprised. Her whisking slows down.

"Yep. I think so. Couple of things."

"First, this does not feel like *your* home. It's not *you*," I say, mentally comparing what we are living in—a dark male thing at least a century out of date—to the well-thought-out space she had created for herself.

"Secondly, I make more money than you do, you have been on your own for a long time, and you don't feel comfortable asking me to spend money on making changes."

I had told Dianna about my first marriage and my mistakes, having been controlling, including about money—I was judge and jury for all of it. In this and other ways, I had damaged everyone around me—my three sons and my wife Shirley, a genuinely fine woman, who did everything she could to satisfy a man unwilling to be satisfied. In short, I had been a jerk.

"I think I know what we need to do."

"You do?"

My first wife and I had separated in 1980, the same year I completed the *est* Training, which, without any exaggeration whatsoever, helped me change the course of my life. I used it to drain my own personal swamp, to reveal my past behavior to myself and gain perspective. I cannot count the number of nights I drove home from one seminar or another at one to two a.m., sobbing much of the way as, piece by piece, I began to see the damage I had done to those I loved and who loved me.

It was painful…, and valuable.

"I can see a way to help you, Dianna…and me, too. See what you think of this."

I have her full attention now. Finally, no more whisking. I slide my feet off the table and sit up straight.

"First, you have carte blanche to do anything you want to make this house your own. I'll pay for everything."

She spins toward me, puts down her whisk and comes over to me, her eyes wide. "Oh, honey! Are you kidding? Do you mean it?" Her eyes are glistening.

I already know Dianna is frugal and more than capable with do-it-yourself projects and decorating (whereas, I might as well add, I can pound a nail with a shoe, but not that well, which is about all there is to my practical skills—or interest, for that matter).

I *was* listening to David's storytelling, and I saw what Dianna did in her own home with very little money. Obviously, Dianna is primarily a creative person, not a shopaholic or spendthrift. So I'm not worried about the consequences of what I'm saying. Thinking back to how I sat on my first wife when she wanted to do something like this, how painful and pointless all that was, I'm determined not to do it again.

"I think something else is important, too. For both of us."

"So far, I have been paying the bills and all that. Why don't we do it a different way? I will hand over my paycheck to you, and it will be your job to manage our budget. My only request is that you forget about saving little pieces of paper in your purse and try balancing our checkbook each month."

Dianna is standing in front of me, her hands cupped around her neck, speechless.

I start laughing.

She is disorganized in an organized kind of way. Record-keeping is not her strong suit. But she also always manages to get it done in her own way. So, this last request is probably just the engineer in me popping out.

"Really? But…why?"

"Why not?"

I stand up and put my arms around her. "Unless you don't want to do it."

"Oh, no, I will do it. I want to do it. I'll do a good job, too."

"I know you will, sweetheart. I have all the confidence in the world in you." And as I am saying these things, I literally feel myself lighten up. This is so much easier than I could've ever imagined.

In the months that follow, Dianna teams up with Marji. They have became fast friends, helped by shared interests in decorating and complementary tastes. They tear through the house like a tornado, dark paneling flying off the walls, dark brooding curtains disappearing. The house, day by day, becomes lighter and brighter and, almost by the minute, turns into Dianna's new hayloft.

I like not having to handle the bills, and Dianna does a stand-up job. It never was about money for me anyway. It was about giving up control. I am amazed at how easy this is to do.

Dianna sells her mobile home shortly thereafter without me mentioning it again. I think she uses the proceeds to fuel her creative fires on our Midland home, but I'm not sure.

We are on a good course.

16

Up North

My ex-wife, Shirley, is in town, visiting from her Florida home. And Sandy McComb, a prior romantic interest of mine and still good friend, lives and works in Midland. I suggest to Dianna it might be nice to take them to the Traverse City area for the day as the weather looks to be perfect.

"Great idea, honey. Would be fun. Why don't you invite them?"

"You wouldn't feel funny about it?"

"Why? Shirley is a very nice person. She has visited us before, and we get along fine. I don't know Sandy too well; but, from what you have told me, she's a nice person. Would be a great way to spend the day."

We had just bought a brand-new, full-sized 1988 Ford van and had a conversion done—carpeted throughout with only four high-end captain's chairs and plenty of windows all around. A living room on wheels, still smelling like a new car.

Early one Sunday morning, the four of us and Breaker head up north.

We spend the day walking empty beaches on the Mission Peninsula, a spike of land sprinkled with boutique wineries poking due north into Grand Traverse Bay, then tour through Traverse City, the crown jewel of the northern Lower Peninsula where "a view of the bay is worth half the pay," a phrase natives use to sardonically describe the startling beauty and economic climate of this bustling tourist magnet situated on south end of Grand Traverse Bay. We cross the relatively narrow, but very hilly, Leelanau Peninsula, also speckled with wineries and cherry orchards, stopping in the small town of Leland perched on the edge of Good Harbor Bay, looking west across Lake Michigan to the Manitou Islands and Pyramid Point. We visit one of the several pristine isolated sand beaches along this coast to give Breaker a walk while we hunt for Petoskey stones.

One of my personal high points of the trip is reveling in the women's predictable consternation as they leap out of the way like jack rabbits as Breaker, dives into the surf, dashes out sopping wet, sidles up next to one of them (of course), expecting to be petted, *then* proceeds to shake himself dry. I see pretty much why dogs do this, but I still think the unbridled joy with which they do it is suspicious.

The other highlight, of course, is dinner at the Bluebird in Leland.

We are barely seated when I begin bragging to the waitress about how I came to own this harem, who each woman is, and how we are related. The waitress stares at us in growing disbelief while she tries to wrap her brain around it all. Never one to miss an opportunity to embellish, I proclaim this just one more simple example of my incredible charm, while Dianna, Shirley, and Sandy roll their eyes, laughing anyway.

Such fun watching, first the waitress serving us, then, one by one, the other waitresses, sneaking glances our way. I can almost read their minds: *What's the matter with these women, latching onto this bozo and seemingly enjoying it.* Obviously, I have no answer for them.

I am pretty sure I would have to search the entire planet to find three men, similarly related, able to pull off what these women are doing with such obvious ease and grace.

17

Body Parts

"I think my breasts are my best feature," Dianna says as she looks at herself in the mirror, naked as a jaybird.

I'm leaning against the wall out in the hallway, flipping through a magazine, waiting for her to get ready. We are going to lunch with friends.

She turns full-face toward me. Her arms are hanging loosely at her sides, like she's posing for a driver's license photo. Her eyes are wide and, absent the makeup, she looks like a little girl…except little girls are not five-feet-ten with breasts like these, or a figure like this.

"Well?"

I look at her breasts and, in plain fact, they are as perfect as I could imagine breasts could be, large, well formed, with just that bit of droop to them that makes breasts look really sexy. As a matter of fact, they are an artistic masterpiece, perfect in shape, size, and carriage.

"Well, what, honey?" I ask.

"Don't you agree?"

"I certainly do."

"I think they are just…well-shaped and balanced—lots of women have one breast larger than the other, you know."

"Really? I didn't know that."

I think I do know that…maybe read it somewhere or…something. But this is just an Italian lie. The ones that make life go better, but do no harm. Italians prefer life to be less brittle, softer, more forgiving.

"Well, it's true."

"I notice you always dress in a way that understates them, though."

"Well, I don't want to be seen as just a blonde with big boobs, John. It's not who I am, so why should I parade around in a tight sweater that says 'Look at me.' Men *will* look at me, but in the wrong way. They'll think I'm saying this is who *I* think I am. I know what I have, and I know who I am—and I'm not a blonde with big boobs. I am a lot more than *that*."

"Well, who are you, then?" I say, egging her on a little.

She doesn't bite.

"I am Dianna," she says without even looking at me.

I am quiet now. Guess I have unconsciously known this about her from the very beginning. And she's right. At the party where I first saw her, I wasn't thinking "blonde with big boobs." I was thinking *mystery*. Maybe she *had* steered my thinking in a different direction with the way she had chosen to dress herself.

"I do need makeup, though…, as you know," she says, laughing, working on her eye-liner and leaning into the mirror now.

"Once, I had to get something at a grocery store and went out without makeup and met a lady there who knew me. Knew me pretty well, actually."

"John," she says, laughing harder now, "*She did not know who I was. She did not recognize me at all!* When I told her who I was, she just stood there, shocked."

Dianna is breaking up, bent over the sink, with both arms holding her up.

"She didn't know what to say," she says, barely able to squeeze the words out.

"What did you do?" I ask, laughing with her. It is true—Dianna is transformed with makeup. Some women don't need it or are even better off without it. Dianna can look pretty washed out, so she needs makeup to look the way she wants to look.

"Well, I gave her a hug, picked up my tampons, and got the hell out of there."

I laugh even harder.

She settles into getting ready, quiet now. I return to my magazine.

"I was never pleased with my legs, though," she muses, apparently done with the breast topic, the makeup topic, and now moving on to the rest of her personal assessment.

I look at her legs and they appear okay to me. In fact, I like them.

"What's wrong with your legs? They look fine to me. Long, slender, nice skin, what's the problem?" This is not an Italian lie.

She looks down at them like she's checking to see whether her shoes are tied or not. Then, she turns around and looks over her shoulder into the mirror to catch a glimpse from the rear.

"They're okay. I just wish they had more of a curve, a better shape to them. Now, Tricia has really nice legs. Mine are straight up and down, kind of like a little girl's legs, only bigger. Know what I mean?"

It's not really a question, and not an invitation for compliments or further discussion. She is flat about it, as if she is evaluating something that does not belong to her.

I look at her legs again. She's right. A tiny insight pops up—this is exactly why I like her legs without having thought about it before. Her legs match her personality—a naïveté that's normally reserved for young girls bounding down the street, giggling, whispering in each other's ears, before boys mean what they will mean later, before sex, before adult thoughts, before innocence is gone, oblivious to a larger world. There is something ephemeral about them then, something delicate and impossible to capture— you can only watch it and enjoy it, and leave it alone, or it will burst and be gone. This quality, I realize, is something Dianna somehow never lost.

I love her legs.

Now, I'm smiling.

"What are you smiling about, honey?" she says, glancing my way.

"You."

"Well, that's nice."

Everything about this moment is nice.

"And no matter how thin I am, I just can't get rid of this belly pouch, darn it. It's just…there."

She turns away from me now, staring into the mirror as she pats her little bump, easy for me to see in profile and in this light.

"Well, right there, sweetheart, you are looking at tiramisu, where you store your 'just desserts'…all those sweets you love so much."

She looks over at me with a raised eyebrow, says nothing, and returns to her work, powdering herself lightly all over.

I know she is not going to trade carrot cake and bread pudding and ice cream and…for a smaller pouch. And why, anyway?

I love watching Dianna in a restaurant. She lights up when dinner is over, and it's time to select a dessert. My guess is she gets as much pleasure in deciding which one as she does in actually eating it. I sip my coffee, watching her go through the entire dance, choosing, the joy when the waitress sets it down in front of her, and her ecstasy as she eats it slowly, appreciating every spoonful, offering me some—sometimes, hoping I don't accept any, which I rarely do.

Nothing makes me happier than watching her being happy.

Still, we have a clash of cultures here. The entire Spence family has an insatiable desire for sugar, and no meal is complete without something sweet to cap it off. This is pretty much an alien experience for me. Like most

Italians, I grew up eating salad after the main course. Salad *was* our desert, except on holidays.

Consequently, another melody of our marriage is, we frequently wind up cooking for ourselves without resentment or fanfare. I like spicy spaghetti followed by olive oil and wine vinegar salad, while she likes meatloaf followed by something sweet, skip the salad. That being said, she is a superb baker and cranks out a pie with greater ease than anyone I have ever known. I am a sucker for pies.

She is lost in her getting ready now, and ignoring me.

"Anyway, you know what my favorite part of you is, don't you?" I ask.

She keeps on powdering. "What?"

"Your elbows."

"My elbows?" she says, turning toward me. "What do you mean?"

"I mean the most erotic part of any woman are her elbows, and yours are just…steamy."

"Are you kidding? Better than my breasts?"

"*Much* more evocative. I can't resist you when you flash one of your elbows at me."

Her skin is silky-smooth and flawless, even her elbows, unlike my own, comparatively speaking, alligator skin.

She stops powdering, turns all the way toward me, bending forward, as if to better understand what I've said, then straightens up and turns back to the mirror.

"Oh, stop it!" she hisses, a faint smile flashing across her face like the shadow from a low, fast-moving cloud on a sunny summer day–here, then gone.

I lean back against the wall and close my eyes, smiling. We will probably not be late…she is surprisingly quick at getting dressed and doing her makeup.

She quickly slips into her watermelon outfit. Not sexy. Just fun, edgy. In every way, it's just more her, an outrageous explosion of color she is absolutely comfortable being in…and being.

"Ready," she states, sashaying out through the doorway with a little flourish.

Part II
The End of the Beginning
1990-1996

18

Stepping Across the Threshold

April 6, 1990

Dianna rushes into the apartment, exhausted. She has just completed a nine-hour drive from Pennsylvania with her Palestinian friend, Najla Bathish. Najla is leaving Mount Pleasant to marry her suitor, Nabil. Like school girls, they laughed and talked and reminisced all the way there and all the way back. Now they plan to finish cleaning Najla's empty apartment for the last time. First, though, Dianna is eager for a shower.

Dianna slips off her clothes, shivering as she slides back the translucent plastic shower curtain, then turns the faucet all the way around to "hot" with an exaggerated flair. Impatiently, she pokes her finger into the spray again, then again, until the water feels right against her hand. She quickly steps into the steamy stall, then leaps back against the wall.

"Yow!"

Getting it right at last, she sighs, dissolving into the thin, steady, shisshing streams of wet heat against her skin.

Lathering herself liberally, she feels every curve of her smooth creamy white skin with both hands. She's proud of her body—at thirty-two, she still looks damn good, is used to turning men's heads no matter what she wears, but she would trade it all and a lot more for just one child of her own, she's thinking as she begins methodically massaging her breasts, checking carefully, an almost unconscious ritual whenever she showers.

Suddenly, she notices something different. She feels it again, freezes, then catches her breath. She forces herself to consciously relax for a moment.

She slowly presses her hand across the area over and over again. It is definitely there, a hard lump, high and toward the inside of her left breast. A different lump squeezes her throat as a feeling of alarm overwhelms her.

"Najla," she yells out. "Come here for a minute!"

As Najla comes into the bathroom, Dianna pulls back the shower curtain. She is standing there, naked, her shoulder-length blonde hair plastered against her neck, water streaming down her body. Dianna guides Najla's hand over her left breast. "Feel this, Najla."

"What do you think?" she asks, as Najla gently runs her hand back and forth slowly.

"It is probably nothing, Dee-anna," Najla says finally. "But you still should have this checked out."

Dianna cannot escape the concern she sees in her friend's eyes.

"I know. But this can't be. I'm way too young to have cancer!"

She bursts through the door of our Midland home with her usual exuberance.

"Hi, honeeee!" She gives me a sweeping hug, a quick kiss, then steps back. "I'm exhausted. Are you glad to see me?" She flops into an easy chair across from me, not waiting for my reply. I'm left standing, my arms empty.

"Well?" she says. "Did you miss me? I would think you did."

"Of course. I really, really, really did miss you. Can't you tell?"

She smiles, her eyebrows arching slightly. She is sizing up the inadequacy of my demonstrated enthusiasm and playing with it. I start laughing.

"Our energies are just different," I say, defending myself. We have discussed this many times before, but we still like to play catch with it. She is immediate and mercurial, almost childlike. One of the things I love most about her. On the other hand, as it so happens, I move through life like a steady hum.

She reaches back under her hair and rustles it into some mysterious arrangement that seems to make sense to her, dismissing my attempt at philosophy, done with it.

"We had such fun, Mom was lots of help, but I'm going to miss Najla so much and I'm so, so happy for her, too."

I will miss Najla, too. When a dear friend disappears from the day-to-day flow of our lives, it's painful. Our lives are never the same.

Before I can reply, the sun disappears from her face as a cloud silently passes through. "Honey, I have something else I want you to tell you about, too." She leans forward. "Feel this." She pulls back her blouse and bra so I can.

I pass my hand gently over the area she directs my hand to feel.

"Hmmmm," I murmur, not sure what I should be saying. There is an unmistakable hardness there beneath her skin, about the size of a grape, but this doesn't mean a lot to me.

"You know, if you were doing your job, you would have noticed this long before I did," she says, turning a little sideways and drooping her eyelids, imitating a sultry glance.

"Yeah, well, I do my best."

We both laugh.

While not completely stupid, I have never had the slightest concern about breast cancer—or any kind of cancer, for that matter—and not being medically astute, and being totally uninterested in medical matters of every kind, and satisfied if I never learn anything about any of it, and disliking hospitals even more than their cafeteria food, I feel neither fear nor the slightest sense of foreboding.

However, being an engineer by disposition and training, my instinct is to swing into action, define the problem, get it fixed, whatever it is, so we can get on with our lives.

April 13, 1990

"We can just watch it for a while," Dr. Yobst says, smiling. "I'm sure, at your age, especially, it'll be nothing." He has been my family doctor for years and what I like most about him is his maturity and experience and, out of that orientation, a tendency to downplay, under-test, under-medicate and, in general, under-react. This is perfect for me. But I decide, not for Dianna, and not for this situation. Dianna is going to want to know everything, right now.

"No, we are not going to watch it for a while," I say flatly. "Let's get it checked out now. What do we need to do?"

He shrugs, still smiling, not the least bit offended. Also what I like about him. "Well, the first step is to get a mammogram. We should be able to get it done in about a month."

I shake my head.

"No, we need to get it done a lot sooner than that."

I know what Dianna and her family will do with the time, and none of it is good. In their world, there can be no circumstance that cannot be construed as *dangerous*, which I find to be both frustrating and amusing at the same time. Still, I can't see the point of waiting, either. "If it's cancer, why give it another month to grow?" I ask. "And if it isn't, no harm done, don't you think?"

Two weeks later, we're told the mammogram is inconclusive. Her breasts are too young and too large for good results. Younger women's breasts are more dense, we are told, frequently making mammograms less reliable, one reason they're not usually started for women until age forty.

Next, an ultrasound (sonogram) is done. This test, using high-frequency sound waves, can better distinguish between a fluid-filled cyst and a solid tumor. The latter result would be a more likely indication of potentially cancerous growth.

The results do indicate a definite solid tumor, but no one can tell us if it is benign or cancerous.

Putting pressure on the system, we get her scheduled for a biopsy at the Mid Michigan Regional Center in Midland within two weeks. A little nail biting is now starting up in earnest for Dianna, while I'm still thinking this is just a nettlesome detour in our lives.

May 21, 1990

Our surgeon, Dr. Sanislaw, meets with us in his office to discuss the upcoming surgery, the biopsy. Dianna and I slide into comfortable padded chairs next to each other as he closes the door and retreats behind his polished wood desk. I like the low lighting and quietness. Everything is neatly in place, books lining one wall, with his many credentials plastering the wall directly behind him. A tall and large man, his very demeanor suggests authority and competence. *I hope so*, I think to myself.

"It is highly unlikely this tumor is malignant. You are just too young. But we will know soon enough."

He comes off as gruff and imperious, but we have learned from friends he is well regarded as a surgeon. We will come to find out, underneath it all, he is a very human, human being, deeply dedicated to his profession and his patients.

"We will do a biopsy. That is, remove the tumor so it can be clinically analyzed to determine whether it is malignant or benign. I have done hundreds of these. Don't worry."

We sit there together in his office, hand in hand, listening to his every word.

I am beginning to feel worried.

I glance over at Dianna. She is sitting up straight, her back away from the chair, listening intently, her eyes a bit wider than usual.

May 28, 1990

It is the morning of the surgery. We are in a pre-op room, and Dianna is looking up at me, her eyes a little shiny. She looks smaller, buried under a single plain white sheet. No flowered prints or plaids here. The room is immaculately clean, the off-white vinyl floors looking glossy in the flood of early morning light.

"Honey, it's going to be okay, no matter what happens."

"I know," she says.

I wish I could trade places with her. She is too young, too alive for all this. Better if it were me. I have lived at least one full lifetime already and willing to leave it all on a moment's notice.

But this is not how it is.

She is so far from the world she knows, I think to myself. No makeup, no jewelry, not even her wedding ring, which she *never* takes off.

Stripped bare.

Waiting.

She closes her eyes.

I study her now, waiting for surgery, buried in white, almost blinding in this sunlight, this light that feels familiar somehow. Mentally, I step back for an instant, feeling weird; then I am right back into where we are, into *this*.

Her eyes are closed, and she seems to be in another world. I take her hand in mine and squeeze it lightly. She squeezes back.

"Well, honey, here we are, exactly where neither of us wants to be. And you know what the food is like here, too."

She opens her eyes, smiles, and squeezes my hand harder.

We are quiet for a few minutes. It is a glorious morning outside. The sun is exploding and the shadows are already sharp and intense, just the kind of day Dianna thrives in. Maybe this is a good sign.

"Is there anything I can get you?" I offer.

She is quiet for a moment, then opens her eyes. "I might want to trade in a breast. I'll let you know later," she says with a faint smile.

"I like the ones you have."

"Well, I do, too…,"she says.

There is an unsaid "but" on the end of this trailing sentence, and I tighten up inside. She has a way of knowing things before she knows she knows them. Sometimes, it's disconcerting.

So we wait.

Two nurses suddenly enter the room. Before I realize what they are up to, one of them deftly slides a needle into a vein in Dianna's left arm. It is a shot of sodium pentothal, the nurse explains, to start Dianna under, and relax her prior to the general anesthetic she will receive in the operating room.

"It'll be okay, honey. This will be over before you know it," I say as I reach over to her. She clenches my hand very tightly, then has to let go as the nurses close in on each side of her and begin wheeling her away. I follow them out of the room, then watch them disappearing down a darkened hall. One is checking Dianna's wristband. With a single sweeping turn, they disappear around the corner into a world I know nothing about.

Unexpectedly, I feel tears welling up and choke back a sob.

Maybe things will be okay.

"She seems to be okay," I say, not knowing what else to say, as I enter the waiting room and slump into a cushioned chair near Dianna's mom and dad, Pat and Bernie, and her sister Tricia. I can see from their worried looks, they're unconvinced.

"I hope so." Pat blinks her eyes a couple of times, then wipes at them.

"They took her in, then?" Bernie asks.

"Yeah. Just a couple of minutes ago."

We fall into our own thoughts, and the room, which is empty except for an older man in a far corner, becomes quiet. Pat fidgets in her chair, and Bernie just stares down at his hands without moving until I wonder if he has fallen asleep. I flip through magazines, looking at them without reading. Finally, I put down a six-month-old issue of *Sports Illustrated*.

"She's a trooper," Pat says, out of the blue.

Pat is a large woman, the commander of her realm, and a no-nonsense Republican, like most people in this part of the country. It's hard for me not to hold that against her. On the other hand, she would walk across the Atlantic under water for her children.

"She is that for sure," I say.

Pat sighs, then falls silent again, slumping back into her chair. She looks calm, but I know she is wound tighter than a drum.

Pat is blessed—or cursed—with a huge "law and order gene," passed down to Dianna in a slightly diluted form. She is very big on the rules. Obey them, and you are in with her. Disobey them, and you must be a Democrat—or worse. Her big word is Responsibility. In a strange way, we have a partial understanding of each other, since it is one of my big words, too. Though I understand it quite differently than she does.

Bernie, on the other hand, is Bernie.

I look over at him. His head is down, his heavily lidded eyes closed, looking at no one and saying nothing, his large hands crossed in his lap. I realize sometimes, when things get tough, when he just can't stand it, he just fades into the background, disappears. Like right now. He might as well be a chair in the room. But looks can be deceiving. Inside, he is in so much turmoil, I can almost reach out and touch it. Anyway, I like him.

We all look toward the doorway when a man and a woman appear and sit down a few chairs away. The woman glances at us, then around the room, her eyes flitting from wall to chair to wall and back again. The man whispers something to her, his head bent toward her. She pulls out a tissue and dabs her eyes.

I start asking Tricia and Pat questions about Dianna, both to take our minds off what is going on, and because I'm curious. I wonder if they see her how I see her.

"What was Dianna like growing up?" I ask.

"Well, she was pretty independent," Tricia says, looking at her mom. "You remember, Mom, after she finished high school and her hairdresser training, she got a job right away, bought that mobile home, and just like that, she was out of the house."

"Well, that was okay," Pat says. She is a strong woman, on the outside anyway, the family matriarch. She likes to be in control and directing traffic. Tricia smiles.

"Then, her boyfriends were different, too, don't ya think, Mom?" Tricia says.

"We don't need to talk about that," Pat says quickly, frowning, folding her arms across her chest. Tricia is enjoying this. Me, too.

"It's okay," I say, "I know about them. I'm absolutely okay with all that. I think it's great to have had Iranian and Saudi boyfriends, relating to different cultures and people."

Tricia nods her head, laughing. "She always was different. Never was interested in dating town boys. And different in other ways, too."

"What do you mean?" I ask, looking at her now, but also watching to see how Pat reacts. Pat picks up a magazine and starts leafing through it.

"Well, she was in her own world. She wasn't like the rest of us kids. Always off by herself, doing her own thing."

I remembered Dave talking about that.

"Maybe so, but since I have known her, it seems to me she loves being with people. In fact, I would say she might be the only true extrovert I've ever known. She seems to gain energy from being with people. I need to get away, to be alone, to regenerate," I say. "She even gets excited about going to funerals, for God's sake."

They both laugh.

"Well, I wouldn't disagree with that," Tricia says. "I guess what I mean is, she never liked doing the same things we liked to do. I don't mean it as a bad thing. Just different."

Pat puts down her magazine and looks over at Tricia. "That's true," she says, after pausing for a moment.

I can see what they are getting at. Dianna's family—not counting Julian—who I don't know very well yet, as he is always traveling around the world, and I rarely see him—are straight-up country folks, the salt of the earth, and pretty typical rural people in outstate Michigan—conservative, Republican, traditional values. Dianna is way left of center from all that.

"I mean, I was a tomboy and we ran in the fields, played ball, stuff like that. Not Dianna. She would rather hang out in her bedroom, practice putting on makeup, rearrange the furniture, decorate her room... *endlessly*...." Tricia laughs.

"Well, nothing's changed there," I say. "Walking into the house after work each day is an adventure. Never know if I will find things like I left them that morning. Most of the time, I don't."

They both laugh.

"She was a normal kid, though," Pat puts in.

"I didn't say she was weird, Mom," Tricia says.

"Remember the loft above the barn? How she turned it into a sitting room, with teacups and tablecloths..., and everything had to be just so?"

"We couldn't touch anything up there, either," Tricia says.

Pat smiles.

"Could you see any of *us* doing that?"

They both start laughing.

"And how she was always playing around with her hair and makeup and clothes...and if anyone messed with her room, look out."

"So, you two didn't have much in common?" I ask.

"We didn't have *anything* in common. We still don't. But don't get me wrong. We love each other very much," Tricia says.

"We all love her very much, John," Pat says.

I am quiet for a moment, looking at them both.

"I know you do," I say.

The room becomes completely quiet again. I notice that ninety minutes have passed and I can see a breeze has come up outside. The trees are swaying back and forth. In here, I can't hear the wind or the trees. I feel trapped and briefly think about going outside.

Suddenly Dr. Sanislaw appears, his tall frame filling the doorway to the waiting room. He is wearing a light-blue gown, his blue mask down around his neck. I can't read his expression, but he's not smiling.

"John?" he says, motioning me to follow him into a dark, little side room. He wastes no time.

"Sit down here," he says, pointing to a metal folding chair tucked under a little wood table. He remains standing. Now, he is towering over me.

"John, I'm sorry. The mass is cancerous. We will have to wait for the pathology report to determine the type, and to stage it, and of course, to confirm it; but I have seen enough of these to know.... Unfortunately, I have to tell you I am certain it is cancer. I'm very sorry." He stares into my eyes, quiet for a moment.

I sit there, frozen in time and space.

"I didn't think, with a woman her age, ...that this would be the outcome," he says finally. He shifts to his other foot and fills in the silence. "I can tell you, though, it is highly treatable, and her chances of complete recovery are excellent."

He stands there, looking at me kind of sideways now, head down, waiting for my reaction.

"Ah...not...not what I expected to..., not what I wanted to hear." I'm in a fog, my stomach churning. I am sliding down into a deep, dark vortex, out of control.

"She will be so devastated," I say after a long pause, trying to gather my thoughts.

"This is not the end of the world, John."

He is wrong there.

Our old world is gone. We have just stepped across the threshold into a radically different world.

Though she does not know it yet, the world as she has always known it has ended forever. Her last moment of life without cancer—BC (before cancer), as we would come to call it—has just ended. And her journey into a new world, AC (after cancer), has just begun. What has not fully sunk in yet is this is *my* last moment of life BC, too.

After Dr. Sanislaw leaves, I sit quietly in this tiny, dark room, grateful it *is* dark, gathering my thoughts.

Deciding I'm not ready yet to face her parents, I turn in my chair and face away from the open door and toward the dark, blank corner of the room. I choke down tears and swallow away the lump in my throat. I don't know how I'm going to be able to tell Dianna. I don't want her to *ever* have to hear this. I want to grab the telling and toss it into deep outer space.

At the same time, I vaguely sense she, at some level, *already* knows, however unconsciously. She is taking me by the hand and leading me on a journey with her. I would so much rather go somewhere else.

When I return to the waiting room, the look on my face says everything. Pat puts her head down and starts to cry quietly. After a brief discussion, we agree I will tell Dianna the news first, before they come in to see her.

I find Dianna in a different bright, shiny room. It is awash in midday sunlight streaming through the large window beside her bed. Outside, there is an open courtyard with scattered crabapples, still in bloom but nearly done now, their little pink flowers limp and wilting. The grass below is dotted with scattered petals, deeply green, almost startling in intensity. A robin skips off a high branch to the green below.

Spring. New beginnings. In some ways, I suppose it is.

Reluctantly, I look back inside. Dianna is still partially out of it, but opens her eyes as I bend over and kiss her lightly on the cheek. She smiles weakly. I don't waste any time; I know she wants to know.

"Honey, the tumor is malignant. But the surgeon says it is highly treatable and your odds of beating it are excellent." The words tumble out, and there is no taking them back. It is now in her universe, and I can do nothing about it.

She drops her eyes, the edges of her mouth turn down into a crumpled pout, then she begins to cry silently. I want to cry, too, as I see a tear sliding down toward her ear. This is my first of a thousand lessons in feeling my heart break while sucking it up and remaining calm. She does not need me to crumble right now. She has to do some crumbling of her own.

She holds my hand tightly for a long time, neither of us speaking.

"We will get through this," I say finally, kissing her on her forehead, then her eyes, then her cheeks, and finally her hands.

"I know," she says softly, after a long pause.

Within a single day, Dianna is back up and running, so to speak, and she is determined to fight back, to do whatever needs to be done and move on with her life. One would think nothing new has happened.

June 4, 1990

We are sitting in Sanislaw's office as he flips through the pathology report, not looking at us.

"Well, the story is this. Your breast cancer is pretty typical. It's called invasive ductal carcinoma (IDC), which means the cancer began in the wall of one of the ducts that connect the milk-producing glands to the nipple and invaded the breast tissue outside the duct. Based on the pathology report, the margins are not clear, which means I did not remove quite all of the tumor, which means we need to go back in to make sure we get it all."

"In other words?" I ask.

"We need to do another surgery. So, now is the time to decide if you wish to proceed with a lumpectomy, which is a partial removal of the breast generally followed by chemotherapy and radiation to the breast area, or we could do a simple mastectomy." He pauses. "In other words, removal of the entire breast."

I look at Dianna. She is motionless, locked in on Sanislaw.

"Maybe we should get a second opinion?" I say.

"That would be fine. I think that's a good idea. Do you want me to recommend anyone?

A few days later, we are in Detroit, sitting across the desk from this old guy, Dr. McNeil, a surgeon who has been practicing for at least a hundred years. He looks permanently tired. His office is gloomy, and I can barely see his wrinkled face in the low light. There is a window behind him, but the shades are pulled. Is this a shady guy, I muse to myself, only half-joking.

"If you were my wife under these circumstances, I would urge you to have a double mastectomy," the old man says flatly, with no emotion whatsoever.

"A *double* mastectomy! Really?" I almost bounce against the back of my chair, as if a huge wind had just pushed me in the chest. *Are you absolutely crazy?* I'm thinking.

Dianna squirms around in her chair, partly turning away from him.

"You would?" she asks slowly, incredulous.

"But...," I say, searching for what I want to say.

We had been counseled toward a lumpectomy and told the survival rates were the same as a mastectomy, so even a single mastectomy was shocking. But a double mastectomy?

He leans forward, his elbows on the desk, his hands clasped together under his chin. He studies us quietly for a moment longer.

"I know they say the cure rate is the same for a partial lumpectomy and a mastectomy; but in all my years of practice, I cannot tell you I have observed this to be the case."

We all sit in silence for a long minute or more. Finally, he sits back and sighs softly. Maybe, he can see our whole story already unfolded.

"Well, you need to do whatever feels best for you."

I turn to Dianna. "Honey, you should do whatever you feel is best."

"Let me think about it," she says to the doctor after a long pause.

Later, at home, we discuss it. A double mastectomy seems archaic and extreme. This old guy must be behind the times.

June 25, 1990

We are back in the Mid Michigan Regional Medical Center. For anyone liking hospitals, they would think this is a pretty good one—impeccable housekeeping, friendly and competent staff. And of course, the food for both patients and visitors is lousy…apparently hospitals are tested and retested to make sure they meet this universal requirement.

I stare out through the heavy plate glass window. I can hear nothing outside. While I watch the wind silently sway a thin row of evergreens in the distance and the sun darting in and out of small scattered white puff clouds, Dr. Sanislaw removes a twelve mm by ten mm by six mm chunk of tissue out of Dianna's left breast, along with fifteen lymph nodes under her arm. Cancer is identified in a couple of the nodes; and that detail, coupled with the size of the tumor, entitles her cancer to be termed stage II–III.

Not the best of news…and not the worst of news, either.

This means Dianna will get six courses of chemotherapy, followed by six weeks of daily radiation to the breast.

She draws the chemo cocktail of cytoxan, Adrimyacin, and 5–FU (Fluoruracil). A battery-operated pump is installed to gradually administer the clear orange liquid, Adrimyacin, into her veins, reducing potential damage to her heart. She gets to wear it for the duration of her chemo treatment period. This is just another conversation piece for Dianna, and she treats all of this as working with her allies in her battle to regain a normal life…and a cure.

Dianna is given Compazine to help with nausea.

19

Jell-O Days and Nights

Compazine does not help Dianna with the nausea. Nothing helps Dianna with the nausea.

Nothing stops all her beautiful hair from falling out in huge swatches, either, which happens while we are on a trip to the East Coast with her best friend, Kathy (Me: "Sure you want to go?" Her: with a look of amazement, "Why not?").

But she is prepared. She has fun picking out several wigs ahead of time.

"In a way, it's kind of neat. I can wear different styles and colors any day I want to—even change hairstyles in a single day!" she says enthusiastically.

I never do get around to liking the red one. There's another one I'm not fond of, either. "Makes your head look like a giant hairy blonde mushroom," I say.

Upon hearing this, she sniffs a little, straightening her shoulders as a faint smile glides across her face like cloud-shadows rippling across the ground.

"Well, I like it," she says.

I think I'm winning, though. Over time, she wears it less and less.

Our routine is quickly established. I'm in charge of the metal bowl. Easy to wash. I use this to catch whatever fluids are left inside of her to vomit as she lies on her side at the edge of the bed. She is pretty much sleeping, vomiting, or in silent misery, for four or five days. Then, she has about a week to recover, followed by another week of near normalcy before we start all over again.

I have no idea what it feels like to be her, right now.

"Honey, the only time in my life I threw up as much as you are right now is when Steve Kridelbaugh and I snitched a fifth of Canadian Club from my dad—might have been New Year's Eve. I almost killed myself—was around sixteen years old. I can still see the bottom of that toilet, wondering if I would see my guts pouring into it—just couldn't be anything else left in there."

Dianna slowly looks up at me, looks back down into the bowl, heaves again, then sinks back into the bed with a disgusted sigh. "Like that?"she asks while using a tissue to wipe her mouth. Then, she closes her eyes and sighs again. Apparently, my little story resonates, but still not all that helpful.

Not so hard for us during the day, but tougher during the night. Gratefully for us both, she is usually so exhausted she sleeps through most nights. But not all of them.

It does not take much trial and error to figure out the only food she can hold down during "vomit week" is Jell-O. I have not eaten Jell-O since I was a kid, and had never made it before. Turns out, any idiot can do it. So, I buy all the flavors available and have batches "jelling" in the refrigerator all the time. We soon learn just plain Jell-O is the only option—embellishments like fruit or nuts are definitely not helpful.

I cry inside when I'm holding the bowl. Then, when she pops out of bed like a cork out of a bottle after each cycle, eager to get back into the mainstream of life again, I want to cry again, this time with joy, amazement, and gratitude.

During one of the later chemo cycles, some friends invite us out to a carnival happening in town. It's right in the middle of one of her "Jell-O weeks." I think this is a very bad idea.

"This is a very bad idea, Dianna. Today has not been a good day. You need rest, not Ferris wheels."

"Oh, honey, I *want* to go. It'll be fun," she says between bouts of vomiting. "I think I have the pattern figured out now. I'll be okay…for a few hours anyway."

Before we leave, she has another short bout of vomiting. Then, we are off to the carnival. She rides most of what is there to ride, including the Ferris wheel, and culminates the evening with a rousing session on the bumper cars, screaming in triumph as she hammers a male teenager in a blue car, rattling his teeth. I watch, laughing from the sidelines. Once we are home again, I hold the bowl for her a couple of times before sleep takes over.

All in all, a good day.

In fact, she misses very few days of work, and even during "Jell-O weeks" she often shows up for at least partial days. I am lucky I have almost infinite job flexibility, so I stay home with her whenever necessary. It works out.

We follow this routine for six rounds of chemotherapy before it is on to radiation, which is a daily, painless routine for another six weeks.

Although there are moments when Dianna wonders if she is going to die from this, she doesn't. One thing *does* die during this period though—her old white Toyota Corolla.

"I have had it, John. Had it! *Had…it!* I…am…*Done,*" she says, exploding through the front door, then flinging her purse across the kitchen table. I watch it skid off the edge and drop onto a kitchen chair.

"Really," I say calmly. "Had it with who…what…?" I turn toward her, my arms folded, smiling, though I'm not sure why.

"It's that damned car! It broke down on me again today! I need a more dependable car." She stares at me, ready to argue.

She drives twenty-five miles each way to work, she is on chemo and her car is a dinosaur…and very light—if she collided with a bicycle, the outcome would be a tossup. I had not thought about it before, but getting a better one is a good idea. We had been having more and more trouble with the Corolla, and it's about ten years old.

My philosophy on cars is simple: buy a good one, often a new one, so I will feel emotionally attached to it, and more likely to want to hang onto it. Then, take good care of the moving parts (appearance doesn't matter to me—a major disconnect between us). Drive it into the ground and, when the cost of maintenance is approaching new car payments, call the junkyard to pick it up and start all over again. This gets me into a new car about once per decade, plus or minus.

In other words, for me, a car is a necessary expense, not an investment or status symbol.

"Okay. So…let's get one then," I say.

"Really?" she says after a pause. I watch the air rushing out of her balloon. "You don't disagree? But I would need your help. I don't have enough money to buy one."

"We're married, Dianna. Your money is your money, and my money is your money, so what's the problem?" I ask, laughing.

"Oh, stop it. I hate using your money, but I'm just so fed up." She still has not come around to the idea all of it is *our* money, I notice. Pride, I guess.

She flops down into the living room couch. I sit down on the floor across the room, legs out in front of me, crossed at the ankles.

"You will never guess what happened today." Her mood is changing from sour to fun, fast.

I raise my hand like a stop sign.

"Stop saying it's *my* money. Not how I feel about it. Wish you wouldn't, either…so, I'm guessing maybe the car broke down?"

"Not only that," she says, already too deeply into her story to be diverted by esoteric topics like our competing philosophies about money.

"It was like someone turned the key to off. I was barely able to coast off M-20 onto the shoulder. Well, the only thing nearby was a rundown mobile home, but I needed a phone.

"Anyway, I slipped while jumping across the ditch to get over there, and my wig popped right off my head and down into the ditch. So, I picked it up out of the grass, brushed it off, and slapped it back on my head—and I had no mirror, of course, and I was in a hurry—and I could see I was going to be late for work. Oh, John, I… was… so… FURIOUS."

Dianna starts laughing as she abruptly gets up and goes into the kitchen to get a glass of water. I follow her.

"Oh, honey, I'm sorry." I'm not sure whether to laugh or not, but start snickering anyway.

She ignores me.

"So, I knock on the door and this older man answers, stares at me like I am an escapee from a mental hospital, kind of hesitates, but lets me in anyway, and points me toward their phone. As I'm talking on the phone, I notice both he and his wife are watching me intently with a look of—oh, I don't know—confusion, concern, disbelief—but they are still very nice to me. When I get off the phone, they offer me a cup of tea, and we end up chatting for half an hour while I'm waiting for the tow truck. I could see they were poor; but John, they were such kind people. I really liked them."

Dianna then starts laughing so hard, she has to put her glass of water down on the table and catch her breath.

"Well, so I get back to the car, take one look in the rear-view mirror and I understand everything. My wig is on crooked, and there is no way anybody could have hair coming out of their head looking like *that*."

"So I'm the eighth wonder of the world as far as they're concerned!" she says, her voice rising precipitously in pitch at the end of this last sentence. As she finishes the story, she folds over laughing, holding onto the back of the kitchen chair while looking up at me.

I'm laughing now, too.

This story goes into the vault. Dianna will retell it too many times to count; sometimes in the oncology clinic during her visits, dissolving other chemo patients into tears, lifting their spirits, changing how they are in life. I can only sit back and watch in amazement as her story becomes another little mini-miracle floating into people's lives, lifting them up, at least for that moment, to the perch she sits on in nearly every moment of her own life.

It becomes funnier with each telling, as she gets her timing down pat, and more hilarious details are added in…and each time, she tells it, *she* laughs harder, living every moment again and again….

She is healing herself, too.

Within a month, Dianna buys a two-year-old, low-mileage, black Pontiac Grand Am with black interior. Her kind of car—has some style, sort of sporty, sleek looking…hopefully no more leaps across the ditches along M-20.

I rarely get to drive *her* new car.

She has another wig episode in late fall on her way to the salon supply store in Midland.

"Well, it was embarrassing, I guess. But I couldn't help laughing… everyone else was."

"What happened?"

"Well, you know how windy it is today. So, I parked the car across from Sally's Beauty Supply out on Saginaw—I always go there when I need stuff—and I was hurrying across the street—it was so cold—and the wind just whipped that baby right off my head before I knew what was happening." Dianna is laughing so hard now, she has to catch her breath. "So, the darn thing was getting away from me, and I started running after it as it tumbled across the road…a lady in the store saw what was happening, and I could see her hand up to her mouth, trying hard not to laugh…and another lady stopped her car, waiting for me to catch up with it…she dropped her head into her hands…I could see she was laughing so hard she was shaking, but trying hard not to show it."

I'm laughing, too, by now.

"Oh, honey. So, what happened?"

"Well, I finally caught up with the damned thing. I had to step on it, for God's sakes. Then, well, what else could I do? I picked it up, dusted it off, and slapped it back on my head, then hurried into the store to get

79

my stuff. The gals in there saw it all and were very sympathetic, but pretty soon we're all laughing about it all over again."

"I'm sorry, honey." It was all I could think to say.

"Guess I just need to get the hang of it," she says, still laughing.

"Well, maybe it's a skill you won't need much longer," I say.

"Hopefully not," she says.

"Hopefully not," I say.

20

Some Dreams Come True

In the BC days (before cancer), we had talked it over and decided we would love to live in the Traverse City area one day—specifically, somewhere on the Leelanau Peninsula, an area of rolling hills that remind people from California of Napa Valley—looks a lot like that. Leelanau, already famous for cherries, is moving fast into grapes and gaining a reputation for wine produced at a rapidly increasing number of boutique wineries.

So, we had started using some of our weekends in 1989 to make the three-hour drive from Midland to check out properties.

On one trip, I have marked out some acreage with hundreds of feet of frontage on Lake Michigan at the extreme northern tip of the Leelanau Peninsula. We drive north on M-22, past Northport onto a bumpy blacktop that eventually dissolves into a desolate sandy two-track. Dianna quiets down as we drive slowly past low grass fields and wind-bent jack pines. When we finally get there, I am *so* excited—this is *exactly* what I'm looking for—lakefront we can afford, secluded, lots of land for gardens, even a vineyard maybe, everything on my checklist. I swing open the door and jump out.

Dianna sits still in her seat, her arms folded across her chest, looking straight ahead. I look back into the car, wondering what's wrong.

"There is no fucking way I am going to live *here*," she says very calmly, glaring through the windshield at the desolate, windswept landscape surrounding us.

Furious, I get back into the car and turn around to head back south. We are swallowed up in a dead silence all the way back to Traverse City.

Finally, Dianna takes the map I have marked with land to look at and, after studying it, says sweetly, "Honey, why don't we take a look at this one—this looks interesting."

So we get through Traverse City, then head back north, this time up the spine of the Mission Peninsula, to locate the land she has identified. Following directions, I turn into a well-developed subdivision, already jam-packed with very nice homes on all sides.

"There it is, honey. That lot there, with the sign on it."

It is a pie-shaped lot stuffed in between two already built homes, and about the size of a postage stamp.

"This is *really* nice—such nice homes. What do you think, honey?"

I could have looked at her as if she had gone completely insane, but instead I very calmly put the car in park, cross my arms over my chest, smile, then say, in the same tone as "pass the butter, honey," "There is no fucking way I am going to live in *this* place."

She turns, looks at me for a moment, stunned. After a long moment, she breaks out laughing. I start laughing, too.

"Why don't we find some place to have lunch? Think we've done enough work for one morning," I say. No woman I have ever known is against lunch.

"Good idea," she says.

We do learn one thing, though. Finding the right piece of land is not going to be easy.

Even though we are living in the AC (after cancer) era now, and even though Dianna is still on chemo, we continue making weekend excursions to the area, creating our future by injecting it with promise. All together, we will spend over a year looking for land that will please us both without compromise.

Finally, in the summer of 1990, we find it.

She stands at the bottom of the hill out in the middle of the sand road, staring up at me through the trees.

"Oh, honey, the view is really terrific from up here," I yell down to her. Only halfway up the hill, I can still see down the entire length of south Lake Leelanau, a ten-mile view. "Dianna, the hills around the lake are just beautiful, too!"

"I can't climb up there, honey," she yells back. "Will just have to take your word for it." During our land search, cancer had come calling and Dianna is now wearing the chemo pump. Her energy is low. She stands down on the road, her legs close together, her arms folded, as she looks up at me, squinting into the bright sunlight.

She had insisted on making the trip. "Why not, John? I need a break, and the weather is nice."

The land is a beautiful ten-acre, fully wooded parcel on a hillside overlooking Lake Leelanau, covered with beech, maples, and oaks, and only fifteen minutes from downtown Traverse City.

After exploring the property thoroughly, I clamber down to meet her, help her into her seat, then hustle Breaker into the backseat of our Ford conversion van. It's about the size of a tank, but we love it. Can camp, sleep, and tour in it.

"Dianna, I want you to see what the view is like—look, right there down the road is a house. Looks like it has about the same view we would have—and we can ask some questions about the area, too."

"Honey, we can't just walk up to someone's home we don't even know, unannounced, and barge in on them like that."

"Why not?" I ask, while driving the few hundred feet to the home.

"I am *not* going to bother them," she says, as I slide out.

"Wait here, then." I shut the van door and walk up to the house.

A petite, sunny, attractive woman answers the door, and we quickly hit it off. Her name is Lynne. I see a couple of golden retrievers nudging her legs from behind her and when I tell her I have one in the car, the deal is sealed. After a few minutes, I retrieve Dianna, who is now almost bursting to join in. We meet Lynn's husband Bill, who is equally welcoming. The dogs surround each other, and everyone falls in love at first sight.

The most important thing of all on this trip is meeting Bill and Lynne Watson, who will become very dear friends and our local B&B, complete with horses and golden retrievers, whenever we visit the area.

The same day we meet Bill and Lynne, I also meet a local developer. Our realtor suggests we see him, telling me this guy has a map of the land we are interested in. When I knock on the door of his establishment, he answers. When he finds out which piece of land I am interested in buying, he looks me straight in the eye and says, like he is telling me the sun is coming up tomorrow, "You will *never* own that land."

Feels like a cold wind hitting me in the face, but I don't show him anything. We will see, I think to myself.

As the plot unfolds, it turns out we can't buy the land because it is mired in a tangle of township politics and a rezoning nightmare...and the developer's friends are on the board we have to deal with..., so the locals are in control and the developer wants the land for himself.

But we do have one ace in the hole. Dianna and I agree we will fight for it.

So, every one of the 3,647 trips we make up there for every single township meeting is just another visit with Bill and Lynne, another time for Breaker to run and play, and another challenge. Long, frustrating meetings at the hall are followed by good times and lots of laughs with Bill and Lynn.

Why should we give up? It's our dream.

After almost five years of polite but persistent effort, and countless six-hour round trips to attend township meetings, the local opposition, apparently in awe of our persistence or just exhausted, finally melts away. Over that time, we deepen our relationship with Bill and Lynne.

We purchase the land in 1995.

Our dream come true.

Well, this is how it feels at the time.

21

And Some Dreams Don't

"I am not willing to trade my life with you for a child without you," I say. Nothing is going to change my mind about this.

Dianna sits quietly at the kitchen table, completely calm. She could be listening to a weather report. She says nothing.

It is her most fervent desire to have a child, and we agreed before we married to have one only. I do not really want another child, but know how important it is to her. She agreed to delay trying for one for a year or so; and after that, it just didn't happen, no matter how diligently she monitored her menstrual cycle.

Then, one day, instead of getting pregnant, she got cancer.

While Dianna is going through chemo, we ask our doctors about the potential effects of pregnancy. They cannot promise the hormonal changes associated with a pregnancy will not re-ignite or promote cancerous growth. It is a possibility, they say.

This is an easy decision for me, and a painfully difficult one for Dianna. She badly wants a baby, but she also wants to live long enough to experience raising it. Looks like a no-win situation.

Though she will later tell me—much later, in fact—that not being able to have a child was the most crushing disappointment of her life, she is, in this moment, weighing her options.

Finally, she lets out a soft, barely audible, sigh. "Okay," she says.

She pops up out of her chair like a cork out of a bottle, looks down at me for a long moment, then leans over and pecks me on the cheek, her face a mask of serenity. No tears.

"What do you feel like having for dinner?"

22

A New Normal

Dianna completes her chemotherapy by late fall of 1990, which is immediately followed by six weeks of daily radiation treatments. She schedules her work to be part-time while that is going on. She does not want to quit.

She sails through the whole thing with flying colors and, as any cancer patient knows, while *it* is always there, sulking in the background, life goes on—and as far as she is concerned, it's over.

Well, she acts like it's over.

Me, too.

Dianna jumps at the opportunity to perform as master of ceremonies for a fashion show at the Midland Center for the Arts auditorium. There are hundreds in attendance. It is a benefit for women cancer survivors who are modeling all the clothes. They nervously parade out on stage while Dianna describes each outfit quite professionally. She is, herself, wearing a long sparkly gold gown and looks spectacular. What is most amazing to me, though, is she is completely relaxed, ad-libs the whole thing with ease and humor, without notes, and makes one nervous amateur model after another feel safe, putting her hand on their shoulder or quipping a joke about herself when an awkward moment shows up. If she flubs a line or a model stumbles, she unselfconsciously laughs at herself or puts the model at ease with a gentle hug, and has the crowd laughing and engaged. She loves being the center of attention, and she has a natural talent for managing the energy of the entire audience, turning it into a fun event for all of us. Just like a very large family gathering for her, I muse in admiration. I'm so proud of her.

As the weeks and months go by, life slides into normal. It is a new normal, though. Once bitten by a dog, you never think about them in quite the same way again. So, every checkup is a mini-adventure. At least, that's how it feels for me.

Time eventually fades that feeling to almost nothing. The checkups happen further and further apart, and eventually stop altogether. We can only think about something scary, something we have no control over, for so long, and then, life goes on, and whatever fear we have left slides into our subconscious.

For Dianna, the eternal optimist, this seems to be a process of hitting the reset button and the new normal *is* the old normal.

She isn't stupid. She knows the cancer could come back. But, as with everything else, she chooses to believe it will not.

That Tooth

"Are you sure you want to give up that part of you?" I ask.

I have always loved the way one of her teeth poked out slightly at an odd angle. Seemed to me it suited the whole of whom I experienced Dianna to be—a bit quirky, all Dianna, and not like anyone else.

"Honey, I've thought about it and I would like to go ahead and get braces. Do you mind the money?"

"Not that. If it's what you want, do it. I just didn't think you were self-conscious about it."

"I'm not."

I study her for a long moment and have to agree. She isn't.

"Just time for a different look," she says, smiling. We are at the dining room table and she is sitting up straight, away from the back of her chair.

I slide down a bit, drape one arm over the back of my chair, and put my feet up on the table.

"Well, I'm just a bit disappointed you'd want to destroy a part of who you are—and *a part everyone happens to love about you*," I say, my voice rising with magnified emphasis.

She studies me for a moment, still sitting up straight, and puts both arms on the table. Then slowly one eyebrow goes up just a little. A faint smile emerges, then disappears.

"I'm not buying any of your bullshit here," she says.

"I'm not *kidding*. Everyone just *loves* that tooth. I do. It just perfectly expresses that specialness about you. It's part of who you are, honey."

She barely hesitates.

"Well, it's time to change that part."

So, she does.

Given Dianna spends about 97.4 percent of her life smiling or laughing, I conclude at least she got our money's worth.

I vaguely wonder if maybe, too, there is something she senses about her role—or her purpose in life—shifting.

23

So Many Changes

In early summer of 1993 Dow cuts 3,000 employees from their workforce and I am one of them.

At first, I feel a sense of rejection and a mixture of shock, shame, sadness, anger (not much). But a friend and former boss, Lee Wilford, who is caught up in the same cutback, takes me aside one day and quickly educates me.

"John, be grateful this is happening—we are getting our full retirement and medical benefits, and they are tossing in one-year severance pay—this cut is just the beginning. Those who follow us out the door—and there will be others (there were) who will never see a deal as generous as this one again, trust me (they didn't). Right now, Dow is just getting used to doing what all corporations have been doing for a long time, but they are not comfortable with it yet. Be happy."

Actually, in short order, I *am* happy. For some reason, I feel both a sense of relief about leaving and an optimism about the future. I see it all as an adventure now. I don't want to stop working yet, so we know we will be moving…somewhere. Dianna is right on board and feels the same way. At times, we are actually almost euphoric.

When I drive out through the plant gate for the last time, I stop the car and get out. I want to use this moment to look back, to remember it. I leave the engine running. How many times had I gone in and out of that plant—I mentally calculate about 6,000. I try to remember the very first time, twenty-eight years ago, but I can't.

Oddly, I feel surprisingly little nostalgia, but I am proud of all I have accomplished, and realize this is exactly the right time to be leaving. I will not miss it.

I won't look back again, either.

After months of muddling around, I pick up work as a team-building contractor while we are still living in Midland, and Dianna continues working at the salon.

In late summer of 1993 Breaker begins to decline, and by fall he is on his last legs. He stops eating, and tests show his kidneys are near failure.

With a heavy heart, I internalize it all. The time has come. I tell our vet she must come out to our house to give him the lethal injection. He is not going to die anywhere but in the surroundings he has known for the past eleven years. She readily agrees.

The day before, Breaker slowly walks beside me out to a little woods at the end of our street, and we spend the afternoon lying on a soft, slippery bed of pine needles, smothered in the scent of pine and the scent of summer dying, watching the sun twinkling through the trees. He is content. I pet him, running my fingers through his silky hair and talking to him occasionally, but mostly I am quiet. Sometimes he dozes off, tight up against me, but most of the time his nose is twitching at new smells or sounds riding the afternoon breeze. Finally, the wind coming through the pines dies off and the sun almost disappears into the underbrush. It is time to go. He can barely stand, so I carry him home in my arms, shocked at how light he has become.

The next day, the vet comes and I have Breaker lay on his side in our backyard, and he readily complies. He is done, and he must know it. I pet him and talk to him while Dianna stands nearby, sobbing. Within seconds after the injection, he just closes his eyes, without moving a single muscle.

Gone.

I sit there for several minutes on my knees next to him with tears that won't stop. The vet leaves and I am left staring at this body that housed my dear friend. A warm gust of fall air flips up a tuff of hair along his chest, flashing in the sunlight. I will always see that bit of hair moving in my mind's eye. I see it today.

I bury him in the woods, not more than thirty feet from where we had lain together for the last time, then scatter pine needles over the grave. I lean up against a tree trunk, shovel in hand, studying it all in a moment of silence. The area looks just like it did yesterday, and it will never be the same.

Just like our lives.

After working as a contractor doing team-building work for about a year, I notice a small ad in the Midland paper advertising for a safety engineer at a chemical plant. It looks interesting, if only because it's in Michigan where we want to stay, still close to our families. Having seen pretty much the whole country, I had long ago concluded there is no other place on earth I would rather live than right here. Dianna agrees.

I take Dianna with me on my first visit to the plant, wearing the full interview regalia, suit, tie, shiny shoes, the whole disaster.

"You can look really nice, honey, when you're cleaned up."

No comment.

I had noticed there are tons of lakes around this area, called the Irish Hills.

"Dianna, I've lined you up with a realtor; so while I'm doing this all-day interview, maybe you can take a look around at some of the best lakes—she will know which ones." We are on US-23, heading toward Adrian, in southern Michigan, where the job prospect is located.

We had talked about all this before. Why not move to a lakefront home and basically be on vacation year-round—we won't have to spend money going somewhere else to have a good time. We figure, too, it will be a good place for our families and friends to gather, giving them a place to vacation on the cheap, and giving Dianna opportunities for entertaining.

Dianna is sitting up straight, excited. The cancer seems far behind us now, and we are both looking forward to life without it.

I do the plant tour, which doesn't take long. While the Dow facility in Midland had probably 4,000 employees and many huge chemical plants, this facility has about 125 employees along with a long list of highly hazardous chemicals I'm used to, having worked with them all my life.

The plant manager, Lehman Klink, greets me as I return from the tour. I drop my hard hat on the chair next to me and sit down in his office.

"Well, John, what do you think of our plant?"

I don't hesitate or even blink. "Well, I can say with complete confidence this is the worst-looking chemical plant I have ever seen anywhere."

He laughs. He has a hearty laugh and I like him right away.

"But, are you interested?"

"Absolutely, ...but only if you are committed to turning it into a world-class facility and will spend the money it takes to do it. Otherwise, I am definitely *not* interested. What would be the point of babysitting a continuing tragedy?"

As things turn out, we design a job that better fits the company's needs than the one originally offered—Safety *and* Environmental Manager, for a higher salary; and on top of that, I negotiate a work contract allowing me to continue the team-building consulting career I had launched while still in Midland.

Much more important to me than all of that, my real agenda is to practice everything I believe I've learned about team building and see what results can be produced. Unlike the huge organization at Dow, there is very little bureaucracy to get in the way here, and essentially *everything* needs to be changed. From the first moment I set foot in this plant, I see it as a golden opportunity to make a difference.

Dianna does a good job narrowing down our home search to Lake Loch Erin. The area and the lake meet what we each want. We make several false starts at buying first one existing home, then another, but the deals keep falling through. Finally, one day, I turn to Dianna. "Enough of this bullshit—people wanting to sell, then changing their minds. Let's just find an empty lot and build our own."

Dianna loves this idea instantly.

Fortunately, in the course of our failed attempts to buy a house, we had the extreme good fortune to cross paths with a young builder high on skill and integrity, Lon Wagenschutz. Even better, he's every bit as gregarious as Dianna. They are both big talkers, quickly take to each other, and form an amazing team.

We locate a group of four lots available on both sides of a single winding road that follows a peninsula jutting a quarter mile out into the lake. We drive there on an early spring day, passing patches of snow here and there, white splotches that belong to winter almost gone. The lots available are near the end of the point, and there are only a few scattered houses along the way.

I want a lot with a good slope to it so we can build a walk-out type home, giving us attractive living space on the lower level for less cost, essentially a basement with lots of windows and air. All the lots have plenty of slope, so it comes down to whether we want to face the lake, looking east or west. We stare out over the lake, but it is so foggy we can barely make out a shadowy tree line on the far shore. Invisible geese are barking back and forth, and a blue heron silently lifts off, disappearing into the fog.

"We can build a walk-out on this one, honey. According to the map, we're facing Goose Bay. Good omen. I love Canada geese, and facing southeast with lots of windows is going to be better, too."

We quickly agree this is the one.

Dianna puts her arm around me and squeezes. She can hardly contain herself. We stand there for a few minutes, taking in the silence, the shadowy shoreline, the cold, damp air. "Oh, John, I do like the feel of this place."

We close the deal within a couple of days. This must be the right thing to do—so easy after months of frustration trying to buy a house already built.

Dianna is bubbling with excitement. She finds a house design she likes, Lon has the skill to build it, and I pretty much step aside—I'm buried at work anyway—and leave them to do their thing...mostly.

Lake Loch Erin is in the middle of open rolling farm country—soybeans, corn, horse farms, and small farmers raising cattle—sprinkled with woods and open fields right on the southern edge of the Irish Hills area. I love this.

The lot we are building on is part of a small subdivision. So our site comes completely equipped with a few nearby neighbors. This means Dianna can walk across the street in her robe with a cup of coffee in hand. She loves that.

We eventually sell our Midland house, Dianna bids a tear-filled goodbye to the Campus Salon and, before we know it, we are driving out of Midland for the last time. I am leaving with excellent memories spread over the thirty years I have lived here...and very good friends, too. For all its Stepford qualities, Midland *is* a nice community with high standards and routinely does things the way things should be done, just like the company that basically owns it. I search for signs of sadness or regret and find none. I will not miss Midland.

"We still have friends here, honey, so we'll be coming back now and then. It's not forever," she says when I share my feelings with her.

Yes and no, I think to myself.

Whichever way I choose to look at it, it feels like a good time for change. As we exit the city and merge onto US-10, I don't remember looking in the rear-view mirror.

Ground is broken for our new home in April 1995, the same year we are finally able to buy our dream-land in Leelanau County up north.

While our house is being built, we rent a tiny basement apartment in Adrian that comes fully equipped with more amazingly large hairy spiders than Dianna can count. They move too fast. We eat dinner on a card table—while Dianna's dream home is literally materializing day by day.

She is in heaven without dying to get there.

24

My First Day at Work

Meanwhile I am in my own version of heaven…at work.

My new job as a safety and environmental manager begins in the fall of 1994. The plant is a leisurely drive from our house over back country roads and farmland interspersed with patches of woods, a drive I will grow to love.

The facility is a 24/7 operation with a separate building for the staff consisting of a few engineers and administrators, including the plant manager. However, my office is located inside the plant, itself.

I will eat and breathe the same air the workers do, so I will also directly experience the results of my own work, for better or worse. For all these reasons, I love this location and, over the years, turn down all opportunities to move into the administration building.

Entering my office for the very first time is a memorable experience. I am instantly immersed in an overwhelmingly irritating haze. The long fluorescent lights overhead are coated with white powder, the corrosive halogenated product this plant produces. So is the desk, file cabinets, chair, floor, ceiling, walls, some old papers lying on the table, and everything else. Obviously, it has been unused and closed up tight for a while.

I cannot tell what color the steel file cabinets holding safety and environmental records used to be. They are entirely rust-colored now, their file drawer faces curled like potato chips from corrosion. I can barely open or close them. I soon discover this doesn't matter much. The records are useless.

The office is a cement box—cement floors, cement ceilings, cement block walls.

In less than five minutes, my eyes are watering profusely and my throat hurts. I quickly deduce, the sooner I clean this place up, the longer I'm going to be able to tolerate being here. I get to it right away.

While engrossed in my cleaning project, I run into several workers.

They pass by me silently with no smiles or hellos. What I do get is a stony look or no eye contact at all. They already know who I am not—I am not one of them—and who I am—the enemy. The "we-them" culture I left behind at Dow is not only alive and well here, it's on steroids.

Perfect.

Clearly, my first and daily challenge will be to create a common vision for what we can be…and be a daily, living example of it.

My dream is simple: We are a world class chemical plant operated by world class employees, where we work without insulting the environment, without endangering workers or the community around us—and we are profitable doing it. Instead of being the laughing stock of the company and community, we are highly respected.

Most of all, we will be a family.

Each day, I will come to work with this dream firmly in mind. It is a culture change based on an ethic these people already know somewhere deep inside themselves, an operating discipline that starts with self-respect.

Finished with a first-pass clean up, I post one of Charles Swindoll's most famous quotes about attitude on the outside of my office door.

Attitudes

Words can never adequately convey the incredible impact of our attitude toward life. The longer I live the more convinced I become that life is 10 percent what happens to us and 90 percent how we respond to it.

I believe the single most significant decision I can make on a day-to-day basis is my choice of attitude. It is more important than my past, my education, my bankroll, my successes or failures, fame or pain, what other people think of me or say about me, my circumstances, or my position. Attitude keeps me going or cripples my progress. It alone fuels my fire or assaults my hope. When my attitudes are right, there's no barrier too high, no valley too deep, no dream too extreme, no challenge too great for me.

I pack up my briefcase and head for the car. This is just about enough work for one day.

When I walk in the door, Dianna is in the kitchen, making dinner. She's in high spirits, playing house in our tiny apartment.

"Hi, honeeee." She comes over to me and gives me a big hug.

"Oh, honey…you…smell….you smell like…."

"Like an over-chlorinated swimming pool?" I suggest.

"That's it…. Wow. Pretty strong."

"Well, I'll never have to worry about bacteria," I say, laughing. "I'll be permanently disinfected every day… and be paid for it, too."

"So, how was it?" she asks, moving back a few steps. I laugh again.

"To tell you the truth, my first thought was, I wondered if I'd made a mistake. The safety rules are pretty ragged and the environmental situation is, let's just say, tenuous. Management and workers distrust each other, …I mean, profoundly."

"Oh, honey, I'm sorry."

She is quiet for a moment. I can see the wheels turning. "Do you think you ought to quit?"

"Quit? Are you kidding? Absolutely not."

When I tell her about the nasty chemicals there, she starts getting nervous.

"I love building our own house, honey, but it's not worth your life. We can find something else. We can move if we have to—maybe this is just a mistake."

I know she means it. As much as she loves creating her own home, she would, without complaint, move again if we had to, make some other place her new castle, make friends with everyone around her within a week, and life would be good.

"Just the opposite, sweetheart."

I walk over to her and give her a big hug, playing with her now. She lets me do that, smell and all.

"It's my dream job, Dianna. It's the challenge I've been looking for, maybe what I've been training for all my life. Dow is a great company, but doing team building under nine layers of management was like trying to melt a glacier with a candle."

I grab a glass of water and sit down on the folding chair at our little card table.

"John, you should change your clothes before you sit anywhere."

I ignore her.

"This place is small and hundreds of miles away from all those layers of management. I can get to know everyone. If I want permission to try something, there is only one person I need to enroll—the plant manager—and he's a really nice guy whose heart is in the right place. This is an opportunity to try out all the ideas I have for changing culture, for building a team that works."

"Well… then… I guess I'm happy, if you are."

I put my feet up on the card table and let out a sigh.

Dianna grimaces but says nothing.

"Dianna, this is my grand experiment, to see if I've learned anything about building teams."

"Honey, I'm so happy you're excited," she says as she walks over to me and takes my hand.

"Now, go change your clothes. And take a shower."

I do as I am told.

25

The Fireplace

The house is going up fast, and many evenings Dianna and I wander around the site, always terminating our visit with the same discussion with the same outcome.

"Dianna, that fireplace mantle is just too high. When we stand in this beautiful living room with this incredible wall of windows overlooking the lake, it breaks up the view. We can't see the lake over that damned mantle."

"Don't worry about it, honey. I know what I'm doing. It *has* to be this way—it balances out the room. All my girlfriends agree it's perfect just the way it is. You'll like it when it's done."

"We're making a mistake here."

"It is all about balance, honey. You don't understand. It'll be fine. Trust me."

Later in the construction and after all the windows have been installed, Dianna takes a trip to see our Saudi friends living in Calgary. Ghalib is working on a project there that I'm involved in, too. She's gone for over a week.

I catch Lon the day after she leaves and ask him to get me a quote on what it would cost to lower the mantle, then reframe and replace the windows above it.

"Are you *sure*, John?" He looks at me incredulously. He and I are good friends by now. I just nod, smiling. He laughs nervously.

One week later, the day before Dianna is due home, the mantle has been cut down more than two feet, so anyone but a midget can now see the lake from anywhere in the living room. The new windows have already been installed.

Dianna and I drive out to the house directly from the airport and we walk in. She's in a bubbly mood, telling me all about her visit with Ghalib and Suzy, and how much fun she had, and on and on.

When we walk into the living room, Dianna freezes in mid-sentence when she notices the fireplace.

What happens next is completely predictable, but I don't care. The deed is done. She is in a rage… I have never seen her this angry before. She rips me up one side and down the other, ending her tirade with her coup de grace. "What really makes me soooo angry is, you didn't consult with me, John. (No "honey" for me right now.) You never gave me a chance to discuss it with you. You just ran over me. That really hurts!"

Oh well.

By the next day, she is acting like it never happened.

Several years later, she will say I was right, even in the presence of others. Not surprising this is so easy for her. For one thing, she doesn't need to do it very often.

I guess somehow, the room got balanced.

Whatever that means.

26

Moving In, Moving On

We move into our new house in November 1995. Dianna is thrilled as she methodically sorts through all the boxes, decorating the entire house, room by room, in the months that follow.

I don't do any of this. I don't want to do any of this, and she does not want me to do any of this.

Besides, I am working sixty-to seventy-hour weeks, writing safety and environmental rules, starting from scratch on blank sheets of paper for our unique chemical environment. I also initiate relationships with our plant neighbors and the city fire department so we can coordinate our emergency response efforts (we are spewing out toxic releases and evacuating the plant about once/month but getting better). I contact the Michigan Department of Environmental Quality (MDEQ) and the EPA guys. I know, for things to work, we must create trusting relationships with these agencies by earning them. From that day onward, I religiously tell them the truth, no matter how embarrassing. They are grateful to have someone they can work with—fact is, our goals are intertwined—a profitable company creating jobs, without killing people or destroying the environment.

And I buy wooden file cabinets so I can open and close the drawers.

While things are changing at the plant, things are changing at home, too. Each day I come home to a different house. Dianna lays up wallpaper here, repaints there, and spends countless hours putting up decoupage in creative, understated, and unusual ways. Day by day, Dianna turns our home into a masterpiece of design and beauty. Female guests, especially, coo in low tones, punctuated periodically with exclamations. Of course, she is very proud when this happens. While I am very happy for her, this is fundamentally mysterious to me. I am in my own world anyway.

That being said, I vaguely notice the house has taken on a highly feminine theme. Slowly, I come to realize this is *her* house. I think I could be, if I'm lucky, a welcome guest in it.

"You can stay, honey," she says, laughing, when I point this out to her one day.

Neighbors and friends begin to ask her to decorate their own homes. She expands into painting unfinished furniture, and I quickly see she could easily turn this into a thriving business. She toys with the idea, but continues making each one a gift of love, transforming nondescript pieces into what will become treasured heirlooms with her quirky, interesting designs and color patterns. Love given, love received. I don't push any other idea about it. It will just be one of her legacies.

Dianna continues her love affair with accent lights, which, as far as I am concerned, serve no useful purpose beyond increasing our carbon footprint and electric bills. I cannot seem to cure her of this malady, so they continue to multiply. We also continue our little dance to another chorus in the song of our life together. She turns them on here, there, and everywhere; and a few minutes later, I trail along behind her, turning them off.

"Goddammit, John, I don't want to live in the dark. Besides, I am coming back into this room in just a bit."

"We're wasting energy. Don't you care about the planet at all?" I whine hopelessly. Of course she does…just not *that* much.

"And 'a bit' will range from four hours to tomorrow," I mumble to myself.

Most of the time, I just sulk. At least our house is well accented, whatever value this has for the universe. *Is this what it means to be enlightened?* I wonder. Or, maybe this is about me learning to lighten up? Hmmmm.

Christmas comes quickly and Dianna takes it to a whole new level. As she does every year, she treats this holiday, her favorite, though Halloween comes in a strong second, as a major opportunity to decorate, to create a sense of all that Christmas, and maybe all of life, is about for her.

Another strange footnote to our marriage, I muse. Even as a child, emotionally, Christmas came and went without much mental or emotional fanfare for me. Christ has been gone for 2,000 years, replaced with lots of stuff meaning nothing to me. In my world, God lives as much in the tiny tree swallows skimming the water outside our house each morning as it does in Jesus Christ. Still, he is an amazing model, so worthy of our attention…and worth emulating, too.

But I can also say this about tree swallows.

Dianna swings into action as soon as Halloween is out of the way, beginning like a tiny snowball rolling downhill, turning into an avalanche. First, nonstop Christmas music shows up, all day long, with Dianna singing along. I notice she has a really nice voice, making me wish she would sing more.

She's singing, but she is also pondering her theme for the year—each year must have a well thought-out theme—some years, predominantly purple. For others, it must be in silver or red or gold or.... Some years are more traditional, others lean toward modern, and so it goes.

Of course, there has to be the main Christmas tree in the living room. I notice it must be copulating somehow, because satellite trees start popping up in almost every room of the house, some tiny, some not. She creates one from scratch that I really do admire.

Then comes the gathering of nieces, as the cookie factory swings into action, and the house becomes saturated with scents of gingerbread and sugar cookies.

Most of all, Christmas, for me, is just the way *she* is, a sparkling childlike spirit many of us abandon somewhere along the line, the gift of embracing the excitement and anticipation of an imagined mood made real. That I'm just about the opposite of all this doesn't dampen my appreciation for all she does. Her energy is, despite my nonchalance, like an infection that won't go away. All of this is just…lovely, that female word no self-respecting man ever uses.

Our first Christmas in our new home gains a special notoriety.

Dianna sizes up the twenty-five-foot ceiling in the living room, sees the drama potential, and sets out to "find the right tree."

I should be paying more attention to this.

One night, she bursts through the door with a "Hi, honeeee," breathless, the way I imagine a six-year-old running down the stairs on Christmas morning.

"Oh, John, I have our tree! It's out in the van. Can you help me bring it in?"

The wind is blowing hard and a few huge snowflakes are twisting in the air. It's already dark, so I bring along a flashlight to see our first Christmas tree for our new home that, itself, still smells new.

When I get to the van, I can't believe my eyes. "Jesus!" I say, but not really in the spirit of the season.

The tree is sticking out about eight feet past the rear doors, tied in place so it wouldn't flap in the wind. It's not hard for me to imagine the six men who loaded it, snickering quietly at whoever is lucky enough to be at the other end of this trip.

This would be me.

The trunk is at least ten inches in diameter. I drag it out of the van because it's far too heavy to lift. I can barely pick up the bottom end of it. I'm getting more steamed by the second.

"Honey, there's not a tree stand on the planet that can hold this…this… monster. It probably weighs 200 pounds…and look how thick it is—what do we put it in—a fifty-five gallon drum, for God's sake?"

"Well…, I'll help you," she says, her voice shrinking.

"Dianna, we can't even get this through the front door." I'm staring at it, wondering what to do.

"Where did you find a tree this big?"

She shifts from one foot to the other and squeezes her hands deeper into her coat pockets. The wind is blowing her hair across her face.

"I special ordered it," she says, her voice getting smaller still.

"What did this thing cost, anyway? Did we have to take out a second mortgage?"

Dianna doesn't answer. The wind is picking up even more now, and the temperature is dropping by the minute. I notice the snow getting heavier, slanting down through the porch lights. She stands there silently, her feet close together now, looking cold.

"Why don't you go inside. I'll do the surgery here."

She does. I do.

After cutting off the bottom trunk three times, slicing six feet off the height and about a hundred pounds off the weight, I finally squeeze it through the front door. By this time I'm really pissed. It takes many swear words for me to finally get it up and in place. Dianna is quiet, contrite. But within minutes, she cannot contain her joy at seeing *her* tree standing in *her* living room.

"Oh, honey, I just love it. I… just… love it. Thank you so much." She gives me a huge hug. She doesn't seem to mind that the tree doesn't come close to reaching the ceiling anymore.

This is the last year we will buy a real tree.

I take her shopping after the holidays, and she finds the artificial tree of her dreams—tall, narrow—and of my dreams—weighs maybe ten pounds and it breaks down into pieces.

This works for her. She can now handle all the decorating for Christmas on her own—and she likes it that way. This works for me for all the same reasons.

Peace and Joy of the season have been restored.

Hi, Honeeee

When I come home and walk through the door, no matter what Dianna is doing, her whole body turns toward me, her face lights up, and I am greeted with an enthusiastic, booming, high-pitched "Hi, honeeee" that proclaims in a single breath how glad she is I am alive and well and home again, and how her life has suddenly been made complete because I am there with her, and there is no one else she would rather be with—the very same feeling I had the first time she showed up at my door so many years ago.

She actually *sees* me. She is *present* to me. Still. After all these years.

My mood, even my consciousness, shifts to another level, enveloped in appreciation, acknowledgment, love, vaporizing my normal illusion of separateness, at least for this brief moment in time and space.

If "Hi, honeeee" could be translated, it would tell a story about this woman we would want to tell our children and grandchildren.

Greetings are vastly underrated and mostly ignored.

I was unaware of this until I met Dianna.

Sometimes I wonder why this simple act of being fully present to another being can be that hard for any of us to do. Yet, somehow, it is. So, each day, most of us endure so many missed opportunities to be alive, to light each other up, to lighten up.

I am one of the lucky ones.

One day, I realize Dianna is this way with everyone, not just me.

Dammit, I think…smiling.

Tongue in Cheek

I don't know whether she read somewhere what it means to be "tongue in cheek" or not.

I doubt it.

Still, she does it to perfection. With regard to this particular habit, she is a lovable cliché.

Whenever she is up to something, designing a way to put one over on me, or concocting a way to get back at me for something I had put over on her (which is easy), she invariably gives it away by poking her tongue into one cheek accompanied by an ever so faint smirk. Her eyes narrow a little, too. Pathetically transparent and a dead giveaway.

I know she does not realize this, which makes it all the more delectable. And I wind up laughing before I know what I should be laughing about.

Her practical jokes are always innocent and harmless, but sometimes unpredictable and creative...and at other times, unconscionably predictable.

Whenever we go out to eat somewhere, she almost always brings home a doggie bag, puts it in the refrigerator with great anticipation of a later treasured snack; and most of the time—but, very importantly, *not always*—I sneak-eat almost all of it, carefully leaving a single bite for her. No matter where I am in the house, I always know when she discovers this.

"Dammit, John!"

One evening, I bring home some leftovers. The next day, as I am going to the refrigerator to retrieve it, she is hovering nearby, watching me, *tongue in cheek*, eagerly anticipating "my surprise."

So, I already know it's gone and start laughing so hard I have to lean on the counter. She puts her hands on her hips and her chin pops out a little.

"Well...I'm still glad I ate it."

27

The Dog from Hell

"Oh, honey, I think we should take this one!" she says, laughing. She's sitting on the floor, holding a wiggling golden retriever puppy. He escapes and scampers across the room.

"Damn. My feelings are hurt. He won't stay with me," she moans, speaking into the camcorder and crawling on her hands and knees after him while I follow her with the camera, laughing.

I'm as excited as she is—a major event is taking place in our lives, and we both know it. It has been almost two years since we lost Breaker and we are settled into our new home. One day, I tell Dianna I'm ready for another dog, which means another golden retriever. I have had no other breed for twenty-five years—the personality fit is perfect; and if carefully selected, they make great hunting dogs, too.

This breed fits Dianna's personality as well. She fell in love with Breaker and feels ready for another dog, too. We both willingly ignore the deadly combination of white carpets, a yard of mud-not-yet-grass landscaping, and the wet spring ahead, not to mention housebreaking a dog in winter.

But we want—no, we need—a dog.

On New Year's Eve, 1995, we drive to Illinois to meet the breeder I've selected—good hunting lines. What I haven't told Dianna is that I have already been forewarned.

"These will be good hunting dogs," the breeder had told me, "But I absolutely promise you, they will be a handful—both parents are quite spicy. So these dogs are not for everyone. You'll need to know how to handle them."

This just excites me. I love a high-spirited dog with good potential for pheasant and grouse hunting. What's the problem?

On the way home, driving through Chicago, our new puppy in Dianna's lap, we debate what to name him. I see a billboard along the expressway advertising the Nutcracker Suite.

"Why don't we name him Cracker—like the sound of that," I say.

"I like that. What about Honey Graham Cracker," she says, laughing. "He's that color. And sweet, too." So we use the full name for his papers, but he will always be Cracker in life.

Firecracker would have been another choice.

As winter wears on, I do all the dog training, but Dianna is home with him all day while I'm at work. She knows nothing about training and, in any case, is not designed that way. She has the same philosophy about it as she does about watering house plants—do it whenever she happens to think about it and feels like she has the time, which is occasionally.

Besides, her voice is higher pitched than mine.

A pattern emerges. When I come home from work, Dianna is often lying across the bed, eyes red, bemoaning his unwillingness to listen, the hem of her white robe increasingly shredded, while myriad cuts keep multiplying on her hands from Cracker's young, needle-like teeth.

The order of our little pack is I'm alpha, Cracker is beta, and Dianna is somewhere around omega. She loves Cracker, wants Cracker; but Cracker is, for her, uncontrollable.

I have created a monster.

When family and friends come to visit, they see all this. Pat, Dianna's mom, never short on opinions, sees her daughter being abused and presses us to get rid of this devil. She labels him "The dog from hell." It sticks.

Dianna defends him with jokes, unwilling to give up.

I have no trouble with Cracker. He is full of energy, and I see early signs he will be a great hunting dog—he attacks a muskrat when he is three months old, comes back to me bleeding, then turns around and goes after the muskrat again. That kind of desire can't be trained into a dog. They either have it or they don't.

One Sunday in late winter, I come to a wrenching decision. Dianna isn't winning. Much as I hate to do it, I decide I must find a new home for Cracker. I tell Dianna I know this guy in town who would love to have a good hunting dog, and I'm going to call him right now. I pick up the phone, serious about this decision, painful as it's going to be.

"No, no, no, honey…please. Don't do this. John, I don't want to give him away. I will work it out…, please. Please don't."

I don't know if she reacts this way because she knows I love him and might resent her later, or whether it is about her unwillingness to give up, to concede defeat. I'll go with the latter.

So we keep him.

We have levers instead of knobs on our doors and, as time goes by, Cracker learns how to open every door in the house, whether he has to pull it toward him or push on it. He even figures out how to open the sliding window on our van. Eventually, he picks up another nickname, Houdini.

As Cracker gets older, things level out; and it seems he and Dianna reach a truce of sorts. But he is still much more my dog than Dianna's.

Each day, when I come through the door, as reliably as day follows night, he greets me with an explosion of joy. When I announce it's time to go, his head tilts, ears popping up to attention, as he strives to understand. When he sees the right clothes coming on, he knows for sure and dances with anticipation. Each day, we head out into the wind and light to find some new fraction of nature we didn't see yesterday.

One winter Sunday morning, while a deep-red sun squeezes into the gray predawn sky, we cross the entire lake in silence. This light is thin, faintly blue, and I don't notice how punky the ice is close to shore. We both break through. I instantly reach down and scoop him up like a loose football and shove him up on good ice, then clamber up after him. We both walk home wet, but alive, satisfied and a bit better educated.

Life is good.

28

Life on the Lake

From the day we move into our home on Lake Loch Erin, life takes on a flow that is everything we thought and hoped it would be...vacations without traveling anywhere, friends and family coming to have fun on the lake with us, Dianna making tons of new friends and playing with her house. Me working.

Dianna, coffee cup in hand, enrolls the entire neighborhood into being a neighborhood. As the years go by, she initiates annual pig roasts where neighbors, shy or not, come together to enjoy a beer and get to know one another. One year, they secretly create a little ceremony, crowning Dianna queen for the day. She sucks up all this attention like a sponge and reflects it back to them in equal measure. People love being around her. She knits the neighborhood into a quilt of valued relationships.

Of course, I come to the pig roasts, too. It's like taking a bath in good feelings. I like pork, anyway.

Halloweens are pathetic, though.

Dianna goes all out. The entire house shifts into orange, white, and black, complete with pumpkins, ghosts, witches, and even orange-and-black cookies produced by enrolling her nieces in baking parties. We scour the countryside for not just one but three, four, or five pumpkins. Bigger is better, carve them, and put them at the front door, complete with candles inside.

And each year, Dianna wears some sort of outfit to amplify the season, purchases several pounds of candy, turns the porch light on, and patiently waits, facing the door.

Most years, zero kids show up. Once in a blue moon, a couple.

We don't have any kids in our sub, and apparently no one thinks to import them. Our little point of land is isolated and out of the way for people. So, each year, Dianna does it all over again, always with the same outcome.

This annual debacle reminds me of seagulls.

So we end up eating all the candy ourselves, satisfying my own candy quota for another year. I also start getting smarter, buying candy useful for our annual deer hunting trip in mid-November.

"Honey?" I say.

I am sitting with her near the front door to keep her company while we wait for the kids who never show up.

"What?"

"Why don't we start giving out ice cream for Halloween?" We both love ice cream.

She turns to me, a blank look on her face.

"That won't work," she says finally, then is quiet for a moment. "What do you mean? How could we do that?"

I start laughing and she gets it, waving her hand at me like shooing me away, then starts laughing, embarrassed she has been taken in, but enjoying the image of it. She shifts in her chair while looking back toward the door. No little faces on the other side.

"We probably should, dammit. The little shits never come to our house anyway." She laughs from deep within herself.

She stands up, goes over to the door, steps outside and takes a last look around, flips off the porch light, then slowly, gently closes the door, walks into the kitchen, and unceremoniously dumps the plastic pumpkin full of candy bars into a Ziplock bag.

"I got dibs on the Milky Ways," she says matter of factly, shoving the bag high up into the cupboard. Like, maybe, I'm not going to be able to reach them there.

Later that evening, I slip into the kitchen, take all the Milky Way bars out of the bag and hide them. A few days later, as I walk through the doorway, home from work, she flagrantly waves a half-eaten Milky Way bar past my face. I'm not surprised. Hiding sweets from Dianna is about as hopeless as hiding a five-day-old piece of spoiling meat from Cracker on the floor of a five-foot-by-five-foot empty room.

Her annual vigil for kids who never come may be silly in one sense, even sad in another, but it's inspiring for me. Her spirit remains unscathed, her optimism undeterred, the past irrelevant, the future always new, while she sits by the door each year, waiting.

She just keeps on *showing up*, doing her part no matter what.

I love her all the more for it even as I relentlessly ridicule her. I would not change this quality about Dianna for the world.

Christmas is always an unmitigated winner, though. Some years, together with other ladies of the neighborhood, Dianna organizes a traveling Christmas party, going house to house, spending an hour or so at each one for cheese and crackers, or cookies, or brownies with spiced apple cider. It is a gentle way to celebrate.

By the time the Fourth of July annual boat parade, organized by the lake owners association, comes around, Dianna has on her game face. During each parade, usually about thirty boats, a panel of judges chooses the most creatively decorated boat. Each year, a general theme for the parade is selected in midwinter. Dianna starts plotting right away, spending months coming up with an idea, creating a design, discussing it with co-conspirators in her family, mostly her mom, then finally collects the needed materials. A day or two before the parade, her family descends upon us. It is a party/project with Dianna as CEO. Just as she did with her "barn loft apartment" so many years ago, she commandeers her entire family to help her decorate our twenty-five-foot pontoon boat, then perform as a dutiful supporting cast during the parade.

I tease her about how silly this all is. She completely ignores me, focused like a laser beam on winning.

In 1996 she dresses herself up in a lavish blue-green sari-type outfit and stands at the bow of the boat as the Statue of Liberty, holding high a huge gold torch made of shiny golden plastic throughout the hour-long parade, her other arm held out in a magnanimous welcoming gesture. Loud cheers ripple along the shore as she passes, and there is sustained clapping at the judges stand. Although she is feeling under the weather and her health is, once again, in turmoil, she is beaming.

She wins.

She wins the next year, too. When she does not win for the third year, there is no doubt in her mind that her idea and execution were the best. She mentions this with a little sniff, confident the judges were obviously obligated to choose someone else to avoid dampening enthusiasm for the competition. Maybe this is for the best, she says, finally, with equanimity, then drops it and moves on.

The best part of the Fourth of July, as far as I am concerned, is the fireworks that start up slowly at sunset, building to a crescendo after dark and not dying off completely until past midnight. Like many other residents, we take our boat into open water, shut off our motors, and just sit, watching the surprisingly professional-quality fireworks go up into a starry sky from all directions. Some people must be spending thousands of dollars, because the displays are spectacular.

What could be better than drinking a nice glass of wine while leaning back into cushy seats on a warm summer night, listening to people oooh and aaah in the distance, the kaleidoscope of colors filling the sky and booming across the water, petting Cracker while having a smoke, and watching Dianna take it all in, each time, as if it is for the first and only time?

When the fireworks die off and the night begins to cool, I put my jacket over Dianna's shoulders, slip my arm around her, and slowly motor back, coast up to the dock, and tie off for the night.

The very best of summer on the lake, though, are sunset boat rides. Even if I drag in late from work, we often grab a bottle of red wine, cheese and crackers, and hurry down to our boat gently rocking at our dock fifty feet from our house. Cracker jumps in ahead of us and instantly begins scouting out spiders scurrying for cover. There are plenty of them. Within minutes, he eats every last one unable to escape, and we are spider-free. This makes Dianna both happy and repulsed. "How can he do that?"

I'm just surprised he finds them so tasty...or something. He is a great hunting dog, so I can only chalk it up to "well, if it moves, I should get it if I can" prey drive.

Once underway, he always does the same thing. Trots up to the very front of the boat, climbs up on the back of the seat and sits kind of side-saddle, one leg hanging down loosely. Up as high as he can get, he settles in for the ride with a good view of everything going on, excited by passing wildlife or an occasional dog on shore, his nose constantly twitching, taking in the infinite patterns of scent we are cutting through as we traverse the lake. But, mostly, he is doing, I think, just what we are doing, enjoying the ineffable sensation of being washed in a warm summer breeze.

Sunsets on the lake are beautiful, every one the only one, just like this one. Best of all is the quiet, with only the low drone of our motor as we barely cut through the water, following the eleven miles of shoreline, in and out of coves and bays, around islands and across stretches of open water. Especially during the week, we are often alone on the lake, joined only by an occasional blue heron, and a scattering of geese and ducks coasting slowly to their nightly resting places while the sun dies into the horizon. If we are lucky, the sun slides through stratus clouds on its way into the western tree line, creating exquisite patterns of yellows, oranges, reds, and finally, purples, as the day slowly dissolves. In Michigan, in midsummer, twilights go on forever. And even after forever, a ghost light with purple traces lingers longer still before reluctantly dissolving into darkness.

"This is such a healing place for me, honey," she says, a barely breeze pushing a wisp of hair across her face.

I silently agree. If we are listening, silence is all we really need to understand everything.

29

Rain

Day is breaking.

Thunder is rippling in the distance and closing in, ragged streaks of lightning crackling across an early morning sky, rolling clouds tumbling over each other on their way to here and somewhere.

Mourning doves. Someone named them well. I hear them mostly in the stillness of early morning, calling, sounding hollow and mournful, a *coo-ahh* followed by *coo-coo-coo*. The first note sounds pleading, begging for attention, and the last three like a longing for love lost. At a distance, the c's are not audible, more like *ooh-ah*, *who-who-who*, even more melancholy, southern Michigan's delicate echoing of loons further north.

Dianna is sleeping. I want to kiss her, but she looks so peaceful I settle for gently adjusting the quilt covering her, then quietly slip away, leaving her to her dreams.

I look outside again. The rain is sliding down the windows, streaks of light against the lightening dark, the wind whirring past the house.

Cracker and I look at each other. We have the same idea. It's light enough to go.

As we head down a straight-as-an-arrow, canopied trail, the rain changes its mind and gradually shifts from quiet steady to coming down in sheets. I can barely see twenty yards in front of me. Soon enough, water is sloshing in my boots.

Every now and then, Cracker looks back at me, shakes hard, throwing water out of his fur, fluffing his coat, reconstituting his insulation, then moves on, sniffing here, sniffing there, checking out our piece of the planet.

Good idea. What else is there to do?

It occurs to me, Dianna does the same thing. When the rain comes down heavy in her life, she shakes it out, reestablishes her "insulation"— her heart, her courage, her optimism, her faith…and moves on with the business of daily living.

As for me, it's different. Rain draws me into my natural melancholy, a feeling I love to traffic in…maybe more in touch with my own feelings, my own heart, my own source?

All I know is, I love it.

Rain.

Being in it.

Being.

Part III
The Grace of Letting Go
1996-2000

30

Another Bump in the Road

In March 1996 Dianna notices a lump almost under her right arm, at the outer edge of her right breast.

"Oh, John, I don't know what this is...."

We head back up to Midland to see Dr. Sanislaw. She is more comfortable with doctors she knows. Another biopsy is done.

It is a very small tumor, only five millimeters.

It is malignant.

Sitting in Sanislaw's office, Dianna's shoulders slump when he tells us the results. Her mouth turns down and a tear slides silently down her cheek. I don't know what to think. After almost five years, I thought we were out of the woods. Dianna, too. It is a crushing disappointment.

Inexplicably, it's a totally different type of breast cancer—classified as stage II, it is ER/PR positive whereas the first breast cancer was ER/PR negative—but, at least, there are no lymph nodes involved. Still, it is confusing and disheartening.

"There is no hurry on this," he says very deliberately. "You might want to get a second opinion and take some time to think about what you want to do."

March slides into April. The ice has gone out early this year, and the wind is whipping the lake into whitecaps, flashing white flecks in the dying light. The house is shuttering, and the aspen I had transplanted from up north, still leafless, are rocking in the wind. It feels safe inside, watching it from the warm side of our windows.

I turn away from the window and sit down across from Dianna in our living room. Even with floor-to-ceiling windows it won't be long before we will not be able to see each other as day fades into night.

"Want me to turn on all your little lights?" I ask brightly. She looks preoccupied.

"I think I want to have both breasts removed. What do you think, honey?" Her face looks calm, and she says this without any emotion I can detect.

She is sitting up straight, perched on the edge of the couch, her hands folded in her lap. She looks like a prim school teacher asking me about my lesson. Maybe she's watching for my reaction. She already knows what my words will be.

"I think that's a good decision, sweetheart," I say without hesitation. I've been thinking the same thing, but wasn't going to say it. What that old doctor told us back in 1990, when we were seeking a second opinion then, has been haunting me.

Still, I'm shocked to hear her say it. Another surprise.

"Well, it seems like the best thing to do," she says, sinking back into the couch with a sigh, her hands still folded in her lap.

We fall into silence, listening to the wind roaring outside. The house creaks now and then. I don't want to say anything right now.

"There's a good side to it, though," she says softly.

"What's that, sweetheart?"

"Well, if I get them removed, at least I won't need chemo or radiation."

She is quiet again, falling back into her thoughts.

"Nothing left to radiate," she says finally. Her face is still expressionless. Then the corners of her mouth turn up a little, and I can just make out her eyes opening, brightening.

"And since the lumpectomy, my breasts have been lopsided. I can have reconstruction and have two new evenly balanced ones," she says, talking faster now. She straightens up, perks up even more, then stands up straight and walks over to the window. She stares out into the darkness for a couple of minutes.

"So…that's a good thing, too," she says finally; but there is a sadness there, a softening and a wistfulness to her voice.

I feel my throat lumping up.

"Well, good point, honey. Hadn't thought of it that way."

I walk over and, standing behind her, wrap my arms around her waist and hold her close to me. I kiss her neck. I am in wonder.

"Just another bump in the road, honey," I whisper.

"Just another bump in the road," she says, putting her arms over mine and pressing hard.

She never does turn her accent lights on.

Before long, we go to bed. She seems to be drifting off, and after reading awhile, I turn out my light. I am starting to fall asleep with my arm around her when she turns over to face toward me. "Will you still think I am attractive? That I'm still a woman?"

I am totally awake now.

I reach over to flip the light back on. I want to see her face, and I want her to see mine. I look her in the eye.

"If I've told you once, I've told you a million times, I married you for your elbows, not your breasts," I say as I pull her close to me. She lets out a little laugh, then starts crying silently. There are tears in my eyes, too, but she isn't going to see them. She has enough of her own right now.

"It just seems like the best thing to do. If I don't, what's next? I want to get rid of this constant worry. I want a *cure*. This seems like my best chance to get one. Do you agree?"

"I do agree, honey. I want *you*. Here. With or without your breasts. I want what you want. This is not complicated for me." She holds onto me even tighter.

It takes awhile to handle all the logistics, because she has opted to have both the breast removal and initial reconstruction done in the same surgery. So there are meetings with the plastic surgeon, and he has to coordinate with Sanislow, who will do the mastectomies.

She chooses saline-filled implants. Too much controversy about silicone.

July 16, 1996

Because the operation is going to take place in Midland, and we no longer live there, Dianna and I are staying with Marji and her husband Scott, who have kindly offered their home as a base of operations. My sister Elena, an experienced and accomplished nurse, shows up to help. She works with Dianna, using visualization and relaxation techniques. It definitely puts Dianna in a better frame of mind.

Early the next morning, we all head over to the hospital. Dianna appears calm, but I know better.

"I love you so much, sweetheart. It'll all be over soon. We're going to be fine," I say, as we wait, her lying in a hospital bed now.

"I know," she says. I lean down and smother her in a long hug.

They wheel her away to the operating room. When she disappears, I turn toward my sister. She sees the look on my face and wraps her arms around me. I fall apart. I have not cried this hard since the night my dad died. I feel so helpless. This is something I just can't fix. It's a devastating feeling.

There is nothing to do but wait.

Dianna comes out of the surgery and I track her down in a recovery room. It is past midday and light is filling up the room, making everything glossy looking. I do like that the Midland hospital is immaculately clean.

She is still completely out. Everyone decides to go down to the cafeteria for a late lunch and to help keep the room quiet. I decide to sit by the bed and wait. I'm thinking, why poison myself with hospital food? Besides, I want to be here when she opens her eyes.

When she finally does, she is dopey, but still in reasonably good spirits, her pain dulled with drugs. Most of all, she's glad it's over.

Within days, though she is pretty sore and still low on energy, she is buoyed by a feeling of new beginnings, the prospect of her new breasts, and her firm conviction that, finally, she has paid the price to be cured. My sense is she has regained trust in her own body.

Over the next two years, Dianna has several surgeries, each one followed by often painful recoveries to complete the reconstruction process, periods of "discomfort," as Dianna is now referring to it—she's talking like the doctors, now. Well, this is bullshit to me. I know pain when I see it. But I keep my mouth shut.

Finally, she has new breasts, but no nipples yet. Nevertheless, she is very proud of them and makes sure all her female friends get a peek, and they reliably coo their reassuring appraisals. Well, she should be proud. She's earned them.

As for me, to be honest, I prefer her old ones. Well, she undoubtedly does, too, but I never hear her say so. She doesn't know how to go backwards. As with everything else, she's always looking forward with optimism, refusing to waste energy lamenting the past or what might have been. Just does not do it.

Even before the fluid-drain tubes are pulled, she bounces back to the Dianna everyone has always known, only more so.

"I think this has turned out really well, don't you think, honey?" she asks.

I have been taking home videos throughout our life together and am behind the camera now as she speaks. When I look back at the videos periodically, I am still amazed at her attitude and demeanor. You would have thought she had just returned from a cruise instead of a series of major surgeries to remove parts of her body, the parts she always felt were "her best feature."

"Absolutely," I say. "Want to get a shot of them for posterity?"

"We aren't doing a porn film here," she says, laughing.

Her eyes are alive with the sound of her voice, sparkling in the bright sunlight of this day. Being with her now, I have to believe, even better days are ahead.

Hummingbirds

We are out in the yard, weeding. Dianna, wearing a flamboyant straw hat with a huge floppy brim, takes the north side of the house—her side—and I take the south side, the wild side, shaded by a cluster of aspen I transplanted from prime up-north grouse habitat. She likes to sit on the little bench I bought her and drill in on each area, pulling every single tiny teensy weed. I am more like a cruise missile, ripping out the big stuff without sweating the small stuff.

Her side always looks better than mine, and over time she disowns my side completely. "Well, if you want it to look like that, you take care of it."

"You like it wild-looking, and I like it looking neat and in order, the way it should look," she says to me, her chin up just a little, as we head off, each to our own side to work.

I feel no judgment in her comment and no desire to copy her way of doing things, either. We just divide up the work and do things in our own way in our own time. Our whole marriage is like this, I muse to myself.

Once in awhile, we take a break and sit together, maybe splitting a beer while cooling off, grateful for the reliable breeze blowing in off the lake. Mosquitoes are not a problem as long as the wind blows, which out on this point is almost always.

This day, I decide it's time for a break, grab a beer and come over to her side, offering her a swig. We are both sweaty but content. The air is cool and the sun is warm. Suddenly, Dianna jumps up, beer in hand, almost spilling it, and stares off toward a flower patch between us and the lake.

"Honey, look at *that*. Look! Quick!" She points, handing me back the beer without looking my way.

"Oh, honey, look…look…there…over there…. See it?"

126

"Yep. Ruby-throated hummingbird."

"Oh, John, I've been hoping and praying they would come. This is the first time I have ever seen one in our yard." She puts her hands on her hips, a look of triumph smeared across her face.

"Finally," she says.

"Yeah. First time I've seen one here, too."

We stand still, watching it flitting from flower to flower, hovering as it reaches into one flower, backing up, then darting off to the next one. Dianna turns, then throws her arms around me.

"Oh, they are my favorite, favorite bird. I planted all these flowers, hoping. I have been hoping and hoping one day they would come."

Well, she does better with hummingbirds than seagulls, I'm thinking, but I don't say this.

"Sweetheart, I'm proud of you—you've won them over to our yard—to *your* side anyway."

"I am so happy."

You'd think she'd won the lottery.

As I am walking back to my side, it occurs to me: she is a lot like a hummingbird herself. She gets her life done in fast forward, darting from one person to another, hovering over each one, accepting their love, nourished by it, while, at the same time, pollinating each person with her love, joy, and optimism, like a key fitting into a lock, then suddenly darting on to the next one.

Symbiosis.

Magic in the air.

The dance of her life.

In the years to come, hummingbirds will reliably show up on her side... just as she believed they would.

31

Wallpapering

Dianna is in the kitchen on the phone with Marji. I'm lying on the bed, reading. I can hear her voice going up in pitch, then quiet, then exploding in full-throated laughter.

"You are?" I hear her say, then "When?," then, "Can I help?" like a child pleading with a friend, "Can I come play with you?" …tentative, hopeful, anticipating, dipping deeply into the holy grail of friendship.

I close my book.

Dianna gets off the phone, shoots past me and into the bathroom. As she scurries around, I lay my book down and just watch her.

"Honey, I'm going up to Marji's…. She's getting ready to wallpaper her bathroom…. I'm going to help her."

"Well…ah…fine. But that's a three-hour drive, Dianna. You really want to wallpaper that badly?"

She ignores me or doesn't hear me.

"Why don't you wallpaper our bathroom?" I say, laughing.

"Again," I cannot resist adding.

"Oh, John, you don't understand," she says, dismissing my little darts as she shoves her clothes and makeup case into an overnight bag.

"It'll be such fun."

She is right somehow. It will be fun for her. Must be like having lunch together or something.

On one hand, I am just as likely to drive three hours one way to wallpaper a bathroom as I am to pull seven perfectly good teeth out of my own mouth with a pair of pliers. On the other hand, I know joy when I see it; and I am looking straight into it as she gives me a kiss goodbye thirty minutes later. She gives me a last quick hug then, with her purse slung over her shoulder, an overnight bag in one hand and coffee cup in the other, she stuffs everything into *her* car and climbs in.

"See you soon, honey," she yells out the window as she backs out of the garage. I wave back, yelling for her to be careful.

Then, she is gone. Cracker and I are left staring into the half-empty garage.

I don't see her again for a week.

The bathroom leads to other projects, helping decorate for a shower with another friend, Linda Muller, many lunches, talk sessions, and who knows what else women do when they do what they do.

How do I feel about all this?

Great.

When she's happy, I'm happy. As for myself, I'm not the least bit lonely. I enjoy the quiet. I also notice Cracker seems calmer. Shows how energy flows in "the pack."

And I am beginning to dimly appreciate what I see going on with Dianna and her friends…their "pack."

What I notice is women, at least the women who have gathered around Dianna, those she has drawn close to her, are an amazing support system, which men are probably not psychologically organized to understand, much less duplicate.

Whenever Dianna needs them most, without being told, with no request being made, one or two or four of them magically appear. When she is in trouble, they know it and they show up for her. They know when to commiserate and they know when to take her out of it and go have fun—Kathy Preston just appearing, uninvited, during a critical hospital appointment; Chris Fowler driving those same three hours to our house, her gardening gloves and tools in tow, to pot flowers or weed Dianna's side of the yard (I have to do my own, dammit); or Sandy Johnson showing up to take Dianna to their Monday night meeting or out to lunch; or…another book could easily be assembled here.

The other side of all this is, of course, when they need "wallpapering" done, or a Christmas tree decorated, or…just need to have some bright, shiny energy injected into their lives, Dianna shows up for them, too. Most of all, she brings herself to every gathering, and that seems to be all anyone really wants from her…and they reliably get it. She inoculates them with a naked and innocent optimism.

I try to think of a time when Dianna said no to an opportunity.

Maybe she has, but none come to mind.

Not too long ago, I remember Kathy thanking me for "letting" Dianna spend time with her friends, many of them single and alone, and how grateful they all are she can be married but still be with them whenever they need her.

I reflect on the idea of "letting" Dianna do anything. Not part of either our lexicon or our relationship. I would sooner cut off my arm than attempt to stop her from seeing family or friends or do whatever she believes she wants or needs to do. Most of all, I revel in the experience of Dianna being Dianna.

It suddenly occurs to me there has not been a single moment in my life with her that I have sensed she feels any differently about me. It feels like being in a state of grace to be both fully committed and fully free.

Standing in the garage doorway, I notice the wind is steady and strong enough to keep mosquitoes confused. Good time for a long walk with Cracker on a trail I normally avoid on windless days.

Soon enough, the garage is completely empty.

32

Dianna Comes to Work

Throughout the mid-to-late nineties, work is huge in my life. So much to do and still working fifty to sixty hours a week, but our progress is remarkable.

Each day, I cruise through the plant, looking for problems; but even more, creating relationships, kibitzing about hunting, fishing, politics, life, our own lives…and listening. Everyone soon knows about Dianna, what she is going through, and are keenly sympathetic.

In the first of my annual employee surveys, in 1994, when I asked the question, "How many injuries should a safe employee have annually." I get answers like four, six, eight, and as many as it takes (wise guys).

When going over that first survey, I introduce them to a radical concept. There is only one right answer—zero—for each and every one of them.

Shocked, they laugh at my ridiculous expectations. But as the years go by, as we improve plant safety, as we spend real money–thanks to a committed management–to correct deficiencies, as we discipline violators, as supervisors are pinned to the wall when their example is lacking, attitudes slowly begin to change and so does our performance.

The routine chemical releases and plant evacuations begin to dwindle until they are rare. Pride and hopefulness begin to replace resignation and hopelessness.

The culture is changing.

One day, I realize it's time to spruce up the old mobile trailer/lunchroom parked outside the plant. I get permission to use Dianna as our unpaid designer/contractor, and she jumps at the chance to come up with a plan within our budget and implement it.

Excited, she tours local stores, picking out new flooring, paint for the walls, new tables and chairs, puts up curtains herself, and turns the rickety mobile trailer into a stylish, fun café, making many friends in the process, endearing herself to everyone.

So, she sprinkles her fairy dust over my work world, too. My job just got easier.

33

Saudi Arabian Adventure

In 1996, while working at the plant, I'm also finishing a team-building consulting project that began in 1994 for our dear friend, Ghalib Alwan, a project manager with ARAMCO, the Saudi Arabian Oil Company. He and his beautiful (inside and out) Saudi wife, Suzy, a pediatrician, have been Dianna's close friends from their days in college at CMU, long before I met her.

Ghalib is managing a huge, multimillion dollar project for the design and construction of oil processing improvements in Saudi Arabia and overseeing the design work in Calgary, Boston, and Virginia. What he needs from me is help improving cooperation and coordination between these far-flung contractors, each with their own design systems and business cultures, each with employees drawn from numerous nationalities and experience levels.

I feel very comfortable with this array of people, being an engineer myself and having been a project manager for the construction of chemical plants while at Dow. I have a good sense of where engineers come from. I start my team-building workshops by discussing my own background, gaining instant respect. I'm one of them. I'm not there to "fix" them.

I make several trips to each work location and find the people to be excellently trained and motivated. All we need are effective organizational interfaces, which, over time, we accomplish. I cap off the project with a visit to the construction sites in Saudi Arabia where the challenge is to create trust and cooperation between the mostly non-Saudi contractors and the mostly Saudi plant personnel, so technology can be safely and effectively transferred. With Ghalib's superb acumen and lots of hard work from the entire team, the project is a huge success.

Naturally, native Saudis experience their homeland as routine. I, on the other hand, disappear into an exotic parallel reality the instant my plane lands in Dhahran, completely enchanted by the explosion of vegetation, their unfamiliar scents more intoxicating than alcohol flooding the heavy, humid air, men and women silently floating by in long robes, the endless scorching desert surrounding Abqaiq, and the salty, bathwater-warm Persian Gulf. I love being here. I only wish Dianna could be, too—she would so deeply appreciate the richness here, especially with Ghalib on one arm and Suzy on the other.

The work at both the Michigan plant and ARAMCO provide me with opportunities to see if I have learned anything useful, anything that might make a difference for people, for producing results.

Work is also an emotional life preserver when things are going south with Dianna's health.

Enough for me, right now.

34

Some Valentine's Days are Better than Others

It is Valentine's Day, 1998.

I pick out a funny card and some flowers—yellow roses, her favorite. Like most women, she loves flowers. And like most men, I figure if she likes them, fine, get them—then I don't have to think too much.

I lay them on the bed while she is showering.

I have agreed to take her out to dinner, which excites her more than I can fully understand, but doesn't matter if I understand. Enough that she is happy. Going out to eat has always seemed a waste of money and time to me, probably due to my upbringing. In our immigrant family, going out to dinner was an alien activity. For entertainment, we visited family, or family visited us. That's it.

I'm already dressed when she steps out of the shower, turns toward me, still dripping, with a look on her face I'm not expecting. She lowers the towel around her, exposing her breasts.

"Honey, come here for a minute. Feel this," she says slowly, deliberately. She guides my hand along her left collarbone and slightly down, almost underneath it. I can feel what she feels, a small, hard lump.

"Do you feel it?"

"I do."

"What do you think?"

"Well…, it's probably nothing to worry about. But I know you're going to worry about it. Why don't we just get it checked out…, so you can stop worrying about it."

She sags into me, dropping her towel. I grab another one off the counter and wrap it around her back, then pull her close for a timeless couple of minutes, her wet skin drying on my shirt. I'm not thinking anything, just wrapping her up as warmly as I can and letting this time be whatever it is.

"I'm so angry, John."

"We don't know if you have anything to be angry about, honey."

"Well, just in case then."

I laugh. She doesn't, managing only a weak, crooked smile.

Back we go to Midland to get the lump biopsied by Dr. Sanislaw, who by this time, in spite of himself, has real affection for Dianna. My sense is he is taken with her sunny disposition and courage. For all his gruffness and sometimes surliness, he is a big man with a big heart. After all this time, I can play with his authoritarian posturing. We all have our ways of protecting our feelings, and I fully understand his way.

On February 25, Sanislaw performs the surgery to remove the lump and some adjacent lymph nodes, but we have to wait for the lab results. Sanislaw stops in to see us in the recovery room afterwards. He is cheerful.

"I don't think you have a thing to worry about, Dianna. I have seen lots of these things, and I don't believe this one is malignant," he says confidently.

Dianna is elated.

I just hope he's right.

He was right the first time, when he removed the lump from her left breast back in 1990. The fact that he would stop in to tell us this ahead of getting the lab results is encouraging. He is trying to minimize this period of uncertainty for us.

Three days later, on February 28, we get a call to come in and discuss the lab results with Sanislaw. As we enter his office, he is already standing and his eyes are glistening.

"I am so sorry, Dianna. I was wrong. We do have a malignancy here," he says, wasting no time on formalities. He walks over to Dianna and wraps his huge arms around her. She drops her head into his chest and cries silently. Sanislaw's head is bowed toward her. I slump back against the wall, crushed.

What now?

The report shows four of the lymph nodes, about five to ten millimeters in size, are malignant. The type of cancer is termed metastatic adrenocarcinoma, and similar to the very first cancer she had in 1990. Apparently, the radiation she had then did not catch these...or...oh, who knows, really? All that matters is, we must deal with this now.

We meet with our oncologist in Midland, Dr. Vellecoop, who waves the white flag. She feels we have reached the limits of what can be done in Midland. Dianna's cancer is now roughly classified as stage 3–4, based both on tumor size and the spread to her lymph system. She tells us the

Midland facility is not equipped to offer her the best treatment modalities available elsewhere. She recommends we begin treatment at one of the major cancer treatment centers around the country.

Fortunately for us, there are two such centers near us. One is the Barbara Ann Karmanos Cancer Center, located within the confines of Harper Hospital, part of a huge complex of hospitals in downtown Detroit, about ninety minutes from our home. The other is even closer, the University of Michigan Hospital System in Ann Arbor, only forty-five minutes away.

Dr. Vellecoop also mentions the possibility of a stem cell transplant procedure currently being done on an experimental basis for breast cancer patients. We would need insurance approval for it. She arranges an appointment through her contacts at the Karmanos facility.

One last thing Vellecoop does is install a port in Dianna's jugular vein under her collarbone, but not without a very painful, bloody probing process done without anesthetic. Vellecoop is embarrassed and extremely apologetic—she has done many of these—it's usually a simple procedure, but not this time; because, as it turns out, Dianna's vein follows a quirky path not found in other patients.

This seems entirely consistent with the Dianna I know.

So we are finished with Midland. We have graduated, as it were, to the big time. On the drive home, Dianna talks about her sadness and the uncertainty of giving up her doctors, and starting all over again with who knows who… and bringing her active cancer along with her.

"I'm going to miss them all, which probably sounds weird," she says as we head south on I-75. As usual, she is sitting up straight, her hands crossed on her lap, looking straight ahead.

"No, I don't think it sounds weird at all. They're good people, every one, and they have done their best for us. The whole hospital experience there has been a positive one…under the circumstances, anyway. We couldn't have asked for better care."

We're both quiet, watching the traffic pick up as we pass through Flint and peel off onto US-23 toward Ann Arbor.

"I just wish it had turned out differently," I say finally.

"Me, too," she says softly, almost like an afterthought, gazing at the woods and fields going by while leaning her head against the window.

The miles go by and the sun is beginning to sink fast. Some drivers are turning on their lights. Why, I wonder? I can see them, and they can surely see me. Dianna seems lost in thought.

As we approach Ann Arbor, she sits up straight again and looks more perky. Then she looks over at me and says, "One good thing, though."

"What's that?"

"Well, maybe, this new experimental treatment will give us a cure. It's like a whole new possibility, you know?"

Always looking for the pony in a room full of horseshit, I think to myself. I reach over and take her hand into mine, hold it up, and kiss it lightly, then lean over and kiss her on the cheek.

"Why don't we stop and get some ice cream, sweetheart? We can hit that place near Saline you're always bugging me about."

"Oh, that's a great idea. Let's do."

"I believe things are going to work out okay for us," I say.

She turns toward me and smiles.

"I think so, too."

Just like that, it feels like a different day than the day we left Midland just two hours ago. I wonder if I'm catching what Dianna has, eternal optimism.

35

Into the Valley

April 1998

I set up appointments a few days apart at both Karmanos and U of M.

The snow is already gone. In Michigan, we can never say gone-gone until late May. Still, it's obviously spring. Feels that way, smells that way. The air has a different quality to it. The sharp, biting edge of winter is already a memory.

We head to Detroit for our first appointment and leave the car, with Cracker in it, in an underground parking garage in the middle of the downtown hospital complex. Everything is concrete, tall buildings, traffic, noise, people, so radically different from where we had just been only an hour-and-a-half ago. I'll be glad to get out of here.

It's a short walk into Harper Hospital. We negotiate the alien internal landscape up to the transplant unit. I notice everything is older, darker, not quite as clean as the Midland Hospital we are used to...and much larger. The main doctors in the transplant unit are Dr. Klein and Dr. Dansey. After checking in, we sit down in the waiting room. A smiling receptionist asks us if we would like coffee, then hands us each a slim booklet, basically a sales pitch for their facilities and their expertise while also explaining the transplant procedure, technically called Autologous Peripheral Blood Progenitor Cell Transplantation, but what we will come to know as the stem cell transplant procedure (SCTP).

With a name like that, how can it fail to cure all of Dianna's maladies? I sardonically muse to myself. We read this document in silence as we wait for our interview. I'm writing down questions in my little notebook. Dianna, as usual, is filing everything into her impeccable memory. As time and events have gone by, she has made herself an expert on breast cancer and has already counseled several friends, and friends of friends, on the subject.

On many occasions, I listen to her talking on the phone with a new cancer patient—friend or acquaintance—and just as often, women she has never met and will never meet. It usually begins with a long period of silence while Dianna listens. Then there are murmurs of sympathy and understanding followed by amazingly adroit descriptions of this or that type of cancer, likely treatment options, the array of likely patient responses, side effects, complications, sprinkled with ways of combating this or that "discomfort," interspersed with her own experiences. Each one ends with a peptalk about the importance of attitude, sprinkled with poignant rays of optimism. Hope sings through the phone line to whomever is at the other end.

She is giving each one an injection of "Diannadopamine."

As the years go by, this pattern only becomes more frequent.

Many letters, cards, even flowers, show up, thanking her for her support. Friends confide in me that newly diagnosed women pick up the phone in tears and hang up filled with hope and determination. Some claim she has saved them—not necessarily from cancer, but from despair. After diagnosis and instantly resigned to a miserable end, Dianna helps them see it all in a more positive light. But I never hear her lecture or try to downplay whatever they have going on. She is anything but a Pollyanna. She is, instead, a hard-nosed realist. It's just that she lives in a different reality. If the situation is serious, she pulls no punches and says so. She never makes predictions or prognoses. But giving up is simply not an option for her.

On one occasion, she gets off the phone and just sits there quietly staring out the window. When she finishes one of these calls, she is usually charged up.

"Anything wrong, honey?"

"Oh, I just talked to this very nice lady. She's just been diagnosed."

"And?"

"I don't think she'll be around long. She's given up already. I can hear it in her voice."

"Well, maybe she will pull out of it."

"I hope so. But I don't think so. I wouldn't give her six months, to be honest. Her condition is serious, and she doesn't have the will to fight it."

Just a good guess maybe, but later we find out her analysis was prescient, which only serves to remind us none of us knows what anyone else's life path is about.

Dianna spends hours reading books, magazines, articles about cancer. I spend many hours researching on the Internet about cancer. She is uncomfortable and unmotivated about using the computer, so when I find something interesting, I print it out for her to read. She pours over everything, highlighter in hand.

Through it all, I come to realize how genuinely intelligent she is—I mean, I have always known she's smart, but even more intelligent than myself? Could this be? Well, when it comes to medical things, no doubt whatsoever. I like to keep it simple. Cancer is bad. That's all I really want to know about cancer…or medicine in general, for that matter.

The receptionist invites us into Dr. Dansey's office. I plunk down the six-inch-high pile of medical files onto his desk, Dianna's medical history that I've lugged all the way from Midland. We shake hands, sit down, and he picks up the top folder and begins to flip through it, obviously chagrined at the sheer volume of it all.

"Would you like me to tell you what's in there, Dr. Dansey?" Dianna asks. Her voice is bright but almost businesslike.

He looks at her and weighs his options. "Well…sure. Why not? Give it a go."

For the next fifteen minutes, Dianna runs through her medical history from the beginning, seamlessly. She looks completely relaxed, completely in control. I look over at Dr. Dansey and watch his jaw dropping minute by minute as he sits there in silence, listening intently, gradually leaning toward her, his elbows on his knees.

When she finishes, she stops, sits back, and folds her hands in her lap.

He is silent for a long moment.

"Are you medically trained, Dianna?" he asks.

She shakes her head no.

"Well…that explanation…was…impressive, to say the least. And genuinely helpful. I must admit, I'm surprised. Every term you used was medically accurate."

She smiles.

"Well, I have always been interested in medical things. And, of course, breast cancer is of special interest for me now. I just believe in being informed."

"Oh, you're definitely informed. I can't tell you how much this helps me, and how much I appreciate your effort."

He sits back and puts aside the files. He does not look at them again, at least while we are there.

"I cannot tell you how refreshing it is to interact with a patient who takes responsibility for their treatment."

Dianna looks ebullient. I'm impressed, too. She doesn't talk that way to me. I suddenly realize she sees me as the rank rookie I am, not worthy of her "full repertoire."

"So, let's talk about the treatment option you are considering here today. I can speak with you in medically precise terms, and that's a plus for us all. Then I'll give you a tour through our transplant floor. It's completely isolated from the rest of the hospital. Patient immune systems are highly compromised during treatment, so cleanliness procedures are extraordinary and comprehensive."

He goes through the drill.

Then he runs through their credentials. They have done 185 transplants to date, with one fatality. Most cancers treated are not breast cancer, which is in an experimental phase, but on the verge of becoming accepted practice for late-stage breast cancer patients. The cure rate is really unknown but estimated to be around thirty percent, based mostly on research studies done in South Africa.

Well, that's not overly impressive, I think to myself, but better than the lottery.

"If you choose us for this treatment, we will submit an all-inclusive package cost of eighty thousand dollars to your insurance company for their approval," Dansey says.

Big gulp there.

I look over at Dianna, but she is listening intently and doesn't blink an eye. I blink several times but say nothing. In any case, this is a first for me. Being told up front the cost of a medical procedure—and capped—so, there will be no itemized bills, no dealing with line item costs for doctor's fees, or hospital fees, or Band-Aids, or surgical gloves, or aspirin, or…

Then he goes into the treatment process itself.

First there will be four courses of normal chemotherapy, three weeks apart, given as an outpatient, which can be done at any appropriate facility convenient for us. The drugs used in this phase will be Navelbine and Taxol. Meanwhile, her stem cells will be stabilized with Neupogen, given by injection, at home, on a daily basis.

Next, when Dianna is ready to enter the inpatient phase, they will install a Neostar lumen catheter into her internal jugular vein under her collarbone with three different ports for administering whatever drugs are in the protocol.

Ouch, I think, remembering what happened with Vellecoop in Midland.

When I mention that mini-nightmare to Dansey and point out the unusual location of her vein, he tells us not to worry. The procedure will be done under anesthesia, guided with a sonogram. There will be no fishing around and no pain, he promises.

Dr. Dansey explains that the catheter also allows continuous high-flow rates to optimize pheresis, a process whereby the blood components are removed, centrifuged, separated, then filtered to harvest the stem cells, with the remainder of the blood components returned to her body.

The harvested stem cells will be frozen, then returned to her body after the high-dose chemo treatment has been completed, a step termed "stem cell rescue," because without those stem cells, she would die from the lethal doses of chemotherapy drugs given to her.

The chemo drugs used for the high-dose portion of the treatment will be cyclophosphamide, cisplatin, and carmustine, each given on different time schedules while she is in the transplant unit.

The potential side effects are numerous and frightening—anemia, infection, bleeding, hair loss, nausea, vomiting, infertility, potential for leukemia, heart damage, severe lung damage, numbness, effects on hearing and taste, liver failure, and even death.

He points out that they provide a hotel next to the hospital used by both the patient and caregivers, after the SCTP is completed. There she will spend two to four weeks in recovery, making daily visits to the hospital for follow-up testing and observation.

He walks us to the transplant unit and, after donning masks, we go partway down the hall, just to get a feel for the place. It is deathly quiet with only a background hum of medical equipment and the low murmur of human voices now and then. The lighting is good, and it does, indeed, look immaculately clean.

We bid Dansey goodbye and exit into the normal world.

Dianna has no doubts. She is eager to do it for one simple reason. It looks like her last and best chance for a cure.

We head home with a lot to think about.

"Can we stop at Ruby Tuesday on the way home, honey?" she asks after a long silence. "You like the salads there." We have escaped the atmosphere of downtown Detroit and are near Saline, a small town on US-12, south of Ann Arbor.

"Sure."

"I'm thinking about a big fat dessert after dinner."

"Tiramisu?" I ask, teasing her about her ubiquitous belly pouch.

"If they have it, dammit." She is way ahead of me. "I think my little belly is the least of my worries right now," she says with feigned defiance.

Her normal body weight has always been 155–160 pounds, about right for her five-foot-ten, large-boned frame. There have also been times, during treatment, especially when on steroids, when her weight has ballooned to 190, and her face puffs up.

"Looks like I'm going to have a lot more chipmunk days. I hate that," she says. I know she is visualizing a chipmunk with too many nuts in its mouth. Then she starts laughing because I'm already laughing. What else can we do?

We visit the University of Michigan Medical Center to see what their program is about, but we are both instantly and totally turned off. We are greeted coldly by a female doctor who seems to see Dianna as another piece of data. The procedure is more complex, requiring Dianna to endure a similarly intense treatment twice, because it is done in two separate phases. And there is no place to stay, so we would have to rent a motel nearby or travel each day. But the coup de grace is the tour of the transplant unit, which we find to be amazingly ill kept. "Dirty" is not a bad choice of words.

"I clean my house better than that," Dianna says as we walk out to our car.

Our choice is a no-brainer, even though Karmonos is twice the distance from home.

We wait to see what our insurance company has to say about all this. Surprisingly, they quickly approve it, no questions asked.

Our next step is to visit with our new oncologist, Dr. Phillip Stella, at Ann Arbor Oncology, which is physically attached to St. Joseph's Mercy Hospital in Ypsilanti, a sister city to Ann Arbor. He will handle the pre-chemo regimen, as well as gradually take over any further oncology care post-transplant.

When we arrive at St. Joe's for the first time, we are impressed. The attitudes are warm and respectful, and the cleanliness is equal to the Midland hospital we liked so much. I notice, given my orientation toward team building, there are signs on the walls with their vision statement, standards, and goals. Their motto is, "Remarkable Medicine, Remarkable Care." Catchy.

Is it true? I wonder.

We sit in the waiting room, filling out papers, then wait…, and wait…, and wait.

We would eventually learn this is normal and for good reason. It will become a joke among ourselves, other patients, and the staff. An appointment time with Stella should be viewed as merely a suggestion—might as well assume it will be "morning or afternoon" and let it go at that.

The good reason, as we shall soon discover, is that Stella does not have a stopwatch sitting on his desk. If a patient has little happening, a routine checkup, his time with them is short and to the point. If, on the other hand, a patient is at some crisis point—a new diagnosis, the need to change treatment or the patient is simply distraught—he will spend as much time as it takes. There are times we will be with him for over an hour. Everyone appreciates and honors this approach to patient care.

We enter his office and meet him for the first time. I instantly like him. For one thing, he is Italian. What's not to like? But most importantly, both of us quickly realize this man has heart, and is not afraid to express it while still remaining highly professional. He actually listens. Then he speaks. Then he records the content of our meeting into his little recorder while we are still sitting there—so we will know exactly what he is putting into the medical record. This gives us a chance to hear what was said a second time, and to clarify and correct, if needed. Finally, he has a great sense of humor. This is a guy we can play with now and then. Soon enough, we learn he is also a strong Catholic, but why hold that against him? I was guilty of that myself once upon a time.

Dianna and Stella hit it off right from the start. We leave feeling reassured.

The transplant process goes into high gear, and one event tumbles into our lives after another.

April 2, 1998

We return to Harper for a procedure to extract bone marrow biopsies, which is done by jamming a small hole-saw device about the diameter of a skinny pencil into each one of Dianna's hips. They have to twist it to literally saw through the bone wall to reach the marrow. This is done without anesthesia, using, instead, a drug called Versed. Dianna is in excruciating pain, and screams while the procedure, far from instantaneous, is carried out, not once but twice, once into each hip.

I am *absolutely furious*. We had no idea what was coming. Afterwards, a smiling nurse walks up to me, and I stand so she can look straight into my eyes. Her smile instantly disappears.

"Listen to me very carefully. You will *never, ever* do this to my wife again. What's the matter with you people?"

She is apologetic and scurries away as fast as possible. I just as quickly figure out what that was about. With anesthesia, they would have to keep someone with Dianna until she comes out of it. Cheaper and quicker to simply pop her a pill and let it rip.

They never do try to do this to her again.

April 27, 1998

The first chemo cycle is started at St. Joe's after a PAS port is installed in her arm. The old port had been removed. Dianna's veins, not great to begin with, are just too compromised now. It's time to end the painful experiences she has routinely endured with the frequent blood sampling and IV-administered chemo drugs. Most nurses want to avoid even doing her.

"Now, you'll be happy to see me again, Jeanie," Dianna quips brightly to one of the oncology nurses.

"Dianna, believe me, we are always glad to see *you*. We just don't enjoy hurting you. Glad you got the port."

"Me, too."

Dianna must have daily shots of Nupogen jammed into her leg to build up her stem cell population. Fortunately, a couple of our neighbors are nurses and they come over to give her the shots each day. I could have done it, but relieved I don't have to.

These shots lead to lengthy periods of severe bone pain, and Dianna often wakes up during the night, crying. I do the best I can to console her. I learn bone pain is one of the worst.

Dianna turns out to be allergic to something in the Taxol, reacting with hives and difficulty breathing. She breaks out in Herpes Zoster on her belly, a nuisance. Stella switches to Taxotere, so now she is getting Taxotere/Navelbine instead, which she tolerates better. There are also improved nausea drugs now, so thankfully there will be none of the brutal vomiting episodes we went through in 1990.

May 1998

By the second treatment, there is no evidence of cancer anywhere in her system. We feel encouraged. I wonder if we even need to go through the transplant at all, but we both know microscopic cancer cells cannot be detected. In any case, Dianna is undeterred, determined to go for a cure.

On the other hand, she gains alopecia, partial loss of her hair, which occurs in patches. She also has her last menstrual cycle and starts having hot flashes.

"Well, guess this is the last nail in that coffin," she says one day. The plaintive tone of her voice is unmistakable.

"What do you mean?"

"No children for me," she says.

Her eyes are glistening. It's not as if we didn't already know this, but the finality of it hits home for her now. Another blow to her femininity, and the certain end to a lifelong dream.

"I'm sorry, honey. You are just doing what you have to do to have a life to live." I put my arms around her, and she buries her head into my shoulder.

"I know. I'm just sad, is all."

"You have a right to be."

The day is winding down and the light outside is going yellow. Canada geese are barking sporadically somewhere on the lake. One plaintive call, then, after a short silence, another, assembling for the night, echoing Dianna's mood.

I help her sit down on the couch. Then I walk around the room, flipping on her accent lights, though it is not really dark out yet.

What the hell.

I sit down next to her and put my arm around her. She leans back into the couch with a sigh.

"My sense of things these days is maybe your life has another purpose. Maybe, in a way, you are being asked to focus all your energy on *that* work," I say.

"You know, John, I've been thinking something like that too lately. I've wondered so many times, why is this happening to me? What am I supposed to do with this?"

She perks up, then decides we need to go for a boat ride. I look outside. The sun is sinking faster now, and the air is cooling. I get her a warm jacket, and off we go.

As we slip slowly away from shore, scores of diminutive tree swallows are sweeping through the air all around us, then gliding on their graceful swept-back wings, their white undersides flashing in the twilight, silently reducing the insect population with their evening dinner dance.

We have a short, quiet ride around the lake, sans spiders, thanks to Cracker, but sans wine, too, thanks to chemo treatments. The western sky slides into spectacular, followed by the rapid blurring into a silver twilight afterglow as we coast silently back up to the dock.

August 1998

By the time the fourth cycle of chemo is completed, Dianna is feeling numbness in her legs and her energy is dwindling. During a chemo treatment visit, accompanied by her friend, Kathy Preston, a nurse notices Dianna's port doesn't look right.

Dianna is immediately admitted to the hospital, and I get a call at work from Kathy. A sonogram picks up a huge blood clot in Dianna's arm, a deep vein thrombosis. She is put on Coumadin and Heparin immediately, and Dianna spends five days in the hospital. A new port is installed.

August 23

We are visiting my brother Ed and his wife Dianne at their new home in Canadian Lakes, a development west of Mount Pleasant. Dianna suddenly starts having severe chills and fever. I have to decide whether to use Midland Hospital, an hour away, or make a run to St. Joe's, three hours away. I opt for the latter because they will have her most recent medical history. I lay Dianna down in the back of our conversion van, cover her with blankets, and take off. This is one of those occasions when my propensity for speeding is an advantage. Dianna isn't in any condition to argue anyway.

She is admitted with a fever of over 103, with chills coming in waves. They put her in an ice bath, diagnose her with Klebsiella septicemia, then start IV antibiotics. She spends another week in the hospital. Most likely this infection was picked up during her last hospital stay.

While she is an inpatient, a CAT scan using a new contrast dye quickly reveals Dianna is allergic to it. She breaks out in hives and has difficulty breathing three hours after the scan is run.

"Well, honey, guess you are in the right place to deal with all this, but in the wrong place; because if you weren't here so often, you wouldn't need to be here," I say. "Confusing isn't it?...Just a few more reasons why I don't like hospitals."

She looks over at me with a wan smile and says nothing.

There is some discussion about whether Dianna is in good enough health to endure the transplant, which is only a week away. Dianna wants to go through with it, so admission to Karmanos is delayed two weeks. Otherwise, the plan remains unchanged.

September 1
The port in her arm is removed and the Neostar triple lumen catheter is installed at Harper. True to their word, everything goes off without complication. There is no pain for Dianna during any of it.

I am grateful. Dianna is probably even more grateful.

September 10
Dianna is admitted to the transplant unit, her new world for now.

We enter through the double-airlock sliding glass doors, and suddenly we are in *that* world. The silence is broken only by soft swishing sounds and the occasional clicking of medical equipment. A nurse shows us the coffee maker, refrigerator, and sink in the snack room. Patients won't be using any of this stuff, though.

I stay with Dianna for the first day, then leave. I don't have enough vacation to stay the entire time, so I plan to visit her in the evenings. This doesn't concern Dianna since friends—Kathy Preston, Kathy Priest (a friend and oncology nurse from Traverse City who amazingly volunteers to take vacation, spending an entire week with Dianna), as well as her mom, Pat,—will be there when I'm not. Dianna will never be without at least one support person.

I opt to work while Dianna's stem cell population is built up with Nupogen (days 1–4), then stem cells extracted (days 5–7).

I will be there around the clock for the next week, when the high-dose chemo is administered (days 8–10), the days that follow when the chemo is doing its thing (days 11–12), and when they give her back her own stem cells (day 13).

I sleep in an easy chair or on the floor in her room. The nurses take pity and find a thin mattress for me. Feels like camping out...sort of.

By the last day of chemo injections, Dianna is in a complete stupor, mostly sleeping or maybe simply unconscious. I decide to lay down for a while.

Startled out of a fitful sleep, I sit up, trying to find my bearings, listening to the low cacophony that has become the familiar background of these days and nights, the sounds of nurses padding down the hallway, their voices low murmurs, the steady clicking of her IV-drip, the chirping of her heart monitor. The bright lights of the hallway stream through our half-open door.

Then I see her.

She is standing at the bathroom doorway, half in shadow, half in light, not moving, one arm tangled in her IV lines, the IV stand behind her.

Wide awake now, I slide past her into the bathroom and flip on the light. Her eyes are wide open and unseeing. There is a steady stream of yellowish-brown liquid running down the inside of both her legs into a puddle between them, slowly spreading around her feet.

"Oh, honey, stand right there. Don't move."

I see a stack of paper towels lying on a little table and grab the whole pile, then quickly wet them with warm water. I steady her against the wall, place her hands on my shoulders, and slowly kneel down with the towels.

"It's okay, sweetheart. Don't move. I'll be done in a minute."

I am not done in a minute, but she is frozen in time anyway. Slowly, carefully, I wipe up every inch and every crevice of her body from her pubic area to her toes, lifting one foot gently, cleaning the sole, then placing it further apart and out of the pool of diarrhea lying between her feet.

She is great. She doesn't move an inch and keeps her hands firmly on my shoulders, saying nothing the whole time.

When I have done as well as I can, and getting worried about how much longer she can stand there, I quickly wipe up the floor, tossing the towels into the corner. I gently take Dianna's hands off my shoulder and leave her leaning against the wall while I rinse my hands in seconds. After untangling her arm from the IV tube, we slowly make our way back to the bed, her arm around my neck, me dragging the IV stand along behind us.

So, we get it done. *What a team*, I think, almost laughing with relief.

I help her back into bed, open the hall door all the way to let more light in, and look her over carefully. There is not a hair left on her body. Her head is bald, her eyebrows—"never her best feature," she would often say, gone, her pubic hair, too. She looks clean, but why not polish her up while she is resting comfortably? Using a package of softer wipes I find in the bathroom, I repeat the whole drill, pat her dry, then powder her.

She looks like a newborn baby and almost smells like one except for a faint metallic scent, probably from all the chemo drugs in her. I don't know how to wipe that away.

I cover her up, then step back to inspect everything. Her face looks flushed and puffy, even in this light, and her eyes are closed. But she seems to be breathing normally, and the machines are making their normal noises.

I lean down, kiss her gently on the cheek, lightly stroke her forehead, then reaching under the covers, I rub her arms and legs. As she drifts off, she murmurs a couple of words I can't understand. Once again, she is somewhere else, in places I cannot go, once again, in places I know nothing about.

Stepping back, as I watch her lying there, I think what a different day this is from that day on the beach, in some other lifetime, when she was hopelessly but relentlessly enticing seagulls that wouldn't come. Yet, her being here now, lying here in this bed, is an expression of that very same determination and optimism.

I am just as amazed on this day as I was on that one.

I toss the soiled towels and wipes into the bathroom hamper, wash my hands again, then flop into my chair.

After awhile, I get up and completely close the door to make it darker and quieter in our room. In the darkness, I notice the moonlight and go over to the window, looking out over the city. It is a paper-thin crescent moon and, barely, stars.

Up north, in God's country, maybe deer hunting or grouse hunting or fishing or just back packing, I could reach up and pluck stars right out of the sky. At home in the Irish Hills, they aren't quite that close; but all the constellations are there, bright in a brilliant black sky. Here in Detroit, probably no one bothers to look up—stars hardly show up at all. One more reason I will never, never, ever live in a city again.

When I look back at Dianna, I can see her moon face in the moonlight. She looks peaceful. She, on the other hand, I muse, would be willing to live almost anywhere if people are close by. Even New York City, for God's sake. I would kill myself first, I think, smiling at the thought of it. Exhausted, I lie down on my little mat and fall asleep almost instantly.

In the morning, when the nurse comes in, I do my little report on the evening's events and ask her to bring me some bleach or something so I can sanitize the floor. She says they will take care of it, thanks me profusely for doing what I am guessing is not their favorite task, then gets busy changing the sheets and giving Dianna a sponge bath.

Almost all the nurses here are black, and almost all the doctors are white. Maybe this is stereotyping, but the doctors are always serious and straight-laced, whereas the nurses and I enjoy banter with each other. We routinely stick one another with gallows humor and trade outrageous insults. It's a way of softening a difficult situation. They do the best they can for us, and I let them know we appreciate it.

Dianna will have no memory of this entire period. A few days simply not part of her life, as she knows it.

I consider this a good thing.

Dianna is left with severe complications. She cannot walk at all because she cannot feel her ankles or feet. "Feels like two pieces of wood at the end of my legs," she says, a result very few patients experience, doctors tell us. Aside from their natural concern, they cannot help being excited in a scientific sense—interesting data for them.

Well.

She also has "gained" a severe loss of lung function, which doctors predict she will gain back, at least partially.

She ends up spending another thirty days at the hotel, mostly with her mom, though friends slip in and out of the picture.

While going through this process, Dianna is introduced by Consuelo, a mutual friend, to a new, to be lifelong, friend, Zena Bianca. They share something very few friends can share—cancer, and going through the SCTP. But they really like each other, too. Zena's husband Frank is a professor at Michigan State University.

I hate visiting the hotel. If there is one thing in life guaranteed to make me cranky, it's feeling too hot. The room is pretty much an oven, the windows don't open very far; and no matter how much we complain, it doesn't get any better. Even the women complain, so it's not just me.

Dianna's condition gradually improves, but her peripheral neuropathy will never go away completely. And there will be other hangovers from this experience, too.

October 23

Dianna is coming home tonight.

I have one of her girlfriends, Marcia, pick her up so I can stay home to prepare a surprise for her.

I pick up a dozen huge pumpkins from a nearby farmer and carve each one with a different, outlandish face, then space them along both sides of our front walk, put candles in each one; and when I get a call from Marcia that they are a few minutes from home, I light them all. By the time they pull into the driveway, it's dark enough for them to show up well.

I help Dianna out of the car. She needs a walker, is very shaky on her feet, and unsure of her balance.

She is like a little kid when she sees the pumpkins. "Oh, honey, who did this? It is beautiful. I love it."

"Well, the master pumpkin carver in the sky did it, of course..., that would be me."

"Oh, honey, I just can't thank you enough. This makes my day complete."

I feel a lump in my throat as I hold onto her. She has changed dramatically. She feels frail, vulnerable. In some way I can't quite put my finger on, a softer, more delicate, more wispy version of herself.

"I'm so happy to be home. I can't tell you how happy I am to be back in my very own home again." Her voice sounds the same way she feels to me...more fragile.

We help her inside; but, after awhile, she wants to go out and look at the pumpkins again. It's pitch black out now and cooling down fast, but the candles are still burning.

I take a video of her "return walk" as she slowly, uncertainly, jerks the walker forward, then takes a step, then jerks again, up and down the walk, studying each pumpkin. She is wearing her blonde mushroom wig. It's perched on her plumped-up steroid face, and her weight has ballooned from the 165 pounds, before the transplant, to 190, now.

Pam Pfau, Kris Forest, and others come to visit her, keeping her spirits up over the next few weeks. The girls laugh when Dianna describes herself as Uncle Fester in *The Addams Family* sitcom with her bald head, puffy face, and dark circles under her eyes.

For me, she is a breath of fresh air. For all her fragility, her being hits me like a bolt of lightning. How much I've missed her energy. She's home. So I'm home, too.

October 31

Halloween night. This time, we are not waiting by the door for the kids that never come. We are on our way back to Harper Hospital. Dianna is swamped with vision problems, frightening her. When I call the transplant emergency number, they advise us to come in.

"It's hard to explain. I keep seeing sparks, flashing lights, and I can't stop it. It seems to be getting worse. I'm scared, honey."

Once there, a series of tests are run, but we don't learn anything new. Consequences of the transplant, of course, but they can find nothing fundamentally wrong with her brain. Wait it out, we are told. It is likely to go away on its own. Dianna is relieved as we head back home in the wee hours of the morning, exhausted.

November 3
Some routine tests done at Harper include an abnormal bone scan that shows nothing definitive. The results are inconclusive.

November 25
While I am off on my annual deer hunting trip, Dianna comes down with a fever and chills. A dear friend and neighbor, Linda Salvador, takes her to St. Joe's where Dianna is treated with antibiotics. It works. What is amazing to me and to Dianna, herself, is the strength of her constitution. She never really gets sick. If it were not for the cancer and the immune system suppression caused by chemo treatments, making her more susceptible to infections picked up in hospitals, she would be the healthiest person on the planet. Good thing. She needs all the strength she can muster to deal with this steady assault on her body.

December 24
Dianna is going to St. Joe's for daily radiation treatments to the area of her chest and lymph system that was cancerous. She is also still experiencing severe shortness of breath due to lungs damaged by the SCTP. She starts getting prednisone to mitigate the inflammation. Her weight bounces up to 204 pounds.

"I feel like a blowup toy," she says ruefully, but laughing. "None of my clothes fit. I will have to go out and buy all—you heard me…*all*…new clothes, you know…. Feel like taking me shopping?"

She knows how I hate shopping. We stopped going together years ago.

She likes to wander around, gradually circling in on whatever she came for in the first place. Maybe two to three hours.

If I know which door is closest to what I want, I go in *that* door, buy it, do a 180, then retrace my own footprints back out the door. I don't look to either side on the way in or on the way out, either. Maybe ten minutes.

I know she's kidding, anyway. She wears comfortable sweats with string ties and loose shirts and jackets. She also knows the steroid effect is temporary, and she will drop back to some more normal weight pretty rapidly.

She is deep into physical therapy now, doing it five days a week, which seems to help with her balance and mobility.

February 1999

Eighteen weeks after the SCTP, she is still greatly irritated by frequent hot flashes, sometimes so severe she almost passes out. Her lung function, a huge concern going into the SCTP, had dropped from 77 percent before the SCTP to 48 percent after, but now is back up to 60 percent and still improving. Guess the doctors were right about it being temporary.

She graduates from a walker to a cane, but the numbness and tingling in her feet, arms, and face continue unabated.

We are told this is a rare complication of the SCTP, called polyradiculopathy, which is just a big name for numbness in the extremity of all her limbs, something only a couple of patients out of hundreds have experienced. Once again, it is confirmed. Dianna is special.

She also experiences seizures regularly, accompanied by an assortment of vision aberrations.

"Hard to explain…it's like I'm looking through saran wrap. Sometimes, I see halos or auras around things, and I get a mint taste in my mouth, too. Other times, I know I'm looking at something or someone, but pieces of them are missing—like when the TV screws up," she says when I ask her how it is for her.

"Like some of the pixels got left out?"

"Yeah. I guess, …what are pixels?"

Eventually, brain scans show she has leukoencephalopathy, a term used by her neurosurgeon at Harper. They conclude this is the source diagnosis of her seizure/vision problems.

To me, this is just another way of saying, "Yeah, you've got some damage to your brain, there." I think we knew that. We just didn't have a big word for it. Now, we do. For me, this is a big "so what?" Still, Dianna actually does feel better once she is given a name for it, providing a degree of certainty she didn't have before—and now she can authoritatively report this condition to all her friends, using the correct term, pronounced correctly, too, I notice.

I'm still going to call it brain damage, providing me with a new avenue for playing with her. Whenever we disagree about anything, my default response is simple. "Well, not surprising you don't agree with me—after all, you *are* brain damaged."

She blows me off completely with a look of disdain and sometimes, if she's being charitable, a little laugh.

The symptoms are handled with a series of drugs, but she will just have to learn to live with some level of seizure activity. And she does.

Pretty quickly, she stops talking about what isn't working, and moves on with her life full force. Though I know it's still going on, I wouldn't know it from talking to her or watching the pace of her life. She does start taking Effexor for her seizures and begins calling it her "happy pill." On the other hand, she is noticeably more fragile somehow—and cautious about doing the various physical tasks of life we take for granted.

"Do you think I can drive?"

"Why not?" I say. "Half the people on the road are brain-damaged. You have an advantage—at least you know it."

She does drive. Even brain-damaged, she's a better driver than I am, but I don't see any virtue in pointing this out.

36

The End of Something

"Honey, why don't we make love anymore?"

We are in bed. Dianna is reading a book about healing cancer, while I'm thumbing through a bird hunting magazine. Dianna lays her book on the end table and rolls over toward me. I lay down the magazine, too. She has my undivided attention now.

"I think we make love every day in some way," I say.

"You know what I mean."

"Sex."

"Yes."

I let out a big sigh. We have not had sex since the transplant. I have been thinking about this for quite a while, and nothing ever comes up making sense to me.

"Don't you find me desirable anymore? Do you still love me?"

"Do you actually have to ask me that?" I'm looking her right in the eye. "I love you more now than I ever have."

"Well?"

"I don't have a way to explain it. It's not that I don't find you attractive or desirable. It's just with everything that has happened to us, to you, I just…I don't know what to say."

"It's because I've lost my breasts, isn't it. You never touch them anymore."

"Well, honey, we've discussed that already. You've admitted you don't have any feeling there anymore. Why would I touch them? I don't fondle doorknobs, either. But, anyway, your breasts have nothing to do with it."

"Then, what?"

"The only way I can put it is, I love you very much, and more and more with each passing year. But expressing my love for you in a sexual way feels…I don't know…just feels inappropriate somehow."

"Like you will hurt me or something?"

156

"I guess so. No matter how much you love someone, if the person you love is wounded and bleeding, you don't try to have sex with them. Feels… just doesn't feel…right. You protect them. You care for them, not have sex with them. Something like that."

"I'm not a cripple, you know. I'm not a piece of glass. I won't break."

"I know that, honey."

"I'm a woman with womanly needs. I still desire *you* sexually. I would love to have sex with you like a normal human being." She slides her arm under my arm. "I feel rejected. That hurts."

"I realize that. I feel terrible about it. Don't you think I haven't thought about how much you've lost? You have lost your dream of having a child. Now your menstrual cycles have ended, reminding you that all you are going to get from now on is hot flashes instead of the child you so dearly wanted. You've lost your breasts, a part of you, you were always so proud of…, and you have lost your hair twelve times. You…"

"Three times."

I laugh. Then, so does she, a little.

"What I'm trying to say, maybe not very well, is I realize all these losses assail your femininity, of what it means to be a woman, …and… not having sex with your partner is just another thing piled on top of all the rest. It's the last thing you need to have happen in your life, right now. I know I can't feel what you feel exactly…, but I do understand these are losses you deal with every day. That's why it hurts me so much to be stuck like this, this way."

"Then, I don't understand why you would want to deprive me of this, too."

My eyes are getting wet, and my heart is thick in my throat.

"Believe me, if I could do anything about it, I would. I just can't. Men can't fake it, you know."

"I don't want you to fake it."

I put my arms around her and pull her close to me. I can't stop the tears now.

"And so I don't. I'm not faking my love for you, either. I would do anything I know how to do for you. I do what I can. I'm so sorry, honey."

She starts to cry, softly, quietly, burying her head into my neck.

"So am I," she whispers.

We fall into silence. There doesn't seem to be anything else to say. I keep my arms around her, and she keeps her arm over me.

We fall asleep that way.

37

The Beginning of Something Else

The next morning, I get up, leaving Dianna still asleep, and go into the kitchen to make coffee. My back is facing the hallway to the bedroom. Suddenly I feel her arms around me as she lays her head sideways against my back.

"I know what love is, John."

"You do?" I ask without turning toward her.

"Yes."

"Look at me," she says.

I turn around and look into her eyes. They look wet, but she's smiling. "Love is the way you are with me," she pauses, then, in a more perky tone of voice, "And the way I am with you, too."

Now I can't help it. I fall apart. She wraps her arms tight around me and I bury my head into her neck.

"It's going to be okay," she says.

"It *is* okay," she says, then adds, "More than okay."

After a minute, she steps back and looks at me with a smirk on her face. "Do you ever desire other women?"

I think about that minefield, but decide to go ahead anyway. "Of course. Once in awhile, I do. Some women are sexually attractive and, …and don't look wounded to me, I guess. Must be about a billion of 'em out there."

She smiles, gives me a little kiss on the cheek, then walks over to the dining room window and looks out over the lake. Finally, she says quietly, without looking at me, "Maybe one day, honey, you'll see we are all wounded."

I stop pouring water into the coffeepot in midstream, about to enlist my skills in mental masturbation, when she darts away to a different flower.

"Oh, honey, I think it's going to be a beautiful day today. In fact, I'm sure it is." She comes across the room and peeks over the bar. "Oh. Are you making coffee for me?"

"Everything is for you," I say with a smile.

We never have sex again, and we never have to talk about it again, either.

38

Dianna's Gratitude Journal

I buy Dianna a gratitude journal, hoping it will help her while she is dealing with the continuing fallout from the SCTP.

A few excerpts, just as she wrote them:

The things I feel blessed for:

January 2	Seeing a winter storm Sitting by the fireplace Talking with my sister
January 3	Making my bed for the first time in months Walking better Seeing better
January 5	My great neighbors, Linda and Howard Ladd, Trudy and Sandy, Clara and Don My bed, warm and cozy Cookies
January 6	A new year filled with hope New lipstick Petting Cracker
January 7	Mom doing laundry Mom cooking Mom cleaning

January 8   Ed, Dianne visiting [my brother and his wife]
Music filling my house
Music filling my heart

January 9   Enjoying the Christmas lights
Enjoying a winter night

January 11   Having a life filled with love
Having faith in myself
Having faith in others

January 14   Being optimistic
Electric carts at KMart

January 15   Loving my new bed [we bought a Tempur-Pedic mattress, so she could sleep better]
Comfortable shoes

January 19   Making sour cream twists
Making my hat boxes
Looking at John
Another day to live my life

January 24   No more radiation treatments
Kissing John goodbye in the A.M.

January 25   Tea & toast in bed
John rubbing lotion on my feet

January 27   The cane Kathy gave me
Petting Cracker

January 30   My hair growing out
Waking up to the promise of a new day. To the promise of a lifetime.

February 8   Such great friends

February 10	Spending the day with John. We go for ice cream
February 11	Going shopping alone Driving again
February 12	Making Valentine cookies for my friends Sending out cards Scratching John's back
February 14	A beautiful Valentine card from John
February 21	Cleaning the van
February 25	Having a clean van Loving my house
March 2	I am alive today Finally off the steroids My hair is growing fast I can walk with a cane I can get up from the sofa on my own
March 6	My husband is so loving and forgiving Having ice cream with Cracker
March 7	A beautiful home A loving husband A near perfect day Cleaning my closet Giving some of my clothes away
March 9	I can walk all the way to Reed Road with Cracker Reorganizing my cupboards My bulbs are coming out

March 16	I can write Very little pain today Had a nice afternoon nap
March 17	John rubbing my back
March 19	I'm grateful Alex and Anna [Vogel] are here for a visit I could make breakfast Anna can still talk [Anna has ALS]
March 21	In bed, watching Regis and Kelly Being able to drive God giving me this day I'm cancer-free.

Note: Not a day during this period is without a sprinkling of seizures, wooden feet and ankles, hot flashes, moving in slow motion, pain, ...oops, I mean "discomfort."

39

The Senna Explosion

The winter of 1998–1999 tiptoes away and spring shows up with two mallards inhabiting a little cove next to our house each morning. Apparently, it's important for them to announce the day…early. I think the same ones have been coming every year. But, to be honest, I can't tell one male (or female) mallard from another, not at a distance anyway.

Dianna mimics their calls so well, I start laughing.

"Every morning, it's the same thing, dammit. They wake me up with a 'quack, quack' here and a 'quack, quack' there." The quack sounds she makes are nearly perfect.

"They're doing their mating rituals. It's a male and female," I say, looking out the window. "Better not quack too loud, you're good enough that you may just entice them right into the bedroom, honey."

She laughs.

"Well, wish they would just do it then, and get it over with," she says, feigning irritation, but we are both laughing now.

"Maybe you should start getting up at 5:30 when I do, so they won't be bothering you, queen bee, …and while you're at it, you could make breakfast for me, too."

I have made my own breakfast, if I have breakfast, for our entire marriage, which began with our different work schedules. Truth is, I like it this way. I can reenter this reality in a quiet way, then, begin thinking about designing my day.

"Believe me, John, I need *all* the beauty sleep I can get these days." She starts laughing again.

"Are you excited?" she asks, changing the subject.

"About what?"

"About your son and Cris having a baby soon. I'm so excited."

It is late spring, and Cris is due around July sometime. Must be like a Christmas thing for her. Start early, so she can enjoy it longer.

Jon calls us the evening of July 21. The baby is a girl and healthy, and Cris is fine. Nothing else matters.

They name her Senna. Where did that come from? Whatever happened to Mary, or Carol, or Barbara, or...? Still, it has a nice ring to it.

We go over to visit them in St. Clair Shores within a week, and Dianna makes many trips there after that, sometimes with me, more often while I'm working.

Around the end of August, we are asked to take care of the baby for four days while Jon and Cris head off on a camping trip (the trip from hell, reports Cris).

Maybe Cris is in hell, but Dianna is in heaven.

The child she could never have is in her arms. It is amazing to watch them together, which is twenty-four hours a day. I videotape them cuddling on the couch, Andrea Bocelli singing in the background. My heart aches, watching them.

"Well, this is Senna, ...1/12 years old," I say.

Dianna starts laughing.

"Too bad you missed it, Jon and Cris. Senna took her first steps today, ...walked across the room," I say, hunched behind the camera.

"And she said her first word, too, ...I could barely make it out but it was 'gran...grand...grandpa.'"

"Oh, John." Dianna is laughing hard now.

Throughout the four days Senna is with us, they are glued together. I might as well be on Mars. Like everything else in life, it's no accident they have each other in their lives right now, right here. I am infinitely grateful.

As the years go by, I will continue to be wonder filled at how their relationship deepens, unfolds, flowers, Senna filling Dianna to the brim. Even more amazing, despite Dianna's powerful feelings and the potential for being overtaken by feelings of "the child she never had" syndrome creeping in, she remains crystal clear about her own role, and effortlessly stays within it, a loving and devoted grandmother.

"It's probably just as well it's the way it is. Given what's going on with me, I wouldn't have the energy to be a mother at this stage of my life," she says one day.

"So, grandmother works for you?"

"It does."

She is quite matter-of-fact about it.

40

The Forum

In the summer of 1999 Dianna and I visit some good friends, Giovanni Sanitate and his wife Susan. He is a superior photographer/artist and I have a good deal of his work in our home. We first met while we were both involved in the original *est* Training in 1980.

More recently, Susan had completed the Forum, an outgrowth of the original *est* Training. We are drinking some Merlot after dinner on their deck, enjoying a pleasant summer afternoon. We talk about our Forum experiences in a casual way, and I really don't know what happens to make her change her mind; but, on the way home, Dianna turns to me. "John, I would like to do the Forum."

"What? I've been asking you to do it for the past fifteen years. What's changed your mind?"

"I don't know. Listening to Susan talk about it, I guess. Maybe I'm just ready now."

"My feelings are really hurt. I've begged you to do it for years and you blew *me* off—me, the love of your life, remember? Then, in one afternoon with Susan, you want to do it? What am I, chopped liver?"

She starts laughing. "Will you go with me?"

"Sure. It's practically free for me anyway. Once you've done it, you can review it for a pittance after that."

"Oh, good, ...but, will it be boring for you?"

"Only if I say so."

We are on I-696 now, and the traffic is actually light for a change. I start thinking about her question.

"I would say anything but boring. If enough time has passed between reviews, it'll always be a new experience, I think. Because the person sitting in that chair is not the same person, ...our listening, our perspective, and our life circumstances have all changed."

It is beginning to get dark enough for lights, and I flip them on. Dianna looks relaxed as she leans back into her seat.

"The only thing I don't like is sitting in a straight-back chair for fifteen hours a day, for three straight days. That's the hard part for me. But I love the challenge of learning more and peeling more of the onion," I say.

"What onion?"

"The one you use to make chicken soup," I say.

She laughs.

A couple of months later, we are sitting in those straight-backed chairs, doing the Forum together in Livonia, about ninety minutes from our home. We commute all three days.

On the second night, we are given homework to complete by the next morning. It's something like, writing out what you want to say to the person who represents the most difficult relationship in your life.

Although it is almost midnight, we feel energized by the events of the day and discuss what we are going to do for our homework as we head home on M-14.

"I've decided to write about my most difficult relationship," she says.

"I think that's what we are supposed to do, honey. Who is your most difficult relationship? Can't be me."

"Not you. Not even who. What," she says. She is looking straight ahead. It's too dark for me to see the expression on her face.

"What? What do you mean, 'what'?"

"I mean my most difficult relationship is not with a who, but with a what. I am going to write about my relationship with cancer."

I'm stunned. I exit M-14 and head south on US-23.

"Do you think that's okay?" she asks.

"Are you kidding? Absolutely. That's very creative, Dianna. What made you think of that?"

"Well, I have feared cancer all my life, long before I was diagnosed with it," she says.

I am quiet for a minute, then look over to her. "Really...I didn't know that."

She seems lost in thought as we drive along in silence until I turn off onto US-12.

"Why?" I ask finally.

"I don't know why. I've just always had this fear, even when I was a child, when I didn't even know what cancer was, really."

I didn't know *that,* either.

"Maybe it was a premonition. Or maybe my fear has drawn it to me. Maybe I actually created it."

I think about an old saying I heard somewhere about whatever you fear most you will bring to yourself. Some spiritualists believe our fear is like any other emotion—it is energy, and whatever we put energy into is what we end up creating. Other spiritualists believe we get to experience what we fear in order to have an opportunity to dissolve it, grow from it. All makes sense to me. We ride along in silence for a while, lost in our own thoughts. We exit US-23 and head west on US-12, the winding, hilly two-lane road that takes us back into the Irish Hills and home.

Long before I-94 came along as the primary route between Detroit and Chicago, the Sac Indians followed a more direct route for traveling between the Detroit River area and the southern tip of Lake Michigan (and actually on to the Mississippi River). White settlers, with their wagons and horses, continued to follow the same path, which came to be known as the Sauk Trail, and eventually US-12.

We don't get home until well past midnight and have to be back by 9:00 a.m. the next morning, but Dianna immediately goes to work on her homework. I do, too.

The next day, we are offered an opportunity to speak about our homework assignment. Dianna immediately throws up her hand, is selected, and walks to the front of the room, which is packed with about 200 people.

She takes the microphone and starts speaking without looking at her notes. She is wearing a honey-blonde wig I like a lot, with some waves, flips up here and there. I like the way it hits her face. And it is not the mushroom.

She starts by saying she has stage IV breast cancer, and there are a couple of gasps in the room. Someone looking like this cannot possibly have advanced cancer. When I look at her, this statuesque blonde with red nails, red lipstick, bright green eyes, and a sunny smile, I can hardly believe it myself.

With absolute aplomb, she quickly runs through a thumbnail sketch of her history with cancer, her fear of it, and her various struggles in dealing with it. She is articulate and magnetic, her delivery emotional but controlled. She pulls no punches, openly telling on herself, her doubts, her foibles, as well as flatly making no predictions about how long she will be here. When I look around the room, I notice people leaning forward, some of them dabbing at their eyes.

"I will end this by saying this experience, this weekend—and your energy—has helped me more than I can tell you."

She pauses and looks at everyone around the room. She is really *with* them, not talking *at* them. She looks radiant.

"I came here Friday morning believing cancer had me," she says, straightening her shoulders slightly and taking a breath.

"I don't know what the future has in store for me, but I will leave here tonight knowing this is not true. The truth is: I have cancer." She steps away from the microphone, then leans into it again and says softly, "Thank you for listening to me."

As she begins making her way toward me, some people start clapping; and soon everyone is clapping. One man stands up, and more follow until, finally, by the time Dianna reaches her seat, everyone is standing and clapping, and some are crying.

She sits down and cups her hands in her lap, back straight, looking like grace incarnated. Several people nearby lean toward her and whisper, and she bows toward them.

I am, once again, amazed by her capacity to speak lucidly, in total control of her own emotions while being so emotionally charged herself. I don't know how someone does *that*. In the entire ten-minute speech, her voice cracked once, and only for an instant. I have no problem making technical speeches before an audience of hundreds—and have—but I could never pull off what she just did. Don't know how to do it, and would not have the courage to try.

On our next break, and later at the end of the Forum, many make it a point to speak to her, hugging her, and wishing her well.

On the way home, I also lavish praise on her. She is quieter than usual, thanking me, but lost in her own thoughts as we enter the Sauk Trail part of our route home.

"Are you okay, honey?" I ask.

"I am."

The road ahead is nothing but a series of hills, valleys, and curves, and a low fog is creeping in as we travel west by southwest.

Dianna, 1987

Author and Dianna, 1987

Dianna and Breaker, 1987

Dianna in wedding dress, June 21, 1987

Breaker, 1989

Portrait of Dianna, painted by Jon Catenacci in 1990

K'Ana Degan, Kathy Davis, Allie Langlois, Chris Fowler, Kathy Preston, with
Dianna seated, with hats, circa 1996

Dianna, circa 1996

Author and Dianna, circa 1996

Dianna's siblings, Tricia, David, and Julian with Dianna in her "watermelon"
outfit

Dianna and friends form a healing circle, Carrie Kram, Suzy Duffy, Linda Muller, Dianna, Marji Noesen, Jenny Noesen, at Dianna's (smile) house on Loch Erin.

Anna Vogel, Dianna, and Kathy Preston, circa 1998

Cracker, circa 1998

Midland women with hats: Carrie Kram, Marji Noesen, Dianna, at Marji's home
in Midland, Michigan, circa 2003

Dianna, circa 2003

Dinner gathering in Rome, 2005. Adnan Al Awami (head of table with his children, Majid, Daniel), Ghalib Alwan, Dianna, Noel Abduljabar, Abubaker.

Gathering in Faleria, Italy, at the Antica Stabia Hostaria with author's father's family: Enza Sperdutti (Santino's wife), Dianna, author, Francesco (son of Santino and Enza), Renato (husband to Marina), and Santino Giannetti.

Dianna and author,
restaurant, Atina, Italy

Chilipeppers, Chili for short, Au Sable River, Michigan, 2006

Dianna, Hank and Jackie Thomas, Seattle, Washington, 2007

Suzy Mushcab, Senna, Dianna, 2007

Dianna C and the Superbs: Chris Fowler, Dianna, Pam Pfau
Dianna's 50th birthday party, June 2007

Donna Miller, Pam Pfau, Dianna, Chris Fowler, Kathy Preston, Allie Langlois, 50th birthday party, June 2007

Dianna and author, 50th birthday party, June 2007

Part IV
Keep On Smiling
2000-2008

41

Alex and Anna

In February 2000 we decide to accept a "come to Orlando for a free cruise to the Bahamas on us—and by the way, take a no-obligation peek at our timeshare program" deal. Dianna has long wanted to go on a cruise as well as to Disney World just like any other kid I know, so we plan it all together as one trip. Just for myself, I'm certain I would never do either one. But I also build in a day trip to the Kennedy Space Center, so I can show her the Apollo rocket I worked on while in the USAF long before I met her.

Just before we leave, we get a sober call from our good friend, Alex Vogel, about his wife Anna. She is in the last stages of ALS.

"John, Anna is losing ground fast. She would like to see you both."

We are scrambling to decide if we should cancel our Florida trip when Alex suggests it will be okay to continue with our plans, but instead of going home, come, instead, to his home in Chapel Hill. We agree and change our plane tickets.

We do our three-day cruise on a boat loaded with local young people, using it as a three-day weekend boat party. Lots of food, lots of people, blue skies, and warm winds. Dianna is delighted and delightful. After an afternoon walk around a super upscale hotel, complete with underground aquarium on Paradise Island, we both know we are visiting a foreign country. We will always be strangers here.

We are blessed to show up at Disney World during the 2000 millennium celebrations. Each night the parade and music are nothing short of spectacular. Later in the evening, we stand, hand in hand, tears in our eyes, watching an amazing explosion of light tracing across the night sky. We return to this celebration every night we are there.

Lastly, we make the short drive to the coast, so I can show her the Saturn rocket and the engines I worked on while in the Mojave Desert in California, fond memories for me.

Needless to say, we do not buy a timeshare.

Our mood change is total as we leave Orlando for the most important part of the trip. When we arrive in Raleigh, Alex picks us up and we drive to Chapel Hill. Dianna and I sit on each side of the bed next to Anna. She can no longer speak, but she is listening. She is glad to see me, but her eyes literally sparkle when she sees Dianna. Dianna leans in, their heads pressed together, whispering inaudibly into Anna's ear for a long time, her arms around her while Anna's smile seems to glow in the bedroom's low light. They hold hands long into the night, while I try to console an inconsolable Alex.

Anna dies during the night.

Through our tears and our breaking hearts, we are infinitely grateful we made it in time.

"She was only waiting for you," Alex says.

Alex has been such a hero in all this. He took care of Anna for years, dealing with one setback after another, tumbling down an ever-steepening slope, with no hope of any other outcome but this one. His courage is amazing.

A couple of months later, Alex holds a memorial service in Midland for their many friends there. Ironically, it is in the Center for the Arts building, the same building where Dianna and I were married thirteen years earlier. Dianna is the first to stand and speak. No notes. Just reaches into her heart and picks the perfect words she finds there. She speaks of Anna's beautiful qualities, and how much she admired and loved her. She says this with perfect composure, while I sit in the audience, listening, unable to hold back my tears.

There it is. A soul gone from our planet, but never from our hearts.

Alex must now go on alone.

42

Redemption

One night, in midwinter 2000, Dianna wakes me up. She tells me she's having a reaction to the drugs she has been taking. I turn on the lights and pull up her nightgown. Huge red blotches cover most of her body.

"Honey, it's getting harder to breathe, too. Do we have any Benadryl?"

I search our medicine cabinets. We have our own private pharmacy filled with every drug sold on the planet. But, of course, we have no Benadryl.

"I'm so sorry, honey, but I think you need to go out and get some, ... tonight, ...now. I would send mom, but I don't want to wake her, and the weather is terrible, too."

Dianna's mom, Pat, is visiting, sleeping in an upstairs bedroom.

"It's okay. Better I go. I know where the drugstores are anyway. I'll do it right now, but I'm not sure what's open this time of night." I look at the clock. It is 3:00 a.m. I make some calls, and the only place I find open is in Adrian. It will take me close to an hour to make the round trip. I head out the door. Fortunately I'm in such a hurry, I leave Cracker home, something I rarely do.

The twisting back roads I normally love so much are just about as bad as I've ever seen them, several inches of unplowed, drifting snow with sheets of ice underneath and the wind howling. I must go slowly—cannot afford to get stuck now. By the time I pull into the garage, Benadryl in hand, I have been gone almost two hours.

When I walk in the door, no one's there, except Cracker. I find a note on the kitchen counter. "Gone to Bixby hospital."

Bixby hospital is a small community hospital in Adrian, where I had just come from. I load Cracker into the car and head back into town.

Dianna is laying on a hospital gurney with an IV going, already looking better. Pat is sitting straight up in a chair next to the bed, looking disheveled but wide awake and alert. A thought floats into my head. So that's where it comes from, that "sitting up straight, ready for anything" gene.

"You will never guess what happened, honey," Dianna says, her voice sounding like her usual high-pitched song. She is breathless now but with excitement, not fear. "Cracker saved my life!"

I look over at Pat, who first called Cracker "the dog from hell" and had always pushed for us to get rid of him. She's not in her usual fighting mood right now.

"What do you mean?"

"You are not going to believe this, honey, but I got to the point where I couldn't breathe. And I didn't have the strength to get out of bed and go up the stairs to get Mom. I yelled for her as loud as I could, but she was dead to the world. I couldn't yell very loud, either. I was so scared, I couldn't catch my breath."

"My door was closed. I couldn't hear her calling me," Pat chimes in.

"Honey, suddenly Cracker jumped up on the bed and stood over me, staring into my eyes. He knew something was wrong. I didn't even say anything to him. Suddenly, he just took off, and I thought, oh my God, he's leaving me in my time of need."

"Would be just like him," Pat could not help adding, but she was laughing.

"John, you know what he did? He went up the stairs and started barking at Mom's door. When she didn't get up, he pulled the door handle down, pushed the door open and went right to Mom and started nudging her!"

"I was so mad at that damned dog when I felt his wet nose splattering in my face," Pat adds, smirking.

"Then Mom heard me downstairs, calling."

"Her voice was so weak, I could barely hear her, even after I was awake,' Pat says.

"Wow. Amazing. Absolutely amazing. Pretty handy having a dog with superior skills, though, isn't it, Pat?" I say, leaning toward Pat and boring a hole through her, milking this moment for all it is worth.

She says nothing, her arms folded across her chest, but she's smiling.

"How did you get here, then? Did you drive, Pat?" I ask.

"Dianna thought to call Steve Capaldi down the street to drive us to the hospital," Pat says. Dianna had done extensive decorating work in Steve's house over the past few years, and we had become friends.

"He was so nice. He was at our house in five minutes. Thank God," Dianna says.

"Well, thank Steve, too," I say.

"Steve stayed long enough to be sure things were under control, but then he had to go—poor guy has to be at work in a couple of hours,"

Dianna says.

"So, Pat, NOW what do you think of my dog from hell, the very same dog who got your lazy ass out of bed and saved your daughter's life?"

We all start laughing.

"Well, I guess he is redeemed, …but I'm still calling him the dog from hell."

We are all still laughing, but she is not going to get the last word. Not about my dog.

"You can call him the dog from hell if you want, but we all know now where he *really* came from."

43

Reaching for Normal

Throughout the year 2000 Dianna experiences such severe hot flashes, she almost passes out. Her feet are still numb, accompanied by cramps in her legs, periodic seizures that last ten to fifteen minutes, showing up as vision problems and a lingering mint taste in her mouth. We talk about it, but are not sure what to do. Are the seizures, in particular, residual effects of the SCTP, or something new?

"It's like I'm looking at things with auras around them, and when people talk, their voices echo. And, John, I'm starting to feel pain in my spine and neck."

Periodic testing and scans don't indicate anything new to worry about.

Spring slides into summer, then fall.

"I've decided," she says one day.

"Really. That's good, I guess, …decided what?"

"I want to get nipples on my breasts."

"Well…, okay, I guess…, but you can have mine, you know. I don't need them for any purpose I can see."

"Oh, stop it. I'm serious. It's important to me."

"Honey, if it's important to you, then do it."

"I just want to look more…normal."

"Sweetheart, you'll always be normal, and you'll never be normal."

44

Look at These!

Dianna is introduced to "The Monday Night Group" by Sandy Johnson, a good friend. It's basically a spiritual study group of eight to fifteen women who meet once a month, aimed at spiritual, mental, and emotional growth.

I don't really know what happens there, but I can see it's good for Dianna. Sometimes they meet at our house, which Dianna likes, giving her a chance to entertain and an excuse to put yet another twist on her home décor. One day I'm watching her lost in meticulous, joyful preparation—it looks like a meditation for her. All her "discomfort" seems far away.

When the women gather at our house, I stay out of their way but can hear laughter sprinkled into long periods of murmuring. Hope they're learning something. Sometimes I drop in at the end to munch on leftovers and kibitz as they are leaving.

Sandy tells me, laughing, about one meeting not long after Dianna's nipple reconstruction process was completed. There are about a dozen women there.

Halfway through the meeting, Dianna makes an announcement. "Girls, I have a surprise to share."

All eyes turn toward her.

"Look at these!" she says, as she nonchalantly lifts her blouse up around her neck, exposing her bare breasts.

"What'd you think?"

Sandy reports Dianna is greeted with a kaleidoscope of reactions with a few women probably embarrassed. But most are just laughing, entrained into Dianna's joy at being "normal" again.

I wish I could have been there.

45

Bombs Away

We are sitting in one of Dr. Stella's meeting rooms on November 21, 2000. He comes in and sits down. His usual bright nature and ready smile looks frayed.

He doesn't beat around the bush.

"Dianna, the cancer has metastasized to your bones. The MRI shows involvement in the thoracic spine, at T7, T10, as well as the left iliac bone—your hip—and some spots on the ribs."

We already know something is going on from a meeting with Dr. Klein at Harper, based on bone scans done there. Since MRIs can offer a more definitive diagnosis, he recommended we follow up with one at St. Joe's. Maybe Dianna already knows what having bone mets mean. I do not.

"Dianna, there is no possibility of a cure at this point."

I feel like someone has just stuck a sharp knife into my heart, then twisted it.

Dianna is sitting a little in front of me so I can see her, but she cannot easily see me. I glance over at her. She looks impassive, her hands folded in her lap, staring intently at Stella. I try hard not to, but I begin to cry silently, tears tumbling down my cheeks. I just can't help it. I drop my head into my hands, my elbows on my knees.

Stella cuts me a break by ignoring me. He focuses directly on Dianna, and he has her rapt attention.

"What we are shooting for now with treatment is quality of life. Whatever protocols I suggest will be focused on hindering the advance of the cancer while providing you with a life you want to live."

Dianna nods her head in agreement, but says nothing. She is remarkably calm. As usual she has been way ahead of me all along.

I get my act together and climb back into the game. "So…what does this mean?" I ask.

"Well, in terms of a prognosis, in terms of how long you may live with this situation, really, no one knows. It's possible Dianna may live with this for years."

Driving home, we are both quiet. When we turn off on US-12, I turn to her. "Why don't we stop at Ruby Tuesday and catch some lunch?"

"That's a good idea, honey. Let's do." She brightens a little.

While she is studying the menu, I go up to the salad bar, the main reason I love this place. When I return, I immediately dive in and suddenly a thought comes to mind. Years? He said years, not weeks or months. "Honey, you know what we are looking at here?"

"What?" she says absently, still studying the menu.

"We have another way to look at this. He said you could live with this for years. I think we need to look at the cancer you have as a chronic disease, not a terminal one."

She looks up at me, and slowly lays down her menu. She is quiet for a moment, her eyes brighten, and I see her first real smile of the day. "I think I'll order the grilled salmon," she says, picking up the menu again. "And I'm getting tiramisu after that, too." She drops the menu down on the table unceremoniously and sits back, looking almost smug now.

"Chronic disease" slides seamlessly into her lexicon and, as time goes by, I listen to her discussing her medical circumstances with friends and family. "Chronic disease" becomes a steady drumbeat that drowns out negative ways of thinking, feeling, and seeing life. She quickly falls back into her natural disposition.

She has, once again, found the pony in the room.

I see the same pony she does, but it's hard for me not to notice how the rest of the room looks, too. Maybe she sees the whole room, too, and it doesn't matter. I wonder about this, but I know I'm never going to ask.

46

The Chemo Orchestra

January 2001

The game plan from now on is to play the quadzillion drugs out there—they are the orchestra—the violins, brass, and percussion instruments. And Dr. Stella is the conductor. Play louder here, softer there, slow the beat here, hasten it there. Try to create the music we all want to hear. Not just survival but, as he put it, a life she wants to live, a life worth living.

He tells me he learned this perspective early on when, just out of residency, he chose to work with Mother Teresa in India. One day, he was attending a dying woman who was struggling to breathe. He knew what to do, jumped on the bed, straddled her, quickly stuffed a tube down her throat, and syringed out the pink foamy liquid impairing her breathing. When he turned to the women standing vigil around the bed, feeling triumphant, he was stunned. He expected trumpets. Something. Instead, there was dead silence in the room and a look of horror in their eyes.

A few days later, when the woman died, as she was in the process of doing anyway, Stella realized all he had accomplished was to extend her suffering by interfering with her natural dying process. He took this lesson to heart and into his oncology practice, and he brings this gift to us now.

His story starts me thinking. Death need not be experienced as a failure for a doctor—or for any of us—but simply the final note in a beautiful piece of music, each life, however lived.

Since we all get to do it, the evidence is pretty overwhelming. Death must be an important lesson in life we all need to experience.

Given I am almost twenty years older than Dianna, I have always assumed I will go before her. I'm not emotionally prepared for it to be any other way. I desperately don't want it to be any other way.

Dianna expected our dying to follow the "normal sequence," too, constantly haranguing me about smoking (while munching down her tiramisu, of course) until I finally did quit—for twelve years. But as the year 2000 slides into 2001, my emotional pain level goes sky high, breaks

194

through my normal hum, and I start up again.

"Honey, I wish you would quit smoking. It will kill you."

"I'll quit smoking when you quit dying. I'm just trying to stay ahead of you," I quip.

She laughs at the twist on words, but follows it with a look that could only be described as scathing. Not at my mention of her dying—she is far too pragmatic to be upset about that—but because I have the health she so desperately would love to have, and I'm squandering it. She has zero patience for the stupidity of wasting life.

Dr. Stella takes a flyer and puts her on Aredia, hoping her cancer is hormone-receptive. He is doing his best to put her on a more targeted treatment less brutal than mainstream hardcore chemo drugs.

"Honey, do you really think you should go to Arizona right now?"

"I want to. I have to. Kris is really down and she needs me to come. I'll be okay. Anyway, it'll be a nice break in the weather, too, don't you think?"

She is going to visit Kris Forest, a close friend who is on her own journey with cancer and feeling despondent.

So Dianna goes, calls me after she has been there a few days and reports, unsurprisingly, they are having a great time. By the time she gets home two weeks later, looking as tan as she ever gets and having given Kris a dose of "Diannadopamine," she also knows the new drug she is on is not working.

"I feel more pain. I think the bone mets are getting worse."

When we see Stella, the latest MRI confirms her suspicions. Nice try, but no cigar.

At this point we don't know whether this cancer is a metastasis from her second breast cancer in 1996 or her very first breast cancer in 1990. About this time, Dianna asks if her original cancer was ever checked for the HER2/neu gene.

Stella is taken aback.

"You mean this has never been done?" he says. Then it dawns on him that the importance of this gene was not generally known back then.

The HER2/neu gene sends control signals to the cells, telling them to grow, divide, and make repairs. Some kinds of breast cancer start when the gene over-produces the HER2/neu protein, resulting in cells dividing much too quickly.

A positive HER2/neu test would indicate her HER2 genes are over-producing the protein, promoting cancer growth. Dianna knows all this already from her incessant study, and she is certain this test has never been done for her.

Stella orders it immediately. I'm surprised tumors removed back in 1990 are still being stored away in someone's refrigerator, but gratefully they are.

The tests are done, and her 1996 cancer is found to be negative, but her 1990 cancer shows up as +3 positive, the top end of the scale, meaning the most aggressive cancer growth.

The importance of all this is that a relatively new drug, Herceptin, has been found to be effective for a HER2/neu positive cancer. It is such a targeted drug; it has very few side effects, a godsend for that quality of life we are after.

But the cancer is spreading so rapidly, Stella feels it will be better to get it under control first with hard chemo, keeping Herceptin, which is still, after all, experimental, in our back pocket for later. He starts Dianna on a regimen of Xeloda, Aredia (to strengthen bones), and Arimidex.

Over time, we confirm this regimen is doing the job, but Dianna is paying the price with "hand/foot syndrome," a predictable side effect of Xeloda. Her feet and hands are cracking and bleeding, and she breaks out in rashes on her arms, legs, and torso. She is also still dealing with SCTP aftereffects—weakened heart function, trouble breathing, dizzy spells, and her feet remain numb from the ankles down. She starts taking depakote to control her seizures, reducing their severity and frequency.

In April, she gets radiation to her spine to slow down the cancer and reduce the pain in those tumor locations. It buys us time.

Kathy Preston delivers an amazing album to Dianna for her birthday. She had secretly put out a call to Dianna's friends months before, asking them to write their thoughts and memories about Dianna. Kathy collected and organized their comments into a beautiful collage of photos and letters. Dianna sits in the living room, silently turning each page gently, slowly, deeply moved by what her friends—over sixty of them—have written, tributes dominated by themes of love, strength, courage, enthusiasm, humor, sprinkled with poignant stories of how Dianna has touched their lives.

Nothing there is any surprise to me.

47

Life Back at the Plant

Meanwhile at the plant, after several years of focused work, things are radically better. Our employee injuries have dropped from 40–50/year to 2–3/year. Instead of having plant evacuations on a monthly basis, frightening our neighbors, we have operated for several years without a single reportable release. The plant is unsurprisingly running much better, too.

This radical change did not happen simply because I thought it was a nice idea. Biolab's upper management poured in the money we needed, our local management spent it well, our engineers automated and improved our processes, federal and state regulators partnered with us to get better, and community support systems embraced us. Not only were we a team inside the plant, but we had created a larger team, a network of support, all focused on a vision we could all share, each for our own reasons.

It's a win–win all around.

We have created a new culture. We are at last the high-performance team operating a world-class chemical plant safely and without damaging the environment, achieving a vision I had dreamed of a lifetime ago, it seems. Most important of all, we have a sort of caring—we could call it love—for each other that no one needs to talk about, but everyone understands.

In late 1999 I am tired of our sister plant in the south, which processes chemicals similar to our own and has a long tradition of few recordable injuries, snickering at us. Like everyone else in the company, they have long thought of us as, well, pathetic. However, I see them as providing an opportunity for us to reach the next level.

I make sure our people hear about our longstanding reputation with those who do not know "the new us." I tell them I have challenged our sister plant to a contest for the year 2000. Whoever ends the year with the fewest recordable injuries wins "the trophy." I post both plant records on the wall next to the time clock, so each day everyone is aware of the score in this game.

As the months go by, the excitement rises. We are neck and neck, both with zero recordable injuries. But late in the year, our sister plant gets one. I hate to admit it, but I—we—are elated. We finish the year with zero, and win the trophy. I have a cabinet made in the hallway to display it. It is our crowning moment.

"To tell you the truth, I didn't believe there was a snowball's chance in hell you'd win," the plant manager says.

"*I* didn't win. *We* won. That's what makes it so sweet."

Of course, I show no mercy. I spend the next year relentlessly rubbing it into the people at our sister plant. They are good sports…but they don't like it.

Our safety standards and environmental permits are in good shape, and our relationships with the EPA and the MDEQ excellent. One day, standing in the hall and looking at our trophy, I realize we have reached all those goals I came here to intentionally accomplish. A sadness leaks into me, and I am not quite sure where it is coming from.

From this moment on, it is a long, slow downhill for me personally. Things continue to go well at the plant, and I love the people there. But… without consciously realizing it, my next important challenge is at home, not at work. Dianna is occupying more and more of my heart and mind while the plant is on cruise control.

During 2001 at almost any time of day, my concentration often and suddenly evaporates. My feelings overwhelm my thinking, and I must escape. Fortunately there is a park nearby with the Raisin River running through it. Sitting on the bank, watching the river rippling around fallen trees, I might burst out crying, creating a river of my own without knowing exactly why. Well, I do know why.

Our HR manager, a woman I like very much, emails me one day in January 2001.

"John, I am concerned about your sudden change in outlook. You were always so up. Everyone is noticing your mood has changed. We have an Employee Assistance Program if you would like to know more about it. What's wrong?"

I email her back.

"Well, it might be watching the person I love most in the world—and the most beautiful human being I have ever been privileged to know—gradually dying of cancer and taking down her Christmas decorations slowly, wrapping each one carefully, then wondering out loud, in a voice so soft it feels like falling snow, whether she will be around to put them up again next year, smiling at me as if she is telling me what's for dinner tonight. But I am old enough to know not all moments in life are the same. Fortunately and unfortunately."

I go on to tell her, "I'm not interested in drugs or counseling. I don't need it. I am fully alive and experiencing this Present. So deeply, sometimes I can hardly stand it. Life is, naturally, both joy and pain, and I am willing to embrace both in full measure. Right now both are happening at the same time for the same reasons, if that makes any sense. But I am not a loose cannon (well, anymore than I've ever been). I would never hurt anyone or myself."

And that's the end of that.

Life goes on, no time-outs.

"Better"

As Dianna wades through choppy waters, "presenting" an ever-changing kaleidoscope of "discomforts," a continuing stream of friends and family visit. So much love, but none of them fully appreciate, understandably so, what she is going through. She doesn't help them much, either. I listen to her when people ask how she is doing.

"Better," she invariably says.

One day I'm thinking about this new word in her lexicon, one of her favorites these days. Is she saying this because she really believes it?

Yes.

I live with her every day, but I can't really know what it's like being in her body. So my appreciation for what she is up against slips through my consciousness, unnoticed, like the wind through the trees. When something is always there, it often becomes invisible.

What I do notice is, with each setback, it may take her an hour or a day to process her anger, disappointment, sadness; but it's never long before she just somehow *changes her mind* about it. Instead of sliding into a pity party, or even doing a "grin and bear it" routine, she reliably chooses to genuinely *let it go*, exiting each valley with renewed optimism and resolve, showcased with the same scintillating smile emerging from deep within her being. She is focused like a laser beam on living her life as fully as possible, on doing her Work.

I am struck full force by the pain she is mastering only when I'm rubbing lotion into her cracking, bleeding feet, or massaging her legs because they hurt so much, or changing her diaper again, or....

In return, I get all the Hi, honeeees I always got.

Her favorite therapy is working on *her* home, or visiting and receiving her huge collection of friends and family. My favorite therapy is to walk with Cracker in some nearby woods or field, and occasional fall grouse and deer hunting trips with my sons and brother.

One winter day, Cracker and I make our way across an open field through a couple inches of snow and into a cluster of evergreens surrounding a frozen swamp. I sit down on a snow-covered log while Cracker drifts off on his own, nosing around. A metallic gray sky spreads a silver patina over everything—the prickly firs and soft cedars surrounding me, the tufts of grass poking through the snow, even the snow itself.

I start thinking about "better." If sometimes her situation looks better to me, and other times worse, why does she always believe things are better?

People thrown to be more cynical or "realistic" may look at her as incredibly unrealistic, even foolish. But it is clear to me, it is *their* attitude that's foolish. She is reliably hard-nosed, deals with the facts as they are, and she can read what she is up against better than anyone I know. So they just don't get it.

But get what, exactly?

Cracker lets out a bark deep into the swamp, and I wonder what he's up to now. After considering all my options, I decide to let him be. He's a big boy.

A flash of insight. Dianna somehow, naturally I think, comprehends the power of creating from a future she can imagine rather than surrendering to current circumstances, whatever they happen to be. She ignores conventional wisdom and lives from her own inner wisdom.

Maybe at some level, she is in touch with her spiritual path and, as long as she is on that path, things *are* "better" no matter what the circumstances look like. This feels somehow authentic. I'm excited. I'm onto something true.

Does she consciously know this? I doubt it. I think it is part of the natural Talent she brought with her into this reality, like red roses bring red, or Cracker, his desire to hunt.

A crow screams its disapproval somewhere on the other side of the swamp. Maybe Cracker. I whistle for him, and a few minutes later he shows up, trotting casually toward me, looking satisfied and content. Who knows what the hell he has been up to, but he looks happy.

Me, too.

I stand up, ready to go. My ass is wet. What I get for sitting in one spot for too long.

As I start back, I'm thinking, no one will ever know how incredibly satisfying it is to live with this woman, no matter what the circumstances. The best part of *my* "better" is her being in my life.

Cracker counts real big for me, too, I'm thinking, as I watch him pushing through some naked dogwood surrounded by died-back ferns, maybe ten yards ahead of me. The light is fading fast now as we follow a deer trail that looks like an expressway, taking us around the swamp and out of the woods.

The days are short now. It will be dark soon.

Diannaisms

"John, it was a horrible crash and when the police finally got there, she was mortally dead," Dianna says, sounding almost breathless, as she recounts the plot of a movie she had watched last night.

We are cruising east on US-12 in *her* Toyota van—she claims ownership mostly because our levels of acceptable cleanliness differ considerably—she is the neatnik—so, if she cleans it and I don't—which is always the case—this is enough to make it hers. She does take excellent care of everything she feels any ownership about: house, car, clothes, and even the simplest things, no matter how ragged she may feel at the time. I do respect her appreciation for stuff. Sometimes I even wish I shared it.

We are on our way to one of her gazillion chemo treatments at St. Joseph's Hospital in Ypsilanti. I can make this drive in my sleep…and sometimes almost do.

I look over at her.

She must have at least a dozen wigs, and the one she is wearing now I like very much. Would be hard to find fault with her appearance most any day. Today she is dressed to the nines, makeup perfect and nails edgy, a bright lime-green this time.

"Dead is enough, honey," I say finally.

She looks over at me, one eyebrow going up a little.

"What do you mean?"

"You don't have to say mortally dead. There's no other way to be dead but mortally."

She pauses, rolling that around in her mind. "Well…I was just emphasizing it."

"But people don't ever say that. You wouldn't say she was dead dead, would you? That's kinda what you're saying when you say mortally dead." I look over to her to see if she is following me on this.

She is staring straight ahead again and shifts in her seat, quiet now, as if she is re-programming some new bytes into memory…and maybe removing some, too. Time goes by in silence.

When I met her in 1985 Dianna had a long list of "coined phrases," turning clichés into non-clichés, her "Diannaisms," as those who knew and loved her came to call them, always with a smile. She didn't do this as a device, but just routinely got it wrong. Everyone knew what she meant, so no one bothered to correct her. Most people counted it as another small blessing among the many she gave them.

Over the years, I routinely brought them to her attention as they popped up here and there like colorful crocuses in the gardens of our conversations—not as a criticism, but because they were fun and it was hard to leave them alone. Unfortunately, once something is in my mind, it is going to come out of my mouth. When she learns they are not normal, she rapidly reprograms her brain to let them go, banishing them into the ether.

Gradually I came to deeply regret this process of attrition I have been materially responsible for over the years. Instead of simply admiring these unique flowers, I had to go ahead and pick them, only to see them die, one by one.

On the other hand, because she happened to be a large-breasted, beautiful blonde, I'm clear she was absolutely determined not to be written off as *that* particular cliché. So maybe she *had* to give up her Diannaisms in order to maintain a kind of credibility, supporting the image she wanted for herself. I really don't know.

Truth is, she is at least as mentally intelligent as I am, can read with lightning speed—and absorb it. She's light years ahead of me emotionally, and in terms of astuteness about people, unmatched. Most of my friends and family were totally thrown off when they first met her—her looks, her bouncing enthusiasm, and her sprinkling of "isms" and other language gaffs were entirely misleading.

In any event, much later, I implore her friends and family to make a list of her peculiar yet delightful ways of expressing things, her Diannaisms. Remarkably, no one can remember a single one of them anymore. Few minds track in those quirky grooves Dianna so comfortably traveled in.

"Well, you know what I mean," she says, long after I had stopped thinking about this particular Diannaism.

I laugh. "Sure, honey, it's okay to say it that way if that's what you want. Not only that, but I love you."

She smiles, still staring straight ahead.

She rarely ever says, "I love you, too." I like this. This is one cliché she ignores for some reason. It adds a tiny, delicious mysteriousness to our way of being together.

In the beginning, when there was still uncertainty in our relationship, it was unsettling for me in those moments when that gap in the air remained unfilled. Maybe she enjoyed creating a bit of uncertainty, too. As time went by and the cadence of our relationship became a comforting song, her non-response became the right note in the right place.

"Can we stop at Ruby Tuesday on the way home, honey?" she asks finally as we approach Saline. She takes my hand and squeezes it a little.

I lean over and peck her on the cheek. "Sure."

This is the last time I remember her saying "mortally dead."

48

Mae West Reincarnates

Dianna's Monday night group is meeting at Garfield's, a restaurant in Adrian, for a Halloween get-together. I'm slumped into an easy chair in the living room, reading, when she shows up in the middle of the room with a mink stole covering a long black, form-fitting dress, bright-red lipstick, and a huge outlandishly puffed-up platinum-blonde wig. Have never seen this one before.

"Well, what'd you think?" she says, spinning around slowly and trying to look sultry. "Think I'll get the prize?"

"There's a prize?"

I decide to videotape her for posterity and get out the camcorder.

"Okay, any words of wisdom for us, Mae?"

"Well, you know, it takes a million bucks to look like this," she says in her best Mae West impersonation as she starts laughing, "and half a day to get ready."

"Yeah, I can vouch for that," I say, speaking for the camera. "I can report she did *not* look like this when she got out of bed this morning."

Dianna is still laughing.

"Do your best Mae West impersonation for the camera, sweetheart."

She exits, slinks back in and fumbles the famous line. I correct her, and she goes back out and does it again, this time, perfectly, and in a husky voice, dragging out the words in a drawl, "Why don't you come up and see me sometime?" then folds over at the waist, dissolving in laughter.

"Last time I had this much makeup on was probably last Halloween."

"Well, she needs every bit of it," I say for the camera. "But I'm guessing all the guys there will be hitting on her."

"They'll probably think I'm the neighborhood whore," she says, still laughing.

I shut off the camera and we sit down at the dining room table together. It's almost time for her to leave.

"Sure you are up for this, though?" I ask, as she starts coughing. She looks tired now that the camera is off. The past few days have been particularly rough with the hand/foot syndrome, and she is just getting over a respiratory infection, and her lungs are still not fully recovered from the SCTP.

"Well..., it's Halloween..., I can't disappoint my followers," she says smiling, "I'm okay. It'll be fun."

I never do find out if she won the prize or not...or even if there was one.

Anyway, she gets my prize for *showing up*.

49

Dianna Tries Them All...with Senna in Hand

Some of our neighbors attend a little white country church, Springville United Methodist, not far from our home, and have taken to praying for Dianna. They start inviting her to services, and of course she goes. The pastor there is a young, vivacious woman, Melanie Chalker, a former artist from upstate who turned minister. She and Dianna take to each other instantly, become fast friends, and Dianna starts going regularly.

November 18, 2001

"Well, honey, feel any different now that you're a Methodist?" I ask her while videotaping her and Senna, now two-and-a-half years old. Dianna had picked her up to attend this seminal event marking Dianna's formal admission to the church.

"Not any different than when I was a Catholic or a Lutheran," she says, laughing.

"Well, why bother then?" I say, teasing her. "I knew this would all come to no good."

She knows I have absolutely no interest, but no animosity, either, toward all organized religions. For me that is their problem. They're organized. Their own survival becomes a motivation conflating with what they are supposed to be about, which is mostly good stuff..., but not all good stuff.

I connect best with God in Nature.

Ralph Waldo Emerson once said, "In the woods, we return to reason and faith." I guess this is how it is for me.

Basically, I'm probably a Pantheist with Buddhist leanings. I deeply believe in Spirit, in life after physical death, in reincarnation—Dianna knows all this about me; and on all these points of faith, Dianna and I use the same playbook. She is just the more social animal, so this little church filled with people is another place for her to play. Okay with me.

"I like this church, John. It's small and they do good things—they have a soup kitchen, help young mothers with a food pantry, do lots of

208

humanitarian things. And after services, we have coffee and spend time together."

"And they've been praying for you for the past two years. You owe them. You had to join."

She starts laughing, and Senna lets out a high-pitched, ear-shattering squeal. Why? How should I know? Because this is a talent little girls seem to be imbued with genetically.

"That's true, too. I need all the help I can get," Dianna says, still laughing.

"Today, we celebrated my good news, too. Had to make everyone feel like their prayers were being answered after all," she says, laughing even harder.

She is referring to the Xeloda working, her bone mets receding, and everything seemingly under control.

She goes on to describe Senna's antics, walking up to the front of the church, sitting on Pastor Melanie's lap, everyone chuckling, Senna's bib pants falling down around her ankles, then cozying up to a four-year-old boy desperately trying to avoid her, sliding down the pew until she has him pinned against the wall. Dianna reports all this while laughing so hard she is bent over.

So it's a good day. Dianna has enrolled yet another support group—people who gladly love and encourage her while entwined in her love, light, and joy of living. I know she will give everything she has to help them in the years ahead.

As I videotape her this day, watching her, listening to her, I am stunned by how effortlessly she gives herself completely away...to everything...to everyone...joyfully, gratefully. She will have left nothing on the table when the game is over.

While all this is going on, Senna is entranced with a huge box of Dianna's jewelry, has about fifteen necklaces around her neck, and going for more. Dianna keeps fishing them out of the box and feeding them to her. I watch them in silence, their heads together, almost touching, as they explore the contents of the box.

Senna wants it all. Dianna gives all of it to her.

In early December 2001, I walk in the door to find Dianna bowed toward Senna, her arm around her, their hair mixed together. They are making homemade Christmas cookie decorations. I get a full but quick "Hi, honeeee," then, just as quickly, I'm abandoned. Senna, sitting on the counter, covered with flour from head to toe, barely notices me. Dianna is offering instructions in soft tones, showing her how to do this and that, while Senna focuses on her. I leave them to their disaster, happy.

Later that day, Dianna takes her shopping, picking out gifts for underprivileged children, explaining to her, these gifts are not for her, but for other kids who don't have very much.

"I want her to learn, first of all, that not everything is for her, and also that there are children in this world who may not get Christmas presents unless we give them. So, we are going to be Santa for them."

"What a great idea, honey. What made you think of that?"

"Well, I'm doing this project for the church anyway and saw this would a good experience for Senna. I picked her up this morning and I'll take her home tomorrow."

"You're willing to drive back and forth across Detroit—twice—to give Senna a lesson in charity?"

Dianna looks at me as if I've grown horns. "Of course. We had such fun, didn't we, Senna?"

Senna laughs, then emits another one of her piercing little-girl screams, bouncing around the kitchen like a pinball.

"And she did so well, John. Once she got the idea, she had such fun picking things out for our cart. I think she is going to be a very unselfish child."

"Guess you're saying she'll never get anywhere in life," I say, laughing.

Dianna looks at me. Idiot. When Senna is not looking, she flips me a big fat finger.

"But I'm not kidding. She is such a happy child," she says.

"I agree. Speaks volumes about Jon and Cris and what a good job they are doing. Guess Jon took notes on his own father."

"What do you mean?"

"Well, apparently, he has decided to do exactly the opposite of whatever I did." I'm both serious and not serious.

"Oh, stop it."

"Senna, want to help me wrap these gifts?" she asks, and they go off together, hand in hand.

It will always be this way with them. Hand in hand.

And with me, lurking in the background, watching this one-act play with a single plot and a single theme.

50

The Doctor from Hell

I start spending a lot more time on the Internet, researching cancer-related topics. One day, I notice an article saying the stem cell transplant procedure Dianna went through does not really work for breast cancer. Turns out there was only a short, two-year window when the medical consensus was that it did. Dianna happened to show up during those two years.

Lucky us.

All of Dianna's peripheral neuropathy, seizures, not to mention the horrific experience she went through, are consequences of this procedure she gladly endured because she was hoping for a cure. So it was a false hope resulting in lifelong damage to her…, and to many others…, not to mention the financial cost to us and to society.

The basis for believing it did work rested almost entirely on trials done by a doctor in South Africa. Turns out he faked the data, was labeled a fraud, and ultimately fired from the university that employed him.

I would love to strangle the son of a bitch if I could. I am tempted to mention his name, just to stick it to him; but revenge is inconsistent with the spirit Dianna represents.

He knows who he is.

When I tell Dianna about all this, she continues pounding a nail into the bedroom wall without even looking at me.

It's almost as if it goes in one ear and out the other. She hears it, she understands it, and it's nothing but history for her. There's nothing she can do about it now. She chooses, without any hesitation, to let it go, put zero energy into it, and refuses to create negative thoughts about it.

"Can't we just make a quick trip over there and break all his fingers." I say.

Dianna laughs, then, just as quickly, becomes serious again.

"There's too much to appreciate in life, John. I don't have time for anger or hatred," she says, looking over her shoulder toward me.

While she's talking, she keeps hitting the nail on the head.

211

"I think the Forum helped me with this, too. And you have, too, sweetheart," she says, finally hanging the print on the nail, then straightening it. "There. That looks good, don't you think?"

"Well, if I've helped at all, you can thank my dad for it. Someone could shoot him in the left eye and he would forgive them. Maybe I was given a little of that."

This is the only time we talk about this excuse for a doctor.

Part of me still wants to strangle the guy. Probably the part that came from my mom, who kept book on anyone she perceived had ever wronged her or, God forbid, any of her family. She had excellent Mafia potential. Fierce. This part of me still thinks we should break at least some of his fingers.

The other part of me says, not really. Like all of us, this doctor has his own private hell to work through.

Dianna is right.

Again.

Dammit.

51

The Orchestra Plays On

By the end of 2001 Dianna is doing pretty well on the Xeloda, based on routine MRIs and bone scans done every few months. She is trading a regression of bone mets and no other signs of cancer for severe hand/foot syndrome. The seizure medication is spacing out her seizures and making them milder. This is a trade she is happy to make, giving us stability for all of 2002.

In March 2003 bone scans begin to show the bone mets are advancing again. The Xeloda is no longer working.

Dr. Stella switches Dianna to Carboplatin and Taxotere, drugs that had worked so well before the SCTP. Dianna soon thereafter begins "presenting" (another euphemistic medical term like "discomfort") with a variety of symptoms: dizziness, night sweats, increased peripheral neuropathy in her legs, feet, and arms, cushionoid swelling due to the adrenal system being overloaded with all the decadron she is taking. Her weight balloons back up to 204 pounds. In July she breaks out in a full body rash and starts taking Benadryl. In exchange for all this "presenting," the bone mets recede again.

In August, Stella gives Dianna a "chemo holiday." Maybe he figures she cannot handle much more "presenting." So he decides to tone down the brass (hard chemo) and bring up the strings. He starts her on Herceptin in late August 2003.

Herceptin is an antibody that binds selectively to the HER2 protein, preventing cells from reproducing uncontrollably. This treatment can increase survival time. However, cancers usually develop resistance to it eventually.

Dianna knows all this already.

"John, I'll just be forever grateful if I can have five more years," she says one day as we are driving home from a chemo treatment.

"Honey, you'll probably live longer than I do."

She looks at me like maybe I have lost most of my brain function.

213

52

Chili Shows Up

Our next-door neighbor, Linda Ladd, catches me walking Cracker down the street and asks me if I would be interested in a second golden retriever. Her daughter is visiting with an eight-week-old puppy they want to sell. This is easy for me. The answer is a firm, emphatic no. I am a one-dog man, period. Settled. Done. Finished.

A couple of days later, Linda invites Dianna over for tea. A couple of hours later Dianna walks through our front door with a squirming little golden ball in her arms.

"Oh, honey, isn't he cute. I just love him."

"No."

"I just want a dog of my own. Cracker is your dog. I love him to pieces, but he mostly ignores me. He hangs on you."

This is more or less true. Plus, Cracker, as advertized, is a handful for anyone who expects a dog to be trained by some sort of magical osmosis instead of daily effort.

"Well, that's what happens when I feed him, I train him, I walk him, I play with him, I make sure he has water, ...you don't even water our house plants, Dianna, ...so of course, by default, he becomes my dog."

"Honey, please."

"Dianna, when I wind up doing all the same things for *this* dog, he will be my dog, too. Will we have to get a third one then?"

"Please."

It takes about a week, but she has that damned cancer card.

So now we have two dogs.

We register him as Chilipeppers, but in our lives he is Chili.

53

Cracker Decides to Leave

It is an uneasy relationship between Chili, who is young, full of energy, and wanting to play twenty-five hours a day, and Cracker, who is almost eight now and used to being the *only one*. I hate it, really. I want to look into one dog's eyes, pet one dog, walk one dog, and not deal with the continual competition. Cracker feels the same way. Chili is young and oblivious. Just the way it is.

By July, Cracker starts acting differently. He stops eating regularly and begins losing weight. The vet locates a tumor in a non-vital location and, with minor surgery, removes it. But his symptoms do not improve. In fact, they get worse.

Deep down inside, I cannot shake the feeling he feels pushed aside and has decided to leave. Is this just me projecting my own angst? Well, I'll never know, will I?

As summer heats up, Cracker takes to lying on the basement bathroom floor where it is quiet and cool. He stops eating. Finally the vet discovers the real cause, an inoperable tumor pressing against his esophagus.

Chili senses the change, stops harassing him and actually takes up a deathwatch, lying just outside the bathroom door near Cracker for hours at a time. It is heartwarming to see the two of them lying there together, both with their heads between their paws, almost facing each other. And it is heartbreaking to realize I must help Cracker leave.

My vet, George, is an old, down-to-earth guy. I really like him. He readily agrees to put Cracker down at home. We pick the date.

Two days ahead of time, I choose a hilltop near home, a place Cracker and I have visited many times together. I dig his grave. We had rarely seen humans here, but plenty of deer, turkeys, an occasional fox or coyote, and once, the fleeting blur of a bobcat. Best of all is the long view of valleys and hills, and the hills beyond those hills, until they fade into faint purple silhouettes. Cracker and I have sat exactly here, in spring grass, catching warm summer breezes, crunching down fallen leaves, and stretched out in the blinding white of winter, during every single year of his life.

When I am done, I gather up a few rocks for marking his grave.

The next day, I buy bottled water for him and an oversized Heineken for me at the corner store, then take Cracker for his last ride. I find a high grassy knoll and lay him down in the dappled shade of some birch trees. I sip my beer and watch him. He takes a little water now and then, looks at me, not moving a muscle, enjoying the warm sun and cool air, turning his head now and then, nose twitching.

"Best hunting dog ever, Cracker, my boy, …best friend ever." He stares into my eyes. There are tears in mine. There are none in his.

The sun is dying as I help him to his feet and carry him back to the car. He's light as a feather. I can feel all his bones, reminding me of another day too much like this one.

The next morning, Eric, my youngest son, comes out to help me bury him and just to be there. Cracker cannot get up, so I gently pick him up in my arms, carry him from his spot in the basement and lay him out in the sun in our front yard. I leave for less than five minutes. When I return, he's gone.

"I can't believe it, Eric. I didn't think he could walk two steps."

"Maybe he went off to die by himself," Eric says.

I search the neighborhood for a couple of hours and finally find him, head-to-toe wet, still dripping, lying in the cool of a neighbor's garage. He has been touring the lake shore, like he has done all his life, taking a last walk on his own.

He reluctantly struggles to his feet. I walk him slowly back to our yard between the house and the lake. We wait.

Just before George shows up, Cracker clambers to his feet, unsteady, then slowly pads down to the lake and nonchalantly walks into the water, swims out about thirty yards, circles back, then calmly walks out of the water and lays back down in the grass.

"Geez, Eric, makes me want to change my mind about this. I can't believe it."

Eric agrees with the sentiment, but we both know Cracker knows more than we will ever know. Just as he lived his life, so will he die, with a last hurrah, a last trip around the point, visiting here and there, seeing all *his* secret places, a last swim, cool now, then resting in the grass. He is doing it all his own way, just as he always has in life.

When I see George walking toward us, my heart tightens. Cracker looks relaxed, sitting on the grass between the house and the lake under a robin's-egg blue sky.

I call Cracker over to a place under a couple of aspen, clattering softly in a faint breeze. Eric and I had dug them out and brought them home on one of our grouse hunting trips…hunting with Cracker that day…and transplanted them here.

I kneel beside him, both of us sprinkled with fractured light darting through the aspen. We are immersed now in our sacred space and moment. Cracker immediately lies down on his side in the cool grass. He *knows*. I put both my hands on his side and lean into him. Dianna is standing way back, sobbing.

The vet injects him while I gently run my hands over his head, neck, and side, then bow into him, my body shudders as his goes still. Just more tears.

In a split second, his life is over, while mine has to start again in some different way I do not understand.

Eric and I take his body out to the grave site, Eric carries him in his arms for me and we bury him, put the rocks on fresh turned earth, then sit in the grass at the top of the hill watching the day breathe.

I will be long grieving this. Well, when is it ever really over?

It's a good thing Chili showed compassion in Cracker's last days or I might not have ever been able to create a relationship with him.

Even so, it will take me awhile to stop looking at him as an interloper.

54

Letter to Zena

In the summer of 2003 Dianna writes a letter to her now close friend and fellow cancer/SCTP traveler, Zena Biocca.

Dearest Zena,

I got the gifts you sent. Thanks so much for the ray of sunshine. What a cute pillow. I will hold it close. I will also pray for you as I hold it every night before bed.

I do this little ritual before I go to bed at night. I belong to this prayer group at church. I am part of a prayer chain. I pray for all those who need it and you and I, of course, are VIPs on it. It is from God I draw my faith. Zena, I believe the holy universe has a divine plan for us. We are teaching others how to live life to the fullest. I know we inspire people. I know we are a fine example for others to let go of small stuff. Get priorities right in life. Love the people you love to be with and even the ones you don't, and most of all, forgive people who have wronged you, with all your heart.

I know I've had the honor to help change people's views on life, how they should never take anything in life for granted.

School Earth is very hard. Classes are full. Lessons are learned, some easy, some not. We are always ready to graduate to the next level. Future? None of us are ever promised tomorrow, just today.

My today is overfilled with appreciation and grace. I feel so humble before the world. Sometimes, I just stare at the wonder of it all and cry, cry, cry.

Life is to feel. I guess you're not living if you don't feel. Why did I pick such a hard class to attend? I want it to last forever.

Zena, I feel so bad you were so close to your goal of five years. You didn't fail. I see it as a harder journey you took because this path of life has more [for you] to learn, more challenges. Not just us but everybody who is a focus around us, who love us, who have any relationship with us. You, my dear, will come to see this and feel this so much more than ever before. Go

218

with it, dear Zena, embrace the all of it. You will gather so much strength and fullness. The healing power will swell within your gut, and soul. And you, my dear, will be such a strong fighter and win!!! It's not win or lose, it's how the game of life is played. Play well, dear Zena, you have the dice in your hand. I love you so much, Zena. I truly believe I was [meant to meet] you and my transplant was delayed to go through that experience with you. John and I will be at the finish line waiting for you. YOU GO, GIRL!!

Blessings abundant always,

Dianna

55

Chemo Clinic Strategies

In December 2003 Dianna again decorates all the trees in the oncology clinic, as she has for the past several years—a huge twenty-five-foot tree in the lobby, and a couple of smaller ones in the waiting rooms. She enlists friends to help, but she is the CEO of Christmas at the clinic. She even solicits donations from various stores to get more lights and decorations.

She is there decorating when a local FOX news crew shows up to interview her. Someone at the clinic must have tipped them off about her story. While on camera, Dianna tells the FOX news reporter about an experience she recently had with another cancer patient.

"She told me she was terminal, and this will likely be her last Christmas with her children and family. She had lost her energy and motivation to decorate this year. Then she said, 'But, you know, Dianna, you have inspired me to make this the very best Christmas for my family that I can. We will have a tree and we will decorate it. I want to thank you so much.'"

Dianna speaks with her usual class, no tears, no voice breaking, but directly from her heart. The reporter is visibly moved. We watch it at home on TV later in the week, and they send us a copy.

Dr. Stella also sends Dianna a personal letter, thanking her for all she has done, not only for her work at Christmas, but also for her consistent positive influence on everyone, including himself, when she comes into the clinic.

"Honey, I can make a difference at the clinic—for myself and for everyone there, too. This is very important to me."

"I think it's the food that gets them," I say. On many occasions, she spends hours preparing food for the nurses and patients.

I am lying across the bed, watching her in the bathroom, getting ready for another chemo clinic visit. She spends a good hour getting her makeup just right, then chooses her wig for the day. She dresses like she's going out for dinner.

I wear a clean pair of shorts, T-shirt, and tennis shoes, so I'm as ready as I'm ever going to be.

"You know, Dianna, no one expects you to get all dressed up. Most of the women in there look like they came to get chemo, not a glass of wine and dinner."

I'm just jerking her chain. How she looks, I have already figured out, is a spiritual exercise for her.

"I have a purpose. I've worked with many abused women and did enough hair for women who were desperate, frightened, lost, without hope. I know what that's about."

She stops doing her makeup and turns to me. She's not laughing now. "I can be an example, John, not only by how I act but by how I look, too. I can say there is hope, that there is a reason to live, without having to say a word."

"Is that how the Swedish meatballs and the brownies and the dessert trays and the vegetable trays you spend hours putting together work, too?"

She smiles, humoring me. "No. Those are thank yous. Those are acknowledgments. Every nurse there works so hard to help all of us stay alive. They do it day in, day out, and they do it with such gentleness and caring. The least I can do, …the very least I can do…is to, once in awhile, say, thank you, bless you."

"Okay, well, what do you think of these shorts? Think they work for me?"

Laughing, she looks over at me. "Honey, nothing's going to work for you. You're hopeless."

I kiss her on the cheek, then take Chili outside to pee before we leave on yet another trip to Ann Arbor.

When we get to the clinic, I walk her in, help her get settled into her La-Z-Boy chemo chair, say hello to everyone, do a quick check in the coffee room to see if there are any treats, then make my escape. By the time I reach the door, she is already lost in conversation. I leave her to all that, and take Chili for a long walk in the woods along the Huron River.

The nurses are really nice. I like them and admire them. She is absolutely right about them. I would just rather be outside.

In December 2003 one of the nurses takes me aside and tells me they are planning a surprise party for Dianna, and could I get her to such and such restaurant without her knowing it.

Sure.

I do.

When Dianna and I walk in under the pretense I'm taking her out to dinner, I lead her around the corner into a banquet room. When she reaches the doorway, they all stand and clap. All this is followed by lots of hugs. After dinner, each nurse has a thoughtful gift and a little speech for her. Dianna is overwhelmed, and it is one of those rare times when Dianna cries.

It's nice to see those kinds of tears.

56

The Promise

In early winter 2003, while in the idea stage about a trip to Italy, I am walking Chili one day when it hits me. What Dianna would like a lot more right now would be a trip to Disney World with Senna.

"What do you think, honey?"

"Oh my God, that's a great idea. It would be such fun. And this would be a nice vacation for Jon and Cris, too. What about going to Italy, though?"

"Honey, I promise you, somehow, we will go to Italy together. I don't know how or when, but we will go." I say this without the faintest idea how this is going to happen and silently hope her health holds up for it.

Paul and Linda Salvador, our friends and neighbors, have a daughter-in-law, Alais, who works at Disney World. She helps us immensely in lining up a good deal at the Polynesian Resort Hotel, right on the grounds, which, in Dianna's condition, will make getting around much easier and give us more time to do things.

In January 2004, just as I am recovering from a bout of viral pneumonia, Dianna comes down with it, probably getting it from me, and ends up in St. Joe's for a week. She has a couple of seizures while there, but recovers quite well.

"Are you up to doing this trip, Dianna?"

"Are you kidding? We're *going*. I'll be fine."

The hotel is fabulous, and it all works out even better than imagined. Jon and Cris are a bit under the weather, have a more laid-back approach to things anyway, and see this as a time to kick back with casual late morning starts. Dianna, on the other hand, is on a mission. She starts off early each day with Senna in hand, determined to make sure she and Senna experience everything. They do.

Dianna supplies one of the mini-highlights of the trip when she loses her wig while on a ride with Cris and Senna. They break up laughing while a befuddled attendant stumbles around underneath the ride structure, retrieving it for her.

The main thing I like about Florida is the fascinating vegetation, so different from Michigan. Nice, but I have zero desire to ever go back. Not my place.

57

Group Dementia

Dementia: a collection of symptoms that include decreased intellectual functioning, interfering with living a healthy life.

My mother, who is suffering from increasing dementia, has been living with my sister Elena for a few years now. There is an old proverb, saying, "Better one daughter than a thousand sons." My sister is living proof of this. She works full-time while caring for Mom, muddling through all those slings and arrows with a startling combination of practical day-to-day consistency and ineffable grace.

I visit now and then. One day Mom goes outside to smoke a cigarette and I find her staring up into the trees and sky. "Isn't it amazing?" she says, her eyes open wide, her face exploding into a huge smile. Her unmitigated joy is impossible to miss.

I follow her gaze into the profusion of nature around us. The light shattering through the maples, the sounds of birds twittering as they race back and forth, a hornet cruising toward some unknown prey, the soft humming of a summer breeze….

"It is," I say.

Yet, I know I do not *really* know. Not in this *exact* moment, I don't. In this moment, she cannot remember a past nor has the slightest inkling of a future. She is totally in the Present. It's all she has. And in this very same moment, the Present is the only place I am not. I am all around it, but not in it. I am in my head, paying bills, wondering what there is for dinner, hoping my sister is holding up okay, thinking about maybe I could, would, should….

Then, if only for a moment, Mom pulls me in as I look into her eyes.

I put my arm around her shoulders and she looks at me, smiling. She does not know who I am, but she loves me anyway. She slides her arm around me, too. I don't know if she notices the tears in my eyes or not.

Funny, I am wondering, as we stand there. We say we are sane and she is demented. In a society suffering from group dementia, how would we know?

Mom dies on January 9, 2004.

58

Time for a Job Change

In February of 2004 Stella, realizing Dianna cannot handle hard chemo any longer, switches her to Faslodex, a drug used for hormone-receptor-positive cancer types, adding it to the Herceptin, an approach Stella terms a dual blockade. That is, it will hopefully prevent cancer growth along two different pathways.

The MRI done in July shows significantly degenerated discs in Dianna's neck and a herniated disc in her back, explaining why she is experiencing tingling in her neck and spine.

Two days later she is packing for a Caribbean cruise with my brother's wife, Dianne, and two girlfriends: Pam Pfau and Pam's sister, Donna Miller.

"How can you do this to me, Dianna? You're going to be lollygagging on a warm sandy beach with a cold Corona, ...*on my birthday,* ...*without me.* Your insensitivity, frankly, is quite shocking."

She stops packing for a moment, turns to me, her tongue poking into her cheek and squinting a little.

"Well..., I'm doing it," she says.

We both start laughing.

She knows I couldn't care less—birthdays—mine or anyone else's—have never meant anything to me, a character quirk that lands me in deep water occasionally. She also knows I would much rather be in a fourteen-foot fishing boat than on a cruise ship. And we both know she will probably have a lot more fun with a bunch of girls on that cruise than she would with me.

These are just the plain facts of the matter.

On her return, she bursts through the door, gushing about all the islands they visited. I enjoyed being alone all week, too. But not being too much of a gusher, myself, I just give her a big hug, then listen.

In late October, she complains about pulsating shocks that start in her right buttock, travel up her spine into her neck, then radiate down into her left leg, ending in muscle spasms. This happens four or five times a day for several days, then disappears for weeks. Physical therapy helps not at all with this unexplained new set of symptoms.

I have been thinking about retiring for a couple of years now. I have climbed out of that scintillatingly painful period during 2000–2001, the plant is in excellent shape, we have not had a chemical release in years, and our safety record is consistently excellent. Really, the challenge is gone. The steady hum of being in maintenance mode is, well, boring. Only the people keep it interesting.

More importantly, I want to spend more time with Dianna. I am dimly aware that my most important job, and the most difficult challenge of my life, is not at the plant. It is at home.

Still, I have worked since I was thirteen doing cement construction work with my dad. I have been blessed all my life with the good fortune of doing work I am passionate about. Deciding to stop is not easy. Plus, do we have enough money, given all the medical stuff going on, and who knows what else? Even with good insurance, our unreimbursed medical expenses are huge, variable, and unpredictable.

"Well, Dianna, what if we start running out of money?"

"Then, we'll just cut back, sweetheart. You've worked long enough. I would love to have you home more." She walks over and gives me a hug.

"What if we have to sell our home? What if we have to move to a mobile home or something? How would you feel about that?" I ask, stepping back and looking at her.

"To be honest, I would hate to lose this house. I have put so much of myself into it, and I love living here, …but I was living in a mobile home when you met me. If we had to do that, I would just make it my home." She says this as if she is talking about whether we should go out to dinner or not. No turmoil I can detect. Guess I'm not surprised.

"Could I be your guest there, too?"

She gives me "the look" all women reserve for husbands acting like idiots, and we both start laughing.

In the end I realize, when it comes to money, "enough" is a subjective experience. Having done the calculations of those things that can be calculated, I'm going to assume we have enough.

In late October 2004, I retire. They toss me a gala retirement party and roast me royally. But I am ready for them, roasting them all in return. Since I firmly believe I am a far more talented roaster than any of them, I claim victory.

What I have learned most of all is the people here are a lot more talented, committed, creative, and magnanimous than even we, ourselves, may have believed ten years earlier. When I first arrived, I was told this is a ragtag group of workers who cannot be counted on. The opposite turned out to be true. They are the salt of the earth, and it has been my privilege to know and work with them.

Feels strange not going to work the next day.

59

My Education in Decor

Now that I am home more, I look around and notice what I have vaguely noticed all along—our home is a lot more "crafty" and feminine than I like. Dianna's taste for style, balance, color, is certainly not in question. Enough people have validated that by requesting her help with their own homes. But I lean toward fine art, and she leans toward craft art. I lean toward less, and she leans toward more. I always thought dishes belong in the cupboard, not on the wall. I bring this up to Dianna frequently, but I might as well be telling Chili, in Latin, to be a cat.

Even more than simple style differences, it feels like just too much of everything everywhere. Are the sides of the house bulging, or is this just my imagination?

Even more than *that*, when I pay the bills, I see "Hobby Lobby" sprinkled liberally throughout every statement. Can we afford to spend so much money on so much stuff?

No.

Either I have to buy stock in Hobby Lobby or stop the bleeding.

I decide to take a stand.

While Dianna is off on a short trip with her parents, I empty the living room of probably ninety percent of its ornaments. The furniture is unmoved and unchanged. I actually really like the way it looks, feels soothing to me. I store the "extras" in the garage on a plastic tarp, making a pile about eight feet by four feet by three feet tall. Maybe subconsciously, I already know it'll all end up back where it came from.

When Dianna and her parents walk in the door, she gives me a hug with a "Hi, honeeee" and starts to tell me all about their trip to Ohio, stopping in mid-sentence as she walks into the living room.

Seeing a storm on the way, her parents sit down quietly in the living room while Dianna looks around the room.

"What have you done to my room?" she asks, her voice trembling.

Then she explodes, which she can do as well as anyone I know. Her parents are rocks, listening in uncomfortable silence. Bernie has no idea what to say, and Pat knows exactly what she wants to say, but to her credit, doesn't say it. Meanwhile I am doing a rope-a-dope the whole time.

After about ten minutes of a nonstop tirade, Dianna pauses to catch her breath. With her hands on her hips and not even looking at me, she says, "Guess you like living somewhere where it looks like no one lives here. This room looks like we're moving out."

I defend myself pretty lamely; sounds like whining, even to me. "I just wanted you to know what my taste looks like. I've tried to explain it to you over and over, but decided this would say it better than all the words I've been using."

She stands there in stony silence.

"Okay, have it your way," she says, finally, without even looking at me, stomping out of the room. She slams the bedroom door, almost shaking the house. End of round one.

Her parents make a quick exit. Dianna does not speak to me for almost a week. Round two.

Finally, one day, she says to me, casually, "Okay, we'll compromise. I'll redo the room to express both of us." Round three.

By this time, I've learned a few things.

First, décor is something that obviously means a whole lot more to her than it does to me. Secondly, it is more important to me that she is happy than for me to have the décor the way I would like it to be. Finally, I know what compromise will look like over a period of the next few months. Everything will eventually glide back to where it was the day before I "transgressed."

And so it does.

End of this little war.

Still, it was a worthwhile war. The huge difference for me, is now I am at peace with it. I created an opportunity to bring my resentment about my house versus her house, my taste versus her taste, to the surface, where I could see it, process it, then let it go. In the end, I choose to let this be one more way to love her.

This is not to say I would ever, in my wildest dreams, miss an opportunity, in the months and years to follow, to recount this episode, exaggerating everything, while everyone laughs. The best part is it never fails to start to wind her up all over again until she realizes what I'm up to, then starts laughing along with the rest of us.

We do have a discussion about Hobby Lobby, and fix that part. She readily accepts a "no explanation personal budget" that is quite modest, so

I no longer need to consider buying stock in the company.

She keeps her word.

Over the years we have all the petty arguments any married couple has, of course, but the "fireplace battle" and this episode are the only two major blow-ups in our twenty years together. Tiny solar flares that burned hot and burned out.

60

It's Not the Same

Shortly after I retire in October 2004 Stella orders MRI brain scans done, searching for an explanation for Dianna's weird symptoms. When Stella calls our home, Dianna is away visiting Senna, planning to stop for a routine appointment with Stella on her way home, so I answer the phone.

"John? Good. I have some bad news. Maybe it would be best if you met Dianna at the hospital today for her appointment." Then he explains the whole thing. After rushing to St. Joe's to get there ahead of her, I am waiting in the lobby when she walks through the door.

"John, what are *you* doing here? I didn't expect...oh, what's wrong?"

She already knows something is really wrong when she sees my face. I waste no time. "Honey, you have three tumors in your brain. One is larger and the other two are small. Stella says they are definitely treatable, though. He sounded upbeat." I don't know that he sounded upbeat. I throw that in on my own. I suppose this is another Italian lie.

She crumbles around the edges, a tear starts down her cheek, her mouth turns down, and she shrinks into my arms. I just hold her for a minute there in the lobby while she collects herself. We make our way slowly to Stella's waiting room and sit down.

She buries her head into my neck, and I put my arm around her. People in the waiting room studiously avoid looking at us while looking at us. I have been in their shoes before. Kind of like being accidentally stuck watching someone having sex when you would just rather not.

Dianna quickly regains her composure, and we sit there quietly for a few more minutes. "This is so disappointing," she says finally.

I make some inane comment about how we are still in the same ballgame here. I am thinking, why should tumors in the brain be any different than elsewhere in the body? Find them, treat them, move on.

Dianna knows better. "No, John. It's not the same."

When we see Stella, he lays out the details, points us toward the next treatment protocol, and we walk through it all together.

Soon after getting home, we walk out on the deck. It is a beautiful fall day. I go over to the railing, while searching for a way to spin this in some better direction.

"Dianna, this is just another bump in the road," I say, reminding her that we have chosen to view her cancer as a chronic disease we can live with.

Two Canada geese suddenly appear so low over the top of the house I can clearly see their beautiful, subtle but distinct markings. After a short steep glide, then skimming low over the water, they plunk into the still surface with surprisingly loud splashes, maybe fifty yards off shore.

She comes over to the railing next to me; but she is quiet for a long time, looking out over the lake. "I know," she says finally, her voice soft, almost inaudible. "I know." She leans into me with a long sigh.

I put my arm around her. We stare out over the water without talking, watching the geese, obviously mates, paddling aimlessly, nudging each other now and then. Resting after a long day.

"I know I've said it before, but it's true. This is such a healing place for me, honey." she says. I kiss her gently on the cheek, grateful we had the good sense and blind luck to settle here.

We watch the two geese slowly swim away, side by side.

"They mate for life, you know," I say.

"I know," she says. She straightens up and a faint smile crosses her face. She is perking up, and I sense something is getting resolved in there somewhere.

By mid-December 2004, she has had whole brain radiation at St. Joe's and disappears into days of interminable sleep. She still does the whole Christmas routine though—music, cookies, home decorated top to bottom…just more slowly, a bit more each day…I help more than usual, but she likes to do it the way she likes to do it.

Her theme is blue this year.

61

Brain Stuff

I wonder out loud to Dr. Henning, the radiologist, why the *whole* brain gets radiated in the first place, thus damaging the *whole* brain. He explains the purpose is to kill off microscopic cancer cells anywhere in the brain that may not be showing up on the MRI. I'm not convinced. But I'm not a radiologist, either.

In any event, the whole brain radiation reduces the size of the tumors, but they are not gone. Henning recommends getting more focused radiation to the tumor sites, using stereotactic radiation (Linac Brainlab Novalis System) at Henry Ford Hospital in Detroit.

We do that.

Not a fun experience. The cage put around Dianna's skull is held in place by positioning sharp, pointed clamps that cut into her skin and poke her skull. She cries out in pain when they put it on.

There must be a better way.

Dianna sleeps away all of January and most of February of 2005.

62

Location, Location, Location

Dianna writes a letter to a friend around this time:

Dearest Gisela,

I wanted to share with you all about my recovery from brain mets.

Before I do that, I want to thank the Nancy Carey Cancer Survivor Group for the beautiful flowers you have given me. They could not have come at a more perfect time. I was feeling so low physically and mentally. It was a lovely surprise!

The last four months have been, shall we say, "a bit of a challenge." I have had radiation to the breast, neck and bone over the last 15 years. I did very well with it.

The brain is a beast of a different kind.

I was informed of all the possible side effects, but still, Dr. Henning, my radiologist, says, "Brain tumors are like real estate. It is all about location, location, location."

I guess, in the grand scheme of things, I am lucky my three brain mets were in places you would move to.

It is so ironic. The one thing I most dreaded with this career in cancer was what I ended up getting—brain mets. "What we fear we bring to ourselves." Who was that smart...who said that?

I have learned, once again, to "buck up" and put in yet another good fight. I did not think the bell would ring again for round five. (Mohammed Ali, I'm not.)

John, my husband, retired on October 29, just in time to be by my side three days later when Dr. Stella gave us the news.

I felt like someone had punched me in the gut.

When I drove to the hospital to get my routine shot and saw John standing in the lobby with this indescribable look on his face... [I knew]...John was the referee. He gave me the blow-by-blow news before we went into Stella's office.

How does one take such news?

You take the good with the bad.

The next three weeks of whole brain radiation took its toll. I became a couch potato, feeling like everything was in slow motion. Nausea, vision problems, chills, feeling so weak, and more.

February, I started feeling a lot better and it helped so much to receive so many cards and letters. I thank God for every one of them.

I'll end this by sharing a poem I wrote during this time:

As I sit here healing my brain
I feel like it is melting my
thoughts like rain.
I know it will be
And soon I can see
My eyes will have a new focus
Of Life's hocus pocus
After all, life's a game
As I sit here healing my brain.

Love always,
Dianna

63

Rug by Dianna

In April 2005 MRIs show a slight residual where the largest brain met had been, which may simply be dead tissue, and the two smaller ones are gone. Dianna's spasms and tingling are also gone.

The dual blockade of Faslodex and Herceptin also seem to be working well. The bone mets are not gone, but have receded and seem under control.

Dianna's weight, which had ballooned to over 200 pounds at various times, is now back down to 172 pounds, making her happy. She looks and feels great even though there are still residual anomalies like an occasional seizure, the permanent numbness in her ankles and feet, and she has trouble with numbers sometimes. She might say thirty hundred instead of three thousand. But math never was her strong suit, and I do all our financial stuff now anyway.

One spring day, I find her surrounded by many little bottles of paint, kneeling on our ground floor cement deck that faces the lake. It's a beautiful Michigan afternoon with a nice breeze coming in off the water.

"What're you doing there?"

"Oh, just felt like painting a rug on this spot, to brighten it up a little, create some interest. Have been thinking about this idea for a while."

Though it's difficult for her to get up and down, and kneeling is hard on her knees, she spends days and days working on it. When I check on her now and then, she barely notices me, lost in the doing.

One day, she excitedly shows up in the doorway to my office. "Come see."

I walk out there with her, and I don't have to fake praise. "Honey, this is really quite beautiful."

The maybe two-by-four rug is pale blue, with an overlay of thin yellow, green, and darker blue stripes. There are large tassels painted at the narrower ends of the rug. Overlaying that design are blue flowers, neatly spaced out. She has depicted one corner of the rug folded over so she could add the inscription, "Rug by Dianna" in very small but legible letters. Painted over one edge of the rug is a pair of black sandals with long, thin brownish-red straps curling out in loose strands to each side.

I murmur appreciative comments.

"You haven't noticed all of it yet, honey."

I look about but notice nothing more. Giggling, she finally points out a tiny black spider painted about a foot away from the rug. "He's my final touch."

"How do you know it's a he?"

"I created him, dammit. It's a he."

She stands there, hands on her hips, a bit of paint on her chin, looking like that proverbial cat that has just swallowed yet one more big juicy canary.

"I'm so proud of you, honey."

I offer to put a couple of clear coats over it to protect it from the weather and scraping chairs.

I will do that every single year I am alive and here to do it.

64

Magic

It is May 2005 when I get a phone call.

"John, are you interested in doing some team-building work for me?" Ghalib asks. He is now the project manager for a multi-billion dollar construction project to build a new gas plant somewhere in Saudi Arabia, near Jabail, on the Persian Gulf, I think.

"Sure. What do you have in mind?"

"Where are you, anyway?" I think to ask.

"I'm in Rome. This is where I'm based right now."

We are in different worlds, as usual.

"I have three teams working on the design of our facilities, but they are in different locations and struggling to work together. We think it will be helpful to focus some effort on bringing them together better."

"Where are the teams located?" I ask.

"London, Rome, and Milan."

"Forget that. I'm not going to any places like *that*," I say, laughing. Ghalib laughs, too.

So, destiny and Ghalib to the rescue, ...and he is offering to pay our way, too, ...for doing work I love to do. I would have done it for nothing.

Magic.

"Would you be interested then?" Ghalib asks.

What a challenge. Though the cultures and locations are different, technical people, particularly engineers, particularly men, are of one world. I know where they come from and where they want to go. But how their particular ethnic and corporate cultural influences play out would be, for me, a discovery process.

"Absolutely. I would love to do that. Thank you for offering me the opportunity, Ghalib."

"You will have to bid on it, though. The other bidders are from England,

and travel costs are included as part of the bid," Ghalib says.

I am going to win this bid, no matter what.

I do.

"Can I go with you?" Dianna asks.

"Are you kidding? I wouldn't go without you. It'll be great to see Ghalib again, …and finally meet my dad's family in Frosinone, and maybe my mom's family in Faleria, too."

"Oh, honey, such fun." Dianna's spirits explode into the stratosphere.

Our plane glides into London Heathrow on the evening of September 24, 2005. As we touch down, I feel like we are passing through an invisible doorway, the beginning of a grand adventure into our own personal Magic Kingdom.

"Do you feel that way, too, honey?" I ask, telling her about my feelings while I help her negotiate the huge main terminal. She is still using a cane and somewhat unsteady.

"Oh, I do. I'm so excited."

A driver from Bechtel, the contractor in London I am working with, is waiting and delivers us to a fine hotel, the Novotel, in downtown London.

My work itinerary involves doing team-building workshops first in London, then Rome, then Milan, winding it up back in Rome with a joint workshop for both the London and Rome teams together. In each of the first three, I have them list what works and what doesn't about their relationships with the other teams. I start the final joint meeting by sharing what each team has said about the others. They discover there is much mutual respect and many positives, and trust levels soar. Then we work out action plans to resolve their understandable disconnects.

The cultural differences are interesting. With Saudi engineers attached to each team, there are actually three interlocking cultures meshing together: English, Italian, and Saudi. Of course, each team is also composed of people of many nationalities from all over the world, adding more spices to the mix.

The English are more formal, punctual (always return from breaks a minute early) and stressed out to the max about meeting the project schedule, concerned about doing it right. I really like their dry and self-deprecating sense of humor. And so welcoming.

The Italians in Rome are casual, boisterous, anything but punctual (rounding them up from breaks is like herding cats), and completely cavalier about the project schedule. No problem, they say, laughing. Just hire more people.

Both teams are basically on schedule, but struggling with communications and moving data back and forth. No wonder. Different operating systems, not close to each other, and different perspectives.

The Milan team already has their act together and really doesn't need my help, but they—in a warm and friendly way—humor me.

All three teams are composed of competent, hardworking people, so it is not surprising, in short order, we are able to shift the trajectory of workability, putting the project on a better course, once everyone has a clear sense of being on one team, playing win-win.

At the tail end of it all, I successfully facilitate a crucial contract negotiation between ARAMCO and Bechtel. Ghalib is smooth as silk, kind, respectful, but more focused than anyone in the room, and brings it to closure. It's fun watching him in action. I see why he has this job.

In London, Dianna does bus tours, taking in the history and beauty of the city. One day, she tells me about missing her bus ride back to the hotel, being lost on the streets of London and rescued by a couple of kindly English ladies. The rescue is complicated by Dianna not remembering the name of the hotel where we are staying. But she can describe the hotel décor well enough, so they all figure it out, laughing the whole time.

One evening we huddle together during a chilly boat ride on the Thames, passing under Tower Bridge. The next evening, we plan to have dinner with Hussain (Ghalib's brother) and his wife, Lena (Suzy's sister).

We are supposed to meet in the hotel lobby. However, there are two lobbies, and Dianna and Lena have not seen each other in years. We are in the elevator, trying to figure out where Lena might be. Standing next to me is a young woman speaking on her cell phone with consternation in her voice, sounding frustrated.

"Dianna, who is this beautiful woman in the elevator next to us—isn't she speaking in Arabic?" I whisper to Dianna. Dianna bends forward to look around me and stares at her for a long moment. Finally, she leans forward and touches the woman on the shoulder.

"Are you Lena?"

We all start laughing and never stop throughout dinner at an exotic Moroccan restaurant complete with belly dancers and great food. We say goodbye too soon, with tears in our eyes. Would we ever meet again?

Hugs all around when Ghalib greets us at Rome's Fiumicino Airport. We accept Ghalib's invitation to stay at his highrise apartment in the city.

One of Ghalib's friends and a coworker on the project, Adnan Al Awami, is married to another beautiful Saudi woman, Nawal Abduljabar, who offers to accompany Dianna around Rome while we work.

Ghalib has lined up a famous guide, Marco, a handsome young Italian, who typically guides movie stars around Rome. From then on we will never hear the end of Marco and his limo, his impeccable dress, his disgustingly good looks, his flawless manners. Dianna and Nawal hit all the sights, tickled by paparazzi hovering around them like flies because—if these women are with *Marco*, they must be worth photographing. It's "Marco this" and "Marco that" for the rest of our time in Rome. We have lots of fun with it while at dinner with Adnan, Nawal, and others in the Saudi contingent.

The Saudis and Italians share at least one quality—the gift of warm, genuine hospitality. Well, others, too—like great food. They're probably pretty skilled with "Italian lies," too.

On the way home from work one night, we pick up fresh-baked Italian bread, *real* tomatoes, and a cheese I would be forever mesmerized by, buffalo mozzarella. Ghalib, Dianna, and I enjoy sliced tomatoes and cheese drizzled with olive oil and a bit of basil, accompanied by a fine Italian red. Good friends sitting on the deck of Ghalib's fourth floor apartment overlooking city lights. Sometimes, simple is impossible to beat.

Life is a necklace strung with pearls like this magical night.

Dianna and I visit St. Peter's Square and Basilica, and I am amazed at the workmanship. The huge marble columns and walls are smoother than silk—it is hard to believe this all could have been done by hand.

As we walk down a busy street away from St. Peter's, we decide to rest at a little outdoor table to enjoy some espresso.

"You feeling okay, honey?"

"I feel great. Just have to take it slow. And the cane helps a lot. But this is just wonderful."

Italy is no place for the disabled. It's a good thing Dianna does not need a wheelchair. But everywhere we look in Italy is a postcard. Everything, down to the smallest detail, is a work of art. And I cannot believe I'm Italian—or that they all are—everyone is impeccably dressed, ...and then, there is me.

We leave Ghalib, and Rome, and fly to Milan for my one-day workshop there. Dianna and I take the train downtown to visit the Galleria Vittorio Emanuele, an enclosed shopping mall formed by two glass-vaulted arcades, at right angles intersecting in an octagon, as well as the famous La Scala Opera House, and the equally famous Duomo di Milano, all within a stone's throw of the huge central square, ringed with outdoor cafes. A light rain is falling, so we sit under an umbrella at one of the outside tables, drinking espresso. But we're not alone. We are joined by a thousand pigeons.

"Here's your chance, Dianna. Now, *these* birds *will* pay attention to you. They're city birds."

Soon enough, four or five are competing for the bits of croissant Dianna is feeding them, almost jumping into her lap.

"Now this is more like it," she says gleefully.

We go into the multi-floor indoor Galleria surrounded by too many upscale shops to count, and Dianna disappears into shopping while I wander off to the top-floor penthouse and sip wine, watching the sun slipping behind the Duomo. She finds everything she is looking for. With the rain gone, leaving behind a constellation of clouds, so do I, moved almost to tears by the spectacular sunset framing the needle-like spires of the Duomo.

My work completed, we say goodbye to Ghalib.

Dianna and I board the train at the huge terminal in Rome and enjoy the short ride to Frosinone, where Francesco is waiting to pick us up, probably stunned by the mammoth amount of luggage he must force into the trunk of his little car. He drives us to his home, where we will be staying. We are greeted by his parents, Santino Giannetti and his wife Vincenzina (Enza) Sperdutti; their daughter Marina; her husband Renato; and their two children, Elisa and Enrico. They all share the same beautiful home on the outskirts of the city with heart-piercing views of the lush countryside.

It is instant love. There is no explaining how Dianna and I could meet this entire family and, within seconds, love blossoms. We don't speak the same language and yet we do.

Magic.

The next four days are a whirlwind of dinners, meeting relatives, day trips to the beautiful and ancient towns of Veroli, Alatri, Atina, Arpino, Isola del Liri, and Castelliri, the town my dad was living in when he emigrated.

Santino and Enza finally take us to the house near Casalviera where my father was born. It is a huge rectangular two-story stone house, standing alone like a sentinel in a velvet green verdant valley. The town itself is in the distance, draped down the hillside like a white stone carpet. A warm breeze floats silently across the valley. Farther away are the foothills of the Apennine Mountains.

I stand in silent wonder. How was it for my dad, age seventeen, leaving this land, going alone to a faraway place he had only heard of but never seen? Was he afraid? Excited? Why hadn't I ever asked him these things? This valley must have been just like this then, …or not? It will always be yes and no.

I don't want to leave, but we must leave. While the others are occupied in conversation, I walk around to the back of the house. Using a rock, I chip off a bit of stone from one of the walls. It's warm in my hands. It's something. Not enough, but something. I wipe away tears before returning to the others.

I cajole Santino, Enza, Renato, and Francesco (who acts as our translator, since he is the only one of us who knows both languages) into taking Dianna and me to Faleria, a ninety-minute drive north, past Rome, and into the hills just to the northeast. I know no one there; but deep within my soul I know I must go there, if only to walk around in the town where my mother's father, a Corradi, was born. In some way, our souls are intertwined. I feel this is how I must honor him. I tell them all I need is an hour or two, and I will be satisfied.

It's a good thing Dianna and I do not try it alone. We might still be looking for it. Once we get off the expressway, there are many twists and turns, all marked by minuscule, sometimes completely hidden, signs. I would have missed every single one. Apparently, everyone either already knows how to get to Faleria, or they don't care if they do.

It is a small town built entirely of stone on a stony hillside overlooking a deep, brushy valley. We walk into the only café (called bars in Italy, but no alcohol is served in them) in town, and Francesco works his own magic, in Italian, of course. Finally, after a lengthy animated conversation, the owner throws up his hands with a "Well, why didn't you say so?" gesture. He points up the hill and we leave, heading in that direction.

"What did you say to him, Francesco?" I ask.

"I told him the only reason you and Dianna have traveled all the way from the United States is to come to Faleria and find your relatives."

We all laugh. Who cannot admire the sublime virtue in an exquisitely placed Italian lie? Truth in it, but not the whole truth. Best of all, it makes everything work, makes everyone feel good…with no harm done. Quite to the contrary.

"He says there are many Corradi people in this town and he will contact them for us while we have lunch at the restaurant up on the hill. Someone will meet us there."

We reach the Attica Stabia Hosteria, perched on the rim of a rocky ridge overlooking the valley. We walk up the stone path, only to have the manager meet us at the door. He tells us there is no room. Today is festival day and all the town's men are there, celebrating and having lunch before the parade.

Francesco swings into his routine. The conversation ends with the owner throwing up his hands in sweet surrender, stands to one side, then sweeps both his arms in a grand gesture toward the entrance.

Same Italian lie. It dawns on me that when Italians lie to each other in this way, they all know it—it is just their polite protocol, a way of making life flow more gently. I love it.

We are directed to a large room where the townsmen, maybe fifty in all, are noisily toasting, laughing, and telling jokes. A waitress swoops up to us, unceremoniously cuts then spreads a sheet of butcher paper across an ancient wooden picnic type table. We all sit down.

Soon every man in the room knows we are from the USA, that I am a Corradi (half true, so a bonafide Italian lie) and before long, they are toasting us, gifting us with bottles of wine. Not too long after that, I am a happy Italian drunk named Corradi. It is one of the best meals we will have in Italy. But, given my condition, I could be biased. The absolute sober truth is, we never had anything but an excellent meal in Italy.

When I go outside to have a smoke, I start talking with a young man, he in Italian, I in English. We understand each other perfectly. We are speaking in the language of joy, love of life, and just the right amount of good wine.

Shortly after dinner, my cousin Roberto Corradi shows up, who I have never met, nor knew existed. We hug and cry like long-lost brothers. He takes Dianna and me all over town, meeting more relatives than I can remember. At each house, I drink another glass of wine, committed to respecting the custom of never insulting the host. In the last house, we are sitting in the living room and the host slaps a VHS tape into the TV, and suddenly there is my sister and mother on the TV screen, talking!

A few hours ago, we drove into Faleria knowing no one, and now I am sitting in the living room of a relative I did not know I had, drinking great wine, and looking at a video of my own family back in the USA.

Magic.

Later, as we watch the parade go by, many of the same men we met in the restaurant, now colorfully dressed in bright shiny gold and blue, break out of the parade line and swing over to Dianna and me, bowing deeply in tribute. Dianna is tickled with the attention. We are taking a warm bath in the energy around us as young men toss huge flags in the air, catching them flawlessly. All too soon, the sun is setting. It is time to leave.

As we are walking back to our car, Roberto Corradi pulls me aside, detouring me down a stone tunnel and into to a low-ceilinged, solid stone wine cellar. The air feels cool as we sit side by side on a stone bench while he ceremoniously uncorks a bottle of wine, turns to me, and smiles. This is his good stuff. We have a toast to each other, alone, in this little cave. He wraps his arms around me, tears in his eyes. And in mine. Somehow we both know we have met for the first time and will never meet again. And it doesn't matter. This moment matters.

Driving back to Frosinone into the fading light, we are all stunned by the day's events. We came ostensibly for an hour to simply drive around the town, and our family bursts open like a fireworks display and fills our lives with Light and Love.

There is just no other way to explain this.

Magic.

Dianna and I take the train back to Rome, then change trains for the Leonardo da Vinci Fiumicino Airport, renting a motel nearby for the night.

The next day, October 13, our plane rises steeply into the early morning sky. I watch the coast of Italy stretching out as far as the eye can see, waves washing white against the long curving gray-brown shoreline. I strain to keep it in sight; but, too soon, we knife into the clouds, still at a steep angle. The coastline fades, then disappears, replaced by a soft and silent white.

After a few minutes, I lean over to Dianna and whisper, "I promised you we would go."

She kisses me on the cheek, her eyes shiny. Before long, she falls asleep, her head resting on my shoulder.

I wish these damn seats were bigger. But I sit there, still as a rock, wanting her to rest. We still have a long way to go before we are home.

65

Selling a Dream

By March 2006 Dianna is experiencing wavy vision as part of a mild seizure sensation along with numbness in her left arm. CAT and bone scans look okay, but an MRI shows a new eight-mm diameter lesion in her right frontal cortex as well as potentially smaller lesions in her posterior and superior frontal lobe. More brain radiation is suggested.

Since retirement, I have been doing intensive Internet research about all aspects of breast cancer and getting up to speed on brain metastases. My research indicates gamma knife is better than other techniques/equipment for brain tumors because it is more precise, thus causing less collateral brain damage and requiring less total radiation to do the same job. It also has a long history of successful use.

Various doctors try to convince us to use the megabuck equipment they have purchased, but I'm adamant. We are going to stay with the gamma knife approach. Dianna agrees, once I explain it all to her.

We head back to Harper Hospital in the Detroit Medical Center because they have good gamma knife equipment, have had long experience using it, and Dianna likes Dr. Lucia Zamorano, a neurosurgeon there with a specialty in oncology. Zamorano looks at the data and believes only one of the tumors is really a tumor and decides to treat only that one.

On March 23, the radiation is done and all seems to go well. By June, her MRIs indicate the tumor has shrunk to half the size, and what is still there could simply be dead tissue. Meanwhile, the dual blockade chemo regimen seems to be keeping the cancer in check elsewhere in her body.

It has been slowly sinking in during the past couple of years that we are never going to build our dream house on the Leelanau Peninsula outside of Traverse City, on the land we worked so long and so hard to find.

Finally, I bite the bullet, emotionally. "Dianna, I think it makes sense to sell it. All your medical needs are down here, not five hours away. What do you think?"

She has wanted to live up there most of her life. We both love the area. We also know if we sell it, we will never be able to afford to buy there again. We will be closing the door to a world where we have long dreamed of living in that cannot be opened again.

Even more profoundly, selling it is also another way of acknowledging she is never going to get better. We do not talk about this at all.

She is quiet for a moment, expressionless.

"I think you should do whatever you think is best for us."

So I do.

In May 2006 we split our ten acres, selling five acres to the couple on one side of our property and the other five to Bill and Lynne Watson, who already own land on the other side.

We use some of the money to buy a Toyota FJ Cruiser. Dianna loves that it "has character." I love that it has a great off-road system. Every time I got myself stuck in some backwoods mudhole somewhere—so many times I lost count—I vowed I would get a four-wheel-drive vehicle someday.

I surprise Dianna by suggesting we remodel the kitchen, something she has wanted to do for years. She has a lot of fun recreating that space.

All nice, but we both know none of this is close to getting up each morning to the sunlight sparkling down the entire length of Lake Leelanau. Well, we all get to play the hand we are dealt, not the one we wish we had.

66

A Sense of Urgency

Dianna's weight is down to 167 pounds and she is feeling better. In May 2006 Kathy Preston invites Dianna to take a two-week trip to the East Coast with two other friends, Chris Fowler and Allie Langlois.

"Think you are up to it, honey?"

"I think so. Do you think I should go?"

"What does your heart tell you?"

"Yes. But…I'm not so sure my body agrees."

"Sweetheart, do whatever you want to do. I'm not in there; you are. So this is not a decision I can make."

"What do you think, though?"

"Well, if you want to know what I think, I think yes. I know you well enough to know, no matter how you feel, you'll feel better doing stuff with your friends, seeing new places, having lunches here, dinners there, pajama parties, all that endless girl talk women seem to wallow in, than you'll feel sitting around here wondering what you missed."

Dianna laughs.

She goes.

They visit Najla in Pennsylvania, go on to New Jersey, spend time in New York City, Newport, then travel up the coast to Maine, visiting Kathy's family and friends all along the way. On the way home, they stop at Niagara Falls.

Dianna flies through the door in late afternoon, tired but happy. She has enough energy for a "Hi, honeeee," a hug, then flops into bed and sleeps all the way through to morning.

By September, her weight is down to 162 pounds and she has an array of symptoms—what she calls her "normal" tingling-type seizures, some visual auras occasionally, but now there is a new persistent numbness in her left arm. She needs a cane to steady herself, but her attitude remains sunny and cheerful.

During one gentle-hint-of-fall-but-still-warm type of day, I take a long, quiet walk in the woods with Chili and return to find Dianna inside the house, up on a ladder, painting something over the front door.

"Jesus, honey. Think this is a good idea?"

"It's a great idea. I've been thinking about the words I wanted to use for a long time."

There is some gold paint on her forehead and she looks frumpy in her old, paint-stained pastel blue sweats. I love the way she looks right now, at this exact moment. I see her most clearly when she is like this, somewhat disheveled…or first thing in the morning, before she's all decked out with the best cosmetics money can buy, before she "has her act together," while she is still wrapped in a sleepy, unadorned innocence so nakedly present when she first opens her eyes.

"But, I mean, up on a ladder like that? You need a cane to even walk, for Christ sake. You can't afford to fall, especially from there."

"I'll be okay. When I start to get tired, I just sit down for a while. Anyway, I'm just about done," she says, not even looking at me.

"Why this sense of urgency?" I ask.

She pauses, then twists on the ladder to look at me. "I have to do it—it's now or never," she says. My throat tightens and I start to say something.

"What do you think? Is it even?"

Her voice is like a song. I swallow it up and read the inscription she has painted in gold, in a double arc, one row longer than the other, over the door:

I am so glad you are here. And below that, *It helps me to realize how beautiful my world is.*

Of course, she has woven some freehand filigree and flowers through it, too.

"Where did you find *those* words, Dianna?" I say, the lump back in my throat.

"I have been working on them for a long time. They are my own words."

"It is…it's just…beautiful." I do think it is beautiful.

I look at her. Her face is smeared with a look of supreme satisfaction as she takes in my reaction.

"Now, let me help you down off that ladder," I say, reaching up to take her hand.

One day, I'm working in my office and happen to glance up at my 2006 New Year's resolutions taped to my bookcase. I break out laughing.

I had written: 1. Quit smoking (not done), 2. Walk Chili every day (done), 3. Replace refined grains with whole grains in my diet (done), 4. Meditate (not really done). 5. Learn Italian (wishful thinking). At the bottom of the list, in Dianna's routinely clumsy handwriting, she has written, 6. Worship your <u>WIFE!</u> (triple underlined)

Laughing still, I think this one is done…and will always be done.

In October 2006 friends at church bring Dianna home early from a service. They say she went into a heavy seizure and was disoriented. She acts dazed, but manages to tell me she is experiencing severe electric shocks and muscle cramps in both her hands and ankles. I take her to St. Joe's immediately. Her neurosurgeon increases her depakote to 1,000 mg/day to help with the seizures.

A brain MRI seems to pinpoint a new tumor, and the bone scans show an increased uptake in her skeletal structure, indicating the dual blockade is not working so well anymore.

By December 2006 Dr. Stella is noticing a decrease in Dianna's mental sharpness, but we all agree she is still quite functional. She is also experiencing pain in her hip from bone mets, but she puts up the Christmas decorations at the hospital anyway. It has become a commitment more important to her now than ever. I have finally realized this is a crucial part of her internal feedback loop, how she keeps herself mentally healthy and in the game. Of course, it is also one of her simple joys in life, and she is adept at enrolling friends to enjoy it with her. Still, she is struggling more with her gait and finding the right words to say what she wants to say.

Stella switches Dianna off the dual blockade and gets her into a trial with Lapatinib plus Xeloda, the old hand/foot syndrome drug. Before long, her hip pain disappears and her bone mets appear stabilized. The only problem now is almost continuous bouts of loose stools that, now and then, graduate into diarrhea.

A PET scan seems to indicate the supposed brain tumor is not really new cancer but simply edema—swelling—from the gamma knife treatment. Anyway, we all agree on no more radiation for now. She can take only so much.

In January 2007 Dianna feels the depakote she is taking is dosed too high and cuts it in half on her own. Within days, her lethargy is gone and her usual brightness comes roaring back. She is like her old self, …well, some new normal, I guess.

67

The Sky is Not Falling

Dianna's friends frequently visit or call to see how she is doing. She invariably still gives them the same report about how she is doing. "Better."

Into February 2007 we struggle with her swinging back and forth between loose stools and constipation as we try to titrate the use of Imodium, which does not help much. I place a portable toilet near her bed, and some nights we are up four to five times using it. Mostly, we get there in time, but not always—I can be a heavy sleeper and she feels bad about waking me. We do this dance for about a month. Good thing I'm not working. Sometimes I'm so groggy I meet myself coming the other way.

In late February, we discover what is really going on. She has picked up Clostridium difficile (C diff), probably from her recent hospital stay. Once she gets on antibiotics, the diarrhea problem disappears and she starts feeling much better.

"Boy, I'm glad to be through with all that. Was getting pretty tired of wiping your ass," I say as I slide into bed next to her.

"Well, honey, it's not like I wouldn't rather wipe my own ass."

"All I can say is, you owe me."

"So, you're saying I have to wipe your ass now?"

We both start laughing, as much out of relief and gratitude, less from dealing with diarrhea than from the continually interrupted sleep.

Life looks "better" to me, too.

A PET scan in March shows the gamma knife treatment was successful and the bone mets are holding steady. So the cancer appears to be in check, but Dianna is left with all the same side effects that hamper her cognition and mobility.

But by April 2007 Dianna is getting wavy vision and more seizures, along with numbness in her left arm and increased weakness in her left leg. Her bone scans have been fine, but a new brain MRI shows two tumors in new locations.

Zamorano wants to do another gamma knife treatment. We agree, and she does on April 30, 2007. In mid-May, another PET scan indicates things look good, but it is becoming more and more confusing—what is a cancerous tumor and what is simply dead tissue resulting from previous radiation? No one really knows for sure.

Dianna drives up to Mount Pleasant to spend time with her family. While there, she falls and sprains her wrist. When Dianna returns, walking through the door, she looks as depressed as I've ever seen her.

"What's wrong, sweetheart?"

"Mom insists I not drive anymore," she says, tears streaming down her cheeks.

"What do *you* think?" I ask.

"Maybe she's right. But, if I can't drive, I can't live my life, either. John, it would be just devastating."

I am quiet for awhile, just hugging her.

"Well, you know how I hate to disagree with your mom, Dianna."

"No, you don't. You love it," she says, laughing a little.

At least she has stopped crying.

"So, *you* don't think you can drive, either?"

"I can *drive*. My big problem is getting in and out of the car. That's when I can fall."

"Look, why don't we take that walker Sandy gave us, and let's practice using it with our van. Oops. Sorry. *Your* van."

Dianna laughs. She is starting to perk up a little.

"I'll bet you can do just fine. Why don't we just play around with it awhile, then do a test run. We can go for ice cream."

Now Dianna really lights up, and not because of the ice cream.

We head right out to the car and spend fifteen minutes figuring out a routine, approaching the car, opening the doors, folding up the aluminum walker, sliding it into the backseat, getting into the driver's seat, then closing the doors. Fortunately our Toyota Sienna van has power sliding doors, and she finds she can do the whole routine safely. When she wants to get out, she just reverses the process. Once she has her walker, she is fine.

Finally I let her do the whole thing on her own a couple of times until she feels confident. I slide into the passenger side, and she drives us into Onsted, a little town nearby, for an ice cream cone. I let her get out on her own.

"You can get your own ice cream, dammit."

Dianna laughs, looking radiant. I get something reliable like butter pecan, and she goes for some disgusting mixture of chocolate, nuts, cherries, and marshmallows with a nontraditional name. She gets back into the car on her own, drives us home, gets out on her own, and goes into the house on her own. It all works.

She has her freedom again, going here, there, and everywhere.

Her mom is furious. Some of her friends think we are using poor judgment. What if this happens, or what if that....

Well? So?

What if the sky falls?

68

The Medical World

I have never wanted to know anything at all about the medical world, ...or hospitals, ...or the medical billing system. And if I meet a doctor, let it be only in the grocery store.

But, alas, this is not how my life is working out.

Over the years I become maize bright dealing with medical bills, which relentlessly swell into four-inch-thick folders each year. I learn to pay attention to co-pays, deductibles, and scour medical bills we receive, almost daily, for obvious errors.

Some are easy to catch: "No, really Denise, she did not have a hip replaced. Am I sure? Yes, I'm sure." But of course, the ubiquitous padding of almost all bills to cover the cost of the uninsured is impossible to catch, and why try? Someone has to pay when others cannot. That is just the way our insane system works, and I am okay with this until we, as a society, find the wisdom and heart to create a system that includes everyone all the time, above the board, where we can see it.

I especially enjoy the countless phone calls to billing departments: "Press 3 if you would like.... please press 6 for...." and then, inexplicably, "You have been returned to the main menu, please press...." sprinkled with a soothing humanoid voice reminding me how important I am to them as a valued customer—and sometimes music—until, finally, after successfully negotiating the gauntlet designed to prevent me from getting there, I actually reach a real human being only to discover, more alas, it is the wrong human being, "Denise is not in today so if you could call back on Thursday...."

I often wonder what would happen if Denise quit, or died, or moved to Malta. Maybe I would *never* escape the phone tree and be trapped in an endless, circular loop, doomed to forever hear how much my call means to someone I will never meet. This is when I realize speaker phone capability is priceless, and I get it. Now I can cook entire meals while waiting.

As the years go by, I refine my system, which helps with tax deductions, complicating our already complicated lives with even more complicated tax returns.

The most important thing I learn is: never, ever pay until the insurance company has paid first or everything crumbles into a major nightmare. Even after the insurance company pays, I learn to wait a bit longer to see what Denise does next.

I realize none of this is easy for Denise, either. To survive, I deduce Denise must certainly be insane to function in an insane system. Oh God, deliver us into a single payer system like Medicare, which is so good, it is nearly invisible to me—and toss in electronic records, too.

I also track our co-pays and deductibles to avoid stumbling into overpaying. If this is about to happen, it is a red flag. I go to war with the insurance company and provider until someone flinches.

This is never me.

Dianna knows little about any of this. She feels bad enough whenever she gets a whiff of what is going on, so I avoid mentioning it. Why? She already knows she is one of those high-maintenance patients who burdens the system. It's not as if she likes it, either. So I keep it as my own private enterprise, …or war, …or challenge, depending on how I choose to look at it that day.

I eventually come to rationalize it in a simple way. If, as a society, we have enough money to kill strangers around the world and bail out rich bankers, I'm not going to feel guilty about Dianna being expensive. She has more class and adds greater value to the planet than all of Wall Street put together. She is what a good investment actually looks like.

All this being said, our own insurance companies, including Medicare, are excellent. I have no complaints. I have no doubt the insurance companies allowed Dianna to receive the best treatment available.

I'm also convinced that, if we had had no insurance, many of the treatment options we were routinely offered would not have been mentioned at all, the care would have been more minimal, and Dianna would not have lived as well, or as long.

69

The Big 5 —Uh Oh

"Honey, I want to have a birthday party this year."

I am sitting on the couch in our living room and she is standing near the windows, the midday sun lighting her up.

"Well...okay." It feels like another shoe is going to drop here somewhere.

"No, I mean a *birthday party*. I want to have a real bash. I want to invite all our friends, all our families, everyone. I want to invite Dr. Stella and his wife and all the nurses at the clinic."

"Really."

My mind starts spinning. We are already into April of 2007, and her birthday is June 10. What will the weather be like? Could we have it in our yard by the lake, rent tents, and what about food and...? In Michigan, it could be sunny and eighty degrees, or rain/sleet and forty-five degrees. This could be a real headache.

"What exactly is the big deal here? Why not a quiet hot dog roast, just you and me with a beer or two? Wouldn't that be a lot more romantic?"

"Oh, stop your bullshit," she says, laughing.

"I have been thinking about this for a while. I want this party to be my gift to all those who have supported me all these years. My way of saying to everyone, thank you, I love you," she says, becoming suddenly very serious.

She sits down on the couch next to me, turns halfway toward me, quiet for a moment. Then she folds her hands in her lap and suddenly looks faintly like that prim school teacher again. "John, ...this is the right time for me to do this. First, it will be my fiftieth birthday, and I've wondered if I would ever live to see it. I thank God every day that I will. I am so grateful, ...and...."

She hesitates again, but looks me straight in the eye. "And, honey, to be honest, I don't know if I will have the chance to see another one." Her voice is steady and matter of fact; but I feel something else, too, almost a fierceness or focus or intensity or....

"Come on. You're going to outlive me. I smoke, remember." But, my heart has already tightened and maybe it shows.

She leans over and puts her arms around me and puts her head sideways against my chest, then says ever so softly, "John, you and I both know that's not going to be true."

I just can't let those words into my brain. Not now. We are in each other's arms for a long minute while I pull myself back together.

"Okay, let's not quibble about minor details," I say finally. "We'd better get to planning it. Let's get a list together and…there's a lot to do."

Getting into action helps.

I create an invitation titled "Dianna's Big 5-Uh-Oh Birthday Bash."

Dianna's good friend, Sandy Johnson, comes up with most of the best ideas—the caterer (food winds up being great), where to have it (perfect rental hall near our home, in a nice country setting, complete with roof in case it rains), and she mentions Don White, a singer/comedian/poet from Lynn, Massachusetts, who she has seen before. I call him, we work it out, and I hire him to do a one-hour show during the party. I like him right away, and he even cuts us a break on the price.

Dianna has her own ideas, too. She asks Consuelo, a professional singer and dear friend, to sing at the party, a real bonus. She also enlists a couple of friends, Pam Pfau and Chris Fowler, to provide entertainment at the party with a performance of their own.

The girls practice a little. The game plan is to dress in long, black-sequined gowns, platinum-blonde wigs, and ten-foot-long fluffy white boas they can hang around their necks and flip around while lip-syncing "Stop in the Name of Love" by Dianna Ross and the Supremes. They call themselves Dianna C and the Superbs. Chris makes a huge sign to put next to them on the stage.

Probably a hundred people show up from all over the country, including many of the oncology clinic nurses, and Dr. Stella with his beautiful wife, Lynn. It is probably a two-to-five-hour drive for most people. Their coming makes Dianna very happy.

Consuelo returns from Rome where she sang for the pope, just in time for the party. She sings her own songs and "The Look of Love," which moves me deeply as the years and the experiences Dianna and I have had together coalesce in my heart.

Don White is outstanding with a mixture of storytelling and singing laced into a moving story titled "I Know What Love Is" that has us crying one minute and laughing the next.

Dr. Stella gives a moving tribute to Dianna, his arm around her. I realize they have traveled their own unique journey together, too.

Dianna C and the Superbs camp it up with their number, singing and dancing to raucous applause. Probably I've had too much wine by this point; but, as I watch her pour out everything she has to give, swinging her bolo, swaying to the music, her smile exploding, drowning us all in joy, I also know how much pain she is experiencing in this exact moment, in too many ways to count. No one else would know it, looking at her. I couldn't help but know it. Tears are sliding down my cheeks, and my heart is breaking with love, loss, but most of all, with amazement as I watch her bringing herself out of herself, rising to the moment. She is all out there with nothing held back, refusing to do anything less than be present with her whole being, which, in some strange way, is also everyone in the room.

Dianna ends the festivities with a moving speech:

"I want to thank all of you so much for coming out to enjoy this day with me. This is certainly a celebration of love and appreciation for all you have done for me throughout the years...." She pauses, gathering herself. "...I can't believe I have been a survivor for seventeen years, ...and still going strong."

There is much applause, but I know she is saying this with more defiance than conviction. We both know she's not going very strong right now. When she mentions her friends who have died recently from cancer, Kris Forrest and Zena Bianco, her voice breaks. Wiping away a tear, she goes on. "But I am still going to stay with it for as long as I can in honor of them. I will dedicate my..."

She stumbles for a moment, tears running down her face. "I will dedicate my pain and suffering for them." She pauses again as the room falls silent, then straightens up, fully back in control again. "You all mean so much to me. So I am honoring you with this party, this celebration of life. This is truly what this is, a celebration of life."

Wiping away her tears, she hands off the mic and smiles to a standing ovation sprinkled with whistles and shouts of encouragement.

I am so proud of her. Again. Still.

After the party, many of the guests return to our house, just a couple of miles away, and party more. I take a dozen people for a pontoon boat ride, getting a ticket from the local sheriff for too many people on the boat with not enough life preservers. He could have taken us right off the water, but he didn't. We finish our ride into the sunset.

Our guests trail off into the night, and finally it is over. Dianna flops into bed, beset with numb feet and arms, on the verge of diarrhea, a tingling up and down her body with incipient seizure symptoms, …but happy.

I adjust her diaper, which she wears at night now. After making sure she is comfortable, I pull the covers up around her.

"It was good, wasn't it, honey," she says, her voice soft, sounding lazy as she begins drifting off.

"It was good, sweetheart," I say. I lean down and kiss her long on the cheek. A faint smile flickers across her face, then gone. Already off to some other reality.

I turn out the lights.

70

Cruising to Alaska

It is late June 2007 when we board the ship. Dianna is using her cane and I steady her as we go up the gangway.

I notice she is wearing rose-colored glasses. I like amber-colored ones when I wear any at all, which is not often. I like the way they make everything look like sunrise or sunset, my favorite times of day. I see the irony in the color she likes to wear. She must have thirty pairs and can never find any of them, but she seems to hang on to these.

"Let me try those on, honey. I want to see what life looks like through rose-colored glasses." She glances at me, takes them off, and hands them to me without comment.

Things look a little softer but not much different than no glasses at all, really.

"Dianna, these don't change the way things look very much," I say.

"They don't have to," she says, a faint smile darting across her face.

We are on this cruise because my dear friend, Steve Kridelbaugh, invited us to go with him, his wife Linda, and another couple, Alan Howard and his wife, Bonnie. Steve had visited us often over the years, so I am long overdue for a visit going his way. Besides, Alaska suggests all that I love: eagles, bears, wild country. Since the ship leaves and returns to Seattle, this is also a golden opportunity for Dianna to visit a part of her family she rarely sees, her nieces, Cary and Megan, and their families, as well as Hank and Jackie Thomas, good friends, all of whom live in the Seattle area.

Our entire vacation is perfect.

The week in Seattle is spent visiting, sprinkled with meaningful conversations and sightseeing. The cruise week is unmitigated good times with best friends. I take off on several excursions, canoeing, rafting, seeing tons of bears, eagles, dolphins, and whales, while Steve and Linda thoughtfully take Dianna on more sedate trips—and shopping—nurturing Dianna, who is using a wheelchair for much of the trip.

In Skagway, one of our port stops, Dianna and I are perusing the shops and I see a fur store. "Let's go in, honey. We probably won't be able to afford any of it but curious to see what's in there," I say.

Almost immediately, I notice a short jacket that is striking, a mixture of pitch-black and snow-white mink. "Dianna, look at this one. Try it on."

"Oh, John, this is way too expensive."

Actually, it isn't that expensive, which is surprising.

"Why don't you try it on anyway. Want to see what it looks like on you."

It looks like it was made for her—the flash, elegance and style is all her, but they have only one and it is too small, which is disappointing.

"I really like it, but it's okay, honey. I don't need to have it. Thank you, though, for wanting it for me."

Awhile later, I drop off Dianna with Steve and Linda, then slip back to the store and order the coat in her size. It has to be made to order, but they promise to deliver it by fall.

It will be a completely unexpected surprise for her.

71

The Dress

In July 2007 Suzy Mushcab makes a trip from Saudi Arabia to visit us, bringing a beautiful, ankle-length dress as a gift for Dianna. She tells us it is one of the Saudi traditional dresses, bluish-green in color, with wide sleeves and gold-colored thread woven throughout a taffeta material, a mixture of silk and other fabrics. She bought it at a shop in Kobar Rashed Mall, not far from where I stayed when I visited Saudi Arabia. Women used to wear such dresses all the time, she tells us, but now they are more often reserved for weddings, traditional parties, and during the time of Ramadan.

Suzy didn't bring me anything.

"What about me?" I ask.

"I brought myself, John. What else could you want?"

Suzy and Dianna are laughing.

Dianna tries on the dress right away, it fits perfectly, and she does look stunning in it. Then she shows Suzy her "Rug by Dianna," and it just gets better after that. We visit Jon, Cris, and Senna, who takes to Suzy like a duck to water. Suzy's visit really lifts Dianna's spirits, and their love for each other is a warm summer rain.

At the airport, saying goodbye, they hug long, bathing each other in tears, knowing in their hearts they will not see each other again, not in this lifetime.

In this moment, I'm not thinking this at all.

A lifetime later, though, I will not have to wonder, what does *that* feel like, to be *that* conscious, to be *that* alive, in a moment like *that*?

72

Buttons

Back in early June 2007, Dianna had been suffering so much with the hand/foot syndrome, we had all agreed it's time to stop the Xeloda and continue with just the Lapatinib, and hope for the best. Maybe part of Dianna's thinking was affected by what she wanted to be able to do at her birthday party and the cruise we had planned.

All through 2007 brain issues seem paramount. She is not moving well with weakness on her left side; worsening balance problems result in a couple of minor falls, even though she is using a cane. Such incidents carry additional risk because her bone integrity is compromised by bone mets. She is also getting strange auras that blur her vision, and new taste sensations that make eating confusing. Still, her optimism and cheerfulness are undaunted, even when she is alone with me.

When we see Zamorano again in late August, the doctor wonders whether the brain MRIs are showing tumors or simply necrosis, dead tissue from previous radiation treatments. She wants to do a craniotomy. That is, to actually go in and remove it to get a definitive diagnosis. We reluctantly agree. It will be done on September 8, 2007.

After our appointment with Zamorano, we are heading west on I-94 toward home. Dianna reaches over and absently takes my hand in hers. I look over to her, but she seems lost in thought. As we get closer to home and back in the country again, she finally looks over at me with a smile. "Do you think she liked the buttons?"

Dianna has a pair of the original croc shoes, yellow, which have all these little holes in them. When Sandy took her out to lunch one day in Jackson, a town forty minutes north of our home, they found a shop loaded with tons of buttons to fit into the holes. During our very first appointment with Zamorano, Dianna happened to be wearing them, the doctor notices, tells us she owns a pair herself and gushes over Dianna's buttons—sunflowers, birds, hearts, and everything else…lots of buttons.

So Dianna makes a special trip to Jackson, buys a bunch of buttons, and gives them to Zamorano during today's appointment.

"Well, I hope she does," I say. Clearly she did. "Maybe you've bribed her into outdoing herself with the surgery. Can't hurt, anyway."

"Oh, John," she says, laughing. "I wasn't sure which ones she would like best. I just thought she would never have time to go find them on her own. She's quite busy."

"It's the thought that counts. Why didn't you tell her you put 100 miles on our car just to get them? Maybe she'll give us a discount on the surgery."

"Oh, stop it," she says, laughing.

The craniotomy goes without incident. The results show no cancer. It is all dead tissue. Good news. Dianna is happy. Me, too.

"Maybe it was the buttons," I say.

"I don't care what it was. I'm just grateful there is no cancer there."

But she has had to give up the cane for a walker now. She spends two weeks in a rehab center next to Harper Hospital in Detroit, and I visit her almost every day. The contrast between where we live, in the country, and downtown Detroit, is jarring to me every single time I go there.

While Dianna is there, she connects with a nurse who is going through a divorce, needs money, and is trying to sell two diamonds taken out of her wedding ring. Dianna is sympathetic and decides to help her.

"Honey, I'm going to buy them. She takes such good care of me."

She's not asking whether I agree or not. She's already past that.

"Do you really need diamonds right now? They're pretty expensive. How do you know they're worth what she claims?"

"I trust her. Anyway, they're not for me. I'm buying one for Cris (Senna's mom) and one for Marie (my youngest son's wife), as gifts from me. They can make them into whatever they like, a ring or pendant. I want you to give the diamonds to them when I'm gone."

"Jesus, Dianna, don't talk that way."

She looks at me for a long moment. Then she reaches out her hand with a faint smile, and I put my hand into hers.

"Can you bring me the money tomorrow?"

I do.

73

Diarrhea Diaries

By October 2007 Dianna is still on lapatinib, the only remaining chemo drug she can tolerate.

She is having trouble getting out of a chair, or walking, and she cannot lift her left leg. We are receiving home healthcare and home rehab three days/week. While all the people who come and go are nice and well intentioned, their visits do little to help her. Their biggest contribution is giving Dianna someone else to kibitz with, adding color to her life. They love seeing her, and several tell me she is routinely the highlight of their day. They always leave feeling better.

So why are they not paying me to visit, then?

Of course, our friends, neighbors, and Dianna's family are steady and reliable in their cards, phone calls, and visits—no one has abandoned her. All that being said, ninety percent of her support comes from me, of course, because I'm the one who's always there. She is essentially bedridden now, so she is my work and my life, which is perfectly fine with me.

In late October, my since-childhood friend, Steve Kridelbaugh, comes for a visit, and he really perks up Dianna. They spend hours together laughing, and making fun of me in one way or the other.

Works for me.

Dianna has never liked my cooking, which is basically peasant Italian with a strong spicy hot twist. On top of that, when it comes to cooking, let's face it, I'm a one-trick pony. I have about five dishes I love to eat, rotate them, making big batches so I'm eating leftovers most of the time. I like cooking and like eating my own food. I just don't want it taking over my life.

Steve introduces us to fish and some convoluted West Coast cuisine, which I, more or less, find...palatable...and which Dianna loves. He takes over as cook. Just before he leaves, he takes me to the grocery store and reveals the mystery contained in those endless rows of coolers—prepared frozen dinners I have never looked at before in my entire life.

"Buy a ton of these and, after I leave, give them to her. Easy to prepare and she'll love 'em. She isn't eating because you've been giving her shit."

"I resent that."

We both start laughing. I buy about a dozen of them and pack our freezer with these overpriced, nutritionally vacant meals packed in pretty boxes. Steve is right, though. Dammit. She starts enjoying eating again.

Steve's visit is a godsend. He cheers Dianna immensely, commiserates with me without being maudlin, and teaches me how to make Dianna happy in an important way.

Then he leaves.

With the reduced chemo regime, her blood work indicates the cancer is becoming increasingly active, but none of the scans show significantly progressive disease anywhere, and the bone mets seem unchanged. Confusing.

I set up a walkie-talkie system so I can get some work done in other rooms or downstairs while Dianna remains essentially bedridden. Fortunately, we bought a TV for the bedroom a few months back, and she loves watching *Regis and Kelly*, *The View*, and various sitcoms. Otherwise, she reads and sleeps.

She is having continuing bowel problems, with wild swings between constipation and diarrhea. One of the visiting nurses tells us to use Imodium and prunes as the balancing tools. This helps, but titrating her stool composition wasn't one of the courses I had in my chemical engineering curriculum, so it's a struggle. Dianna is in diapers 100 percent of the time now, and we have a Porta-Potti next to the bed.

We come up with a good way to handle getting in and out of bed without hurting her. She puts her arms around my neck and hangs on while I put my arms around her waist and gently, slowly, pull her out of bed, then swing her over so she can sit on the potty. I clean her when she is done, using these nifty wipes that are impregnated with some sort of aloe lubricant, helping to keep her bottom from getting sore. We just reverse the process for getting back into bed. Works like a dream. No bedsores at all.

Of course, we don't always make it to the potty in time.

I'm downstairs working in my office when I get a frantic call on my walkie-talkie.

"John…Jooohhhnnnn…come here, *nooowww*."

I rush upstairs. She is half sitting up against a pillow and slumped over to one side. She was probably trying to get up on her own. *Regis and Kelly* is just coming on.

"Honey…I'm so sorry, …I just had an oops," she says, looking at me sheepishly from her sideways position.

"No big deal, sweetheart. It happens. Or did you do it on purpose?"

She laughs and becomes a little more at ease.

I straighten her up on her pillows, then undo her diaper. I am amazed. She is almost swimming in a brown-yellow liquid. Could float a mallard on this pond. This is an engineering problem I have to think about.

"Geez, honey, this is going to be a challenge…to clean you up without messing up the sheets and spilling it all over the carpet. I can tell you one thing, though—there's no point in worrying about front to back on this one."

We both start laughing as I study the problem. She had to teach me what apparently all women already know—at birth? When wiping one's ass, always wipe from front to back to minimize the possibility of vaginal or urinary tract infections. Makes sense—just never occurred to me. Never was my issue.

"Maybe I can use a turkey baster to suck up a lot of it before I try to move the diaper."

"Don't you dare!" she says, laughing, but making a face.

"Well, I *am* going to use a ladle. I promise to run it through the dish washer before I serve you soup with it, though."

"Oh, honey…." then she pauses. "I'm so sorry to put you through all this."

"Look, you need to listen to me here." I lean down and look straight into her eyes. "This is *not* a big deal. If I can gut a deer, I can do this. And I don't have to drag you a half-mile out of the woods when I'm done, either. Trust me, this is easy."

She smiles and sinks deeper into her pillow, relaxed now.

What amazes me most, even now, even in this moment, is she is not one bit less a lady with as much grace and dignity as any woman I have ever known. She could just as well be in an evening dress seated at a concert. I take a long look at what class looks like, then get to work.

I get it done, step by step and without messing up the sheets or carpet. After sliding a second clean diaper underneath her, I spend a long time cleaning her thoroughly. The home aides did put us onto some really good disinfectants and the importance of using powder for drying.

When I'm all done with the cleaning, I slide a third diaper underneath her while she lifts up a little, then shoot some powder into it and on her with a triumphant flourish and pull the Velcro closed around her.

Done.

By this time, *Regis and Kelly* is almost over.

Would you like some coffee, honey?"

"Oh, I would. Thank you."

I put a spoonful of cocoa in it and top it off with a big squirt of whipped cream. When I bring it in on a tray, she lights up in joyful anticipation, wiggling to slide up higher against her pillow.

"Oh, honey, thank you so much. This is so nice. I feel so much better."

"Good. What're you watching here....ah, *The View*. I can hardly wait to hear what these women will say next."

I lie down next to her, give her a kiss, adjust her pillows, then grab a book.

We have a really nice morning together.

74

The Wedding

"I don't know, Dianna, we have enough of a challenge handling your diarrhea right here at home. I don't know if we should do it." I am not keen on this *at all*.

"John, this is something I want to do. I sat for Jackie when she was baby. I held her in my arms. It's important for me to be there for her wedding."

Jackie Bailey, daughter of Dianna's good friends, Dick and Elaine, is getting married...near Sutton's Bay, a measly five-hour drive from our home. It means getting up there without, hopefully, rushing Dianna into a MacDonald's restroom, if there happens to be one, doing a clean-up in there—or maybe even in the car. Then we would have to stay overnight in a motel...and then, there is the drive back...not to mention the wedding and reception.

"Okay," I say. "We'll do it. Think you can hold it for seventy-two hours straight without going?"

She laughs. But she is also determined. We pack up everything, including a suitcase full of cleaning supplies and a boatload of diapers, the wheelchair, and most important of all, the dress Suzy brought her.

"Is wearing the dress behind all this determination, Dianna?"

She looks at me, and one eyebrow goes up. "True, it may be the only time I will get to wear it. But I would want to go if I had to wear a burlap sack."

"It won't be the only time you wear Suzy's dress, sweetheart. Trust me."

She just looks at me without saying anything. Her face is a mask.

We make the journey up there without a stop, getting to the wedding in plenty of time. The Baileys and many other people there take perfect care of Dianna. Jackie's brothers carry her up the stairs in her wheelchair into the reception hall. Her many friends hover around her all night. She is in a circle of love, and she revels in every minute of it. When she needs to use the restroom, there is enough help around her to handle an army. I don't have to do anything but watch.

I take Chili for a walk up the hill behind the reception hall. It's easy to see my way with a three-quarter moon. I trace the jagged pattern of Cassiopeia across the black northern sky. While Chili noses around, I revel at my own party, the main guests being this sharp, cold, clear October air and this blessed stillness.

Our ride home is equally uneventful.

"Why can't you do this all the time?" I say, as I wheel her into the house on the new aluminum ramp I'd recently purchased over the Internet. Works great.

"I don't know. I wish I could. I can't explain it. I guess I just do what I have to do, when I have to do it."

A week later, the mink jacket I ordered in Alaska shows up at the door. I sign for it and open the package. Makes me very happy to see how great it looks.

"Dianna, close your eyes. I have a surprise for you," I yell into the bedroom without going in.

She's in bed, reading. I peek around the corner as she lays down her book on her lap.

"Oh, honey, what is it?" She's really excited now and squinches up higher against her pillow.

"Well, close your eyes and I'll show you."

She does. I bring the jacket in and hold it up high.

"Okay, you can open them now."

She opens her eyes, then puts both hands to her chipmunk cheeks.

"Oh, my God! I can't believe it. Where did you get it? How...I don't understand. They didn't have my size...I never expected...oh my God, honey, I can't believe you did this!"

"They made it just for you. When I told the man at the factory about your situation, he said he would make a special run just for you. Normally, they make them only once each year."

This is true. The man was so moved by Dianna's circumstances, he decided to go out of his way, and promised it would be done. I am deeply moved that he kept his word.

"See how much you affect people. You don't even have to meet them anymore," I say, as I tell her about the factory man's attitude.

She smiles, though there are tears in her eyes.

I lay it across her. It is soft as silk...well, soft as mink. She strokes it slowly, while I explain the whole story.

It is a happy day.

She never does get to wear it.

No regrets.

75

The Fall

We develop a routine when I have to leave her alone, whether to walk Chili or run errands. I make sure she has everything she needs, does not need to pee or poop, and I always lay our cordless phone next to her. It's something of a gamble, but life is full of gambles.

On December 8, I'm in a hurry and forget to give her the phone before leaving. So it's still on the other side of a king-sized bed, my side. I keep it plugged in there so if the phone rings, she doesn't have to struggle to reach for it. I can get it instead. Dumb. We have several phones. I could have very easily put one on each side of the bed. Just never thought of it.

When I get home, I find her sprawled out on the floor on my side of the bed. Maybe someone called. Maybe she wanted to call someone. Obviously, she was trying to get to the phone.

I lie down next to her, talking to her; but she is dazed, crying softly, confused and incoherent.

Never occurs to me to call 911, either. I just lie there beside her, with my arm around her, stroking her, talking softly to her. We lie there together on the floor for probably half an hour. Finally she starts coming around, recognizes me, and is able to respond to me. I help her up and back into bed.

In an hour or two, she seems back to her most recent normal self, but she still cannot remember what happened. When the physical therapy people show up later that day, they think she is okay. We go on like this for another week until we all begin to notice her progress in physical therapy has stopped. She has lost considerable use of both her left arm and left leg, so can no longer use the walker.

On December 15, I drive Dianna to St. Joe's, and they do a series of brain tests. The doctor concludes she probably has had a stroke, but admits he can see no evidence of one. I think she had a concussion in the fall. But who knows?

They move her to the physical therapy floor and her initial evaluation is quite optimistic. They think she will make progress and admit her to the unit. Our spirits rise.

At home, I'm busy getting the house ready for her homecoming. She and I have always assumed if and when that day comes, she would die in the home she created and loved so much. My idle visions are of her out on the deck, watching a hummingbird sipping at a feeder, enjoying a summer day… maybe with a helping of tiramisu in her lap…or something. I guess all this falls into the category of delusions—or, at least, wishful thinking.

I buy a huge cabinet for all the diapers, cleaning supplies, and medicines, then stock it with tons of wipes and cleaning stuff. While movers come in to rearrange everything so it will fit in the bedroom, I have new carpeting installed. Dianna is *not* going to spend her last days in a room with carpeting stained by too many accidents to count. I bring sample carpet swatches to the hospital for her to choose from. She barely looks at them.

"This one is nice, honey," she says, looking up at me with a half smile.

At some level, I know she is humoring me now. Has she started some other process I'm not included in? Is she thinking I am a complete idiot but doesn't have the heart to burst my bubble? Knowing her, though, she is likely to be making a more gentle assessment than that.

I sort of get all this somewhere inside, but I can't stop myself. I feel impelled to get extra railings for the shower, toilet, double railings for the stairs to the lower level—what could I be thinking? And Lon Wagenshutz, our builder, though he's really busy, responds immediately, installs it all in no time, and refuses to accept money for it.

I create an elaborate Microsoft Word table for her medication schedule, what tasks will need to be done and when, which ones I can do alone, which I can't, better ways to handle leaving the house, and….

A brass sign I had forgotten I ordered shows up in the mail. It says, "Dianna's Garden." I pound it through the snow and frost near the front door into the middle of the mums Dianna planted and cared for with such devotion for so many years. How many times had I seen her perched on her little bench, patiently picking out every single miniscule weed, lost to the world in a silent meditation?

Would she ever see it? I must believe she will.

Finally, I have everything ready for her homecoming.

It's as if I'm two people. One is watching the other from a distance, seeing how pathetic he is acting, but unable—or unwilling—to stop him from doing all the doing that promises she will come home. My head is operating on some sort of engineering track while I put my sinking heart "over there," somewhere far.

Everything I do is at least a step or two, or three, behind what is really going on. Things are changing so fast now. I feel like we are standing frozen on the tracks with a train hurtling through our lives. Somewhere inside, I know it doesn't have any brakes.

Within days after starting intensive physical therapy, her progress, which is good at first, nosedives. She is trying so hard, but she can do less and less each day. I sit with her through her therapy, my heart breaking. Her attitude is still, even if in a more foggy way, optimistic. She is so proud of a primitive painting she has taken painstaking hours to complete, smiling the whole time, barely able to control her fingers and hands.

"What do you think of it, honey? Nice, isn't it?"

One day, I'm asked to attend a meeting about her situation. There are about eight women in the room, including the lead orthopedic doctor…and me. They run through the entire mini-drama we have been watching, then put a document in front of me. They want me to sign it, saying Dianna is no longer qualified for physical therapy, that she is in a stable state, and that she can be discharged to a nursing home.

I refuse.

After politely and quietly delivering my logic for not signing it, I stand up and walk out, leaving them all sitting there in the room.

Inside, I am absolutely boiling.

My reasoning is simple. They are the ones who said she was a good candidate for therapy the first day she showed up; and now, a few days later, she is not. How could this be called a stable state?

Before I leave, I travel the length and breadth of the hospital, getting correct names for each of the department heads involved with Dianna's care. I finally reach home near midnight and immediately type up a letter to all of them—the stroke guy, the female therapy doctor, department heads, and Dr. Stella.

Basically, my letter says you can move her to a nursing home if you want, but a) her condition is *not* stable, and b) she does *not* have a diagnosis that explains the sudden changes everyone agrees have occurred, and c) you now have these facts in writing…*and so do I.*

I end the letter by thanking everyone for the remarkable care she has received so far—which I mean to be sincere. They *are* all dedicated, ethical people simply following Medicare rules like robots, but missing the point.

Not a crime. Not acceptable, either.

The next morning I travel about ten miles inside the hospital, hand delivering copies of my letter to every single doctor on the list. Then I go sit with Dianna. On the way to the hospital, I had picked up a serving of tiramisu at Ruby Tuesday, and put it in a cooler. Tiramisu is, more or less, Italian for "lift me up" and it always seems to do exactly that for her. It works this time, too. She is happy. I help feed it to her. I'm just satisfied to be with her.

She will always be my tiramisu.

The next morning, when I show up, there are four or five doctors huddling in her room, discussing her situation and figuring out what tests are needed to achieve a diagnosis. I ignore them, saying nothing. I'm not going to rub it in. I just want results.

Dianna is moved to the oncology unit on the 11th floor. Okay with me. Obviously, she is in no condition to do physical therapy, anyway. A series of tests are run, and she is given a dose of radiation on her pelvis to relieve pain that is now becoming severe.

And we wait.

On December 29, around 11:00 p.m., Dr. Stella appears in the doorway of our room, looking somber, and sits down next to her bed. Then he cups Dianna's hand with both of his. He is struggling to hold back tears; but I can see, even in this weak night light, his eyes are glistening.

"We have found what the problem is, Dianna. You have metastatic cancer throughout your liver. I am so sorry, but there is nothing else we can do at this point."

Dianna's face is frozen, her eyes unblinking, staring at Stella. I am stunned. Neither of us say a word.

"I suggest you consider hospice as your best option," he says finally, after a long pause.

Dianna begins to cry softly, and tears are streaming down my cheeks, too. I drop my head and take Dianna's other hand in mine.

After another pregnant silence, Dr. Stella sits up straight and lets out a barely audible sigh. "I can offer you one other option, if you want it. There is another chemo regimen we could try; but I have to be honest with you, I give it a very small chance of success. The only reason I even bring it up is because you have beaten the odds so many times, for so long. In the end, who am I to say, you shouldn't have another chance, to say you may not be able to do it again?"

He slumps back in his chair. He looks tired. Obviously, for him, it has been a very long day with a lousy ending.

"Thank you, Dr. Stella," I say. "Let us think about this overnight. Thank you so much for all you have done for us."

He stands, leans down, gives Dianna a long hug, kisses her on the cheek, glances at me with compassion and genuine sadness in his eyes, then leaves. Dianna and I look at each other. She looks so vulnerable, so fragile.

"What do you think we should do, honey?" she says, staring at me.

For the first time I see unvarnished fear in her eyes.

I do not hesitate for a second. I don't have to think about what to say. I know what she wants to do, and I know what she wants me to say. This is her parade, and I am *never* going to be the one who rains on it. Only she is going to decide when this parade is over. Her journey is my journey.

I smile and squeeze her hand. "Well, what do we have to lose, sweetheart? Why not give it a shot?"

Dianna lights up like someone has plugged her in and turned the switch to "on."

"Okay. I do think that *is* a good way to look at it. Where there's life, there's hope," she says, wiggling to sit more upright against her pillow.

For just an instant, the sun peeks out.

76

Into Winter

On January 7, Dianna is moved to the Heartland Nursing Home, very close to St. Joe's, so she can be easily transported by ambulance to the hospital for her last-ditch chemo treatments. For me, this is about forty miles from home. In the dead of winter, the drive on US-12, a winding, hilly, black two-lane road, can be treacherous. But Dianna begs me to be there every day, and to stay as long as possible. I do. I want to be there anyway. It helps enormously that the nursing home has no objection to me bringing Chili in with me.

The central problem now is bone pain. Dianna is getting lots of it now; and at the nursing home, it has to be managed with morphine in pill form. They are not qualified to administer it as an IV drip. The problem with pills is gauging how often they are needed and, once given, the inevitable delay in the onset of pain mitigation. What's worse, the staff is overworked and not really trained to deal with this condition—they do their best, but Dianna begins to experience periodic episodes of excruciating pain. I have never seen Dianna cry much, but I see her crying now. It is sapping her natural enthusiasm.

When I'm there, generally sixteen hours a day, we prevent this from happening. But when I am gone, sometimes the staff drops the ball. It is simply the nature of this particular game.

Chili makes friends on the floor and becomes a minor celebrity. We go for short walks along the Huron River nearby; but mostly, he lies next to me, listening, nose twitching, in this whole new world of sounds and smells.

"Honey, they took off my wedding ring. They said my ring finger is too swollen."

I study her fingers. They always were fatter than mine, and I would tease her about that now and then. Not now. I have never worn my own wedding ring. Hate rings. Maybe, in part, due to all those years of watching safety films with people's fingers shredded to the bone when their ring caught on something. But she loves them and she loves wearing hers, no matter what.

"Want me to wear it for you?"

She looks at me, vacantly at first, then smiles. But it doesn't last long. She turns very serious again. "Honey, it's very important to me. I want it on, especially now. What can we do? It doesn't fit."

"Where is it?"

"I have it here in the drawer next to the bed. They said you need to take it home. I want to wear it, John."

I find the ring and test it on her ring finger. Not a chance. It does fit perfectly on her baby finger though.

"How about we put it on your baby finger?"

She breaks out into a big smile. "Oh, honey, that would be wonderful."

I put it on carefully, kiss the ring, then lean over and kiss her firmly on the lips. "How's that?"

"Thank you so much. You don't know how much this means to me." She relaxes into her pillow and closes her eyes, smiling.

"I do know, sweetheart."

I sit back in my chair and Chili pushes his nose into me. Touch me, he says.

Soon Dianna is sleeping and she looks content.

One morning, I am in the car on my way to the nursing home, and Rod Stewart is singing, "Smile." Suddenly the tears just explode out of me and won't stop. I can hardly see the road. Chili is sitting in the seat next to me and instantly puts his paw on my arm and presses hard, boring a hole through me.

> *"Smile though your heart is aching*
> *Smile even though it's breaking"*

My heart *is* breaking. Relentlessly. So, I'm getting lots of practice.

Soon after Dianna's move to the nursing home, I bring some things from home to keep up her spirits. In particular, we have a print by Brian Andreas called "Dark Garden," a combination of primitive art and philosophy of life that is so perfectly Dianna. The words say:

> *I once had a garden filled with flowers that grew only on dark thoughts.*
> *But they need constant attention and one day I decided I had better things to do.*

I put it on the wall and she looks over to it, recognizes it, smiles, then closes her eyes again. I sit looking at her with a heavy heart, thinking back to that sunny summer day in Leland, up in Leelanau, when we first bumped into Andreas' work and were enthralled. We wanted to buy them all. We ended up buying quite a few. She liked this one best.

One day I reach inside her diaper and notice it is wet. Just then, an aide pops in and offers to change her.

"No. Thanks, but no, I'll do it," I say quickly. "You can help me turn her, though."

I have done this so many times, I could do it with my eyes closed. They are good people, but they are busy and constantly moving from room to room. The first day we are there, one of them is cleaning her, and I can see her butt and vaginal area are red and raw. They do it too quickly, with wipes that feel like dry sandpaper to me. Cheaper, obviously. Dianna cries out softy while they are wiping her, and tears come to her eyes.

Enough of *that*.

I immediately run out and buy some wipes with aloe in them. I crack open a package in the drugstore while a clerk eyes me, frowning. They are slightly damp, and soft as a baby's ass. Good. I buy a whole bunch of them.

When I get back, I put a big note on the boxes of wipes,

PLEASE USE <u>ONLY</u> THESE WIPES. SLOWER HURTS LESS THAN FASTER. DIANNA WILL APPRECIATE IT. SO WILL THE MANAGEMENT (ME). THANK YOU SO MUCH.

The aides smile when they see the note. They don't show up too often when I'm there, but the wipes gradually disappear as the days go by, so either they are using them on Dianna when I'm not there, or stealing them. I choose to believe they are using them.

When I'm there, I let the aides assist me—hurts her less if she can be gently rolled and held, and more hands help with that. But I prefer to do the wiping myself. Good as they are, they don't love her the way I do. They have many asses to wipe; I have only one, not counting my own, of course. They appreciate the help, and I always treat them with the respect they deserve. With most of them, we tease each other with abandon.

There is one black aide from Jamaica who I do allow to do the wiping. He is a happy young man, always sporting a smile with no tears hidden behind it. Dianna likes him, too.

He pops into the doorway one day and says, in his delightful accent, his voice rising at the end, "And how are you today, Dianna?"

Dianna opens her eyes, slowly turns her head toward him, and smiles. "Better," she says.

Better now that he has *shown up*. He is actually *present* to her. So in this particular moment, she *is* being accurate. I begin to think about this as I help roll her to one side. What other moment is there besides *this* one?

I watch him do the diaper change. He is very gentle with her. He uses the correct wipes. He handles her lovingly. She enjoys his attention. It's like a mini love affair. I feel blessed to be in the presence of their wisdom.

"Hide any trace of sadness
That's the time you have to keep on trying"

I do try. I do my crying when I'm alone.

It's funny. Consciously, mentally, I never think about her dying. Mentally, I'm in total denial. Yet many of my actions support the knowledge she is, in fact, dying. I spend most of my away time reviewing hours of our home videos, marking out bits I want to put into a funeral tribute video. A good friend, Hank Adkins, a professional at these things, is taking my mark-ups, editing it into a piece, and putting it to music. When I review his work, often in tears, he chokes up, too; but he is doing an excellent job. I'm so grateful. I want it done with the same class that represents the Dianna we all know, the class with which Dianna is living her life, even now, in these pain-laced days and nights.

While I keep my mind busy, my heart betrays me when I least expect it—a song, some idle thought of better times past, the way the light fractures through the trees.

Each day, I drive the forty miles to the nursing home to be with her, mostly sitting, watching, making sure stuff is handled, petting Chili. As light slides into dark, I wait until she is sleeping for the night, then kiss her gently on the cheek and slip away—and return to a cold, empty house. The nursing home feels too hot, and the house feels too cold, and too…something. It is almost as if no one lives there now. Not even me.

As the days go by, she talks less and less. Hours go by without a word being said. She finally stops eating completely, no matter how we adjust the menus—the staff tries their best to entice her, but her menu shrinks to zero. We are down to occasional ice cream. Eventually she closes her eyes and rarely opens them anymore. The only thing she still likes is listening to music, thanks to Jeff Rahl, who so kindly loaded a list of her favorite songs on a MP3 player for her. This turns out to be a godsend. Jeff is a big heart that happens to have a body wrapped around it.

I have several meetings with the resident doctor about morphine dosing, but because Dianna's situation is constantly changing as the cancer progresses, we are trying to hit a moving target. In all her years of dealing with cancer, this is, ironically, the first pain Dianna has experienced from the cancer, itself. Until now, all her suffering has been due to the treatment modalities she has endured.

It is really hard to anticipate the pain, and sometimes the staff is distracted or late with the pills. Consequently, Dianna goes through long periods of being comfortable sprinkled with short periods of pure agony. I get in the habit of calling her every morning as soon as I get up to check her pain status. As often as not, I have to call the desk to tell them she needs her pills immediately. The desk gal doesn't like it, but I tell her I'm staying on the phone until she tells me they have been given. It takes me an hour to get there, so they just have to do it.

It's not a good situation.

Looking back, I can see it is during this time that Dianna's body and mind are coming into alignment with her soul wish to leave her body. Life, finally, even for this eternally optimistic being, is no longer worth living.

Not that I recognize this consciously in the moment. On the contrary, I can't even put two and two together and come up with four. As usual, my mind is just running as fast as it can, taking care of business while immersed in a dense emotional haze. The balls just keep on coming, and I just keep on swinging.

It is time for her second chemo treatment.

77

No More Pain

On February 10, 2008, Dianna is transported to St. Joe's for her second chemo treatment. I follow the ambulance in my car, then sit next to her in our all-too-familiar oncology clinic, in a side room. All the nurses there know what is going on and wave hello.

By the time we get there, Dianna is starting into another peak pain period. Melanie, one of the nurses, comes in to set her up for the chemo treatment, then stops in her tracks, looks at her, then at me, and back to her again. She instantly comes to a decision.

"John, we are not going to let her suffer like this. This has to stop. She is in no condition to have a chemo treatment."

I'm stunned. Dianna is in too much pain by now to discuss anything.

"I just want you to do something," Dianna blurts out.

"John, I'm going to get the doctor right now."

Turns out Stella is not in this day, and another doctor I do not know comes in a couple of minutes later, takes one look at Dianna, and flatly kills the chemo treatment. They give her an injection of morphine, then start her on a morphine drip. Within minutes, Dianna is relaxed again.

I am furious.

"How can you stop her chemo? It's what she wants. Without it, what else is there?"

Melanie and the doctor look at me, then at each other, without saying anything. They know what I refuse to know.

It is over.

"I will work on getting her admitted back into the hospital, John." Melanie says. "She needs pain management that works. I cannot allow her to go through this. She just can't get the treatment she needs in the nursing home."

The doctor agrees. They aren't discussing this with me, they are telling me in as nice a way as they can.

I give in. I don't want her suffering, either. It is just such a rapid reversal of "The Plan," I can't mentally catch up with it. And throughout all of this, Dianna has not been consulted, either.

We are back on the 11th floor, the oncology unit, the top floor in the new wing of the hospital. It is the penthouse, so to speak. Room 1105.

By now, I'm calm. I just needed time. Seeing Dianna finally relaxed and sleeping is worth everything. How could I have been so blind?

The rooms in this wing are brand new and are, for a hospital room, classy. There is a floor-to-ceiling window that looks almost due east. I walk over to it. The sky is clear and, even with a bare quarter-moon, I can make out the tree line along the Huron River that twists and winds around the hospital perimeter. I stare out at the lights twinkling here and there through the darkness. Finally, I collapse into a large La-Z-Boy-type chair, exhausted. I have to do something about Chili out in the car. It's way too cold to leave him there.

Here she will get all the attention and pain treatment she needs and deserves. No calls at 6:00 a.m. to discover her crying. That is over, too. I am grateful and relieved.

Dianna is dead to the world and looks completely at peace. It finally hits me, like a stone falling on my chest, staring at her, awash in this silver light. She is *never* coming home again.

She wanted so much to die in her own house, in the home she created. At this point, though, her highest priority is my highest priority, for her to not to die in pain. Moving her now, and moving her from a place where she is getting that need met better than anywhere else would be cruel.

I study her in the moonlight. Well, in a way, she *is* home now. Home is where she can get the care she needs. And unlike me, she always seemed to treat hospital visits as social events, just visiting a different set of friends. She has come to love the people at St. Joe's, and they have come to love her. So this is going to be how it is.

This room will be the home she dies in.

After giving Dianna a light kiss on the cheek, I drive back home with Chili, crying on and off all the way. Once there, I start making phone calls and writing emails. Our neighbor, Howard Ladd, readily agrees to take care of Chili each day while I'm at the hospital. I warn him some nights, I may not come back at all. He's okay with all of it.

Family and friends begin showing up, and Dianna's room is never empty of visitors. The nurses are terrific. They know how to do all this with efficiency, unobtrusiveness, and kindness. Dianna's pain episodes are over.

Mine are not.

I ask one of the nurses for her prognosis.

"John, I have seen this process many times before; and of course, one never ever knows exactly. But it won't be more than a week, maybe two."

To hear her say this is shattering. Reality keeps crashing in on me in waves but begins clearing away the fog, too. My mind and my heart come together on the same page, into some sort of alignment I hadn't experienced until now.

So I start mechanically doing all the things of death, and the engineer in me takes over. I decide right away we will have two funerals. There are too many friends where we live, many of them too old to travel, and too many friends and family in Mount Pleasant, again, many of them too old to travel. When I am not with Dianna, I hire the funeral homes and even go out and buy a suit, shirt, and tie. I haven't worn a suit in years.

Dianna asks for her "fluffy," a soft white robe someone had given her, to be put over her covers. She wears a favorite white knit stocking cap day and night to cover the remnants of her hair, maybe for style reasons, wanting to look her best, even now. She smiles at friends and family now and then, and likes listening to their chatter when she is more alert. But mostly, especially as the nurses gradually increase her morphine dose to keep up with her increasing pain, she rarely opens her eyes and says less and less.

One day, a young doctor, looking increasingly uncomfortable and frustrated, is standing over her bed, firing questions at her like a machine gun while she simply lays there, saying nothing, refusing to open her eyes. She is done with all that.

Finally, I decide to rescue the doctor. I lean down and kiss Dianna firmly on the lips for a long few seconds, then step back. Slowly she turns toward me, opening one eye, lifting her eyebrow more than a little.

"Are you trying to get a sultry kiss from me?" she asks very clearly as a faint smile crosses her face.

"Indeed I am, sweetheart. Indeed I am."

I break out laughing, and even the embarrassed doctor has to smile. He beats a quick exit.

These are the very last words I remember her saying—out loud—to me.

78

7:04 A.M.

I am going back and forth between spending time with Dianna and making arrangements. I fervently pray, and silently beg, actually *demand*, that Dianna not die without me being there. It is crucially important to me, and I worry about it constantly.

The evening of February 19, Dianna's family leaves for the night to sleep at Linda Salvador's home nearby. Only my sister Elena stays, and we both fall asleep in Dianna's room. As I am drifting off, I glance out the window. The moon is full, and everything is silvery, shiny. I silently but firmly instruct Dianna to wake me if she decides to leave. I must have this moment with her, I tell her. I fade off into a fitful sleep.

Hours later, startled, I suddenly sit up straight as if someone has shaken me. Dianna's breathing is much more labored, louder, rasping. I stumble to her side. I *must* be touching her *now*, I am thinking, laying my hands firmly against the warmth of her arm. Each breath is like a hammer beating against my heart. I sit paralyzed, not holding her back, not wanting her to go, tears exploding out of me in a torrent. What can I do?

A final rasping for air, then deafening silence.

Death is digital. In a single instant, someone flips the switch. Spirit is gone. I am stunned by how sharp and distinct this is.

I notice the clock. 7:04 a.m.

I drop my head down against her arm and sob silently as I feel warm go cool. Finally, I lean over her body and press her mouth closed so she looks like she is sleeping. Then, I kiss each cheek, which feels like kissing something else besides Dianna. She is not here anymore. I step back. I do not want to wake or speak to anyone. I want this time for myself.

The light draws me to the window.

Winter's thin icy light floods the room while I watch the Huron River Valley beginning to take shape, a tree line of black filigree, the leafless trees of February, stand out against the snow, still blue white in this light. Through

287

the trees, the horizon is purple with faint hints of reds and oranges.

I cannot comprehend it.

How can there be light showing up, just as the Light of my life has gone out? She has left me with a rising sun, a new day, facing an empty page. A day Dianna will never see.

All my eggs are still in her basket, as I always wanted them to be. Now the basket is tipped over, every egg scattered, every egg broken.

Her life is over.

Frozen in this moment, so is mine.

Part V
Dianna Still Teaching
2008-2011

79

The Daze Phase

I'm standing in the funeral home, looking at an array of caskets, and he's droning on about how this one is that, and that one is this. And I'm thinking, why not a pine box? Better yet, cremation. But this is Dianna I am serving, not me.

I point to the classiest one. "I'll take that one." She would like that one.

"Do you know which dress you want her to be wearing?" he asks.

"Yes," I say, without hesitation, surprising even myself. *Where did that come from?* I hadn't thought about this before; but, somehow, I didn't have to, either.

Dianna and Suzy laughing, their heads together, on that warm July day, Dianna admiring the traditional Saudi dress in the dazzling sunlight, running her hand gingerly across the fabric, almost with tenderness.

Later, and not so long ago, and in another lifetime, I also remember promising her she would wear it again, then the way she looked at me when I said it. I quickly turn away so he cannot see my face fracturing like china hitting a ceramic floor. "Think I'll go outside for a while," I say.

For some reason, I think to phone a neighbor and friend, Pam Moriarty, who attended Dianna's 50th birthday party and works in a salon.

"Pam, the funeral home can supply someone, but wonder if you would like to do Dianna's hair and makeup and all that?"

"Oh, John, I would just love to do that for her. It would be an honor," Pam says.

I feel a huge lump starting in my throat. "I have a bunch of wigs to choose from. I'm not sure which one would be best." I barely squeeze this out.

"Bring some over to the funeral home and we can pick one. Bring whatever jewelry you would like her to wear, too."

I won't be bringing the blonde mushroom. *Dianna smiles somewhere.* In my head, I suppose?

She will want to wear her wedding ring.

Yes. I can almost feel her nodding in agreement.

I sit down on the edge of the bed, the ring cupped in my hands. Chili instantly leaps up on the bed next to me, pushing his nose hard into my arm. Get your act together, he's saying. But I drop my head into my hands and crumple up anyway.

I decide to bring all the jewelry I can find.

Pam picks the right things.

"Where are you going to hold the funeral, John?" Pat, Dianna's mom, asks. I can hear the trembling in her voice over the phone. She's afraid I'm going to have it where we live, over a hundred miles away.

"Pat, we're going to have two funerals. One here, then transport her body to Mount Pleasant for a second one."

A long silence at the other end of the line.

"Are you there?"

"I'm here, …Thank you so much, John, for doing this. You don't know how much this means to me…. Do you need any help?"

"Nope. Everything's arranged. I picked down-home, Midwest, mom-cooked-type food—no Italian stuff. Just the junk you guys eat."

I feel her smiling on the phone. We have routinely disparaged each other's cuisines over the years, each confident our own is better. Which, of course, is utterly ridiculous. Clearly, mine *is* better.

Kathy Preston, a rock in Dianna's life, had some time ago offered Dianna a burial plot near Kara's grave in a Mount Pleasant cemetery. She now wants to know if this is what I still want to do.

"Yes," I say.

"There's only one plot there," Kathy reminds me. "But Dianna knew you wanted to be cremated, so she decided on this one, near Kara's grave."

"That'll be fine, Kathy. Thanks for offering it."

"She also said she hoped you would have at least half your ashes buried with her one day," Kathy adds, almost a question.

"She did? Did she say which half?"

Kathy laughs.

"The half with your heart in it, I would guess," Kathy says without hesitation, a smile in her voice.

Later, I decide to have all my ashes buried in Dianna's grave site. I tell my sons, Eric and Jon, to simply slip into the cemetery one day, don't ask, scoop out some dirt, toss in the ashes, and go have a beer…on me, of course.

Consuelo Campbell calls. "John, I am not sure if you know this or not, but a few years ago, Dianna and I were walking to our car after lunch one day and she asked if I would sing a particular song at her funeral. Do you want me to do that?"

"She *did*? When did she say *that*?… I mean, I guess so,… if you would. I'm so grateful, Consuelo… ah… which song?"

"She wanted me to sing 'Over the Rainbow' from the *Wizard of Oz*."

"Well…okay. Will you sing at both funerals, Consuelo?"

"I will."

"Wonder why she never told *me*?"

A question left hanging. Probably didn't want to go there with me. Maybe just forgot.

I begin thinking about this. She loved life, wanted to live it as long as possible, and did not want to die with a lot of pain; but there's nothing I ever saw in her suggesting she feared death. So planning for it would not be morbid for her. Just getting it the way she wanted it, like decorating *her* house. A certain pragmatism I guess I knew was there, and yet, still jolting when it shows up like this. Is she smiling right now, knowing she's tossed me yet another surprise?

Oh, yes.

After getting off the phone with Consuelo, I immediately look up the lyrics. Reading them is just one of many moments I will come undone during these days. I cry and I laugh as I imagine how she came to select exactly **this** to be her signature swan song.

Dreams you dare to dream come true… Of course. Dianna dared every day. She lived each day, knowing it *was* a dream; so, completely unafraid of looking foolish or idealistic—her sophistication lived at another level. She trusted things would work out—not necessarily how she thought they should but rather, embracing whatever way they did.

Bluebirds flying over a rainbow is another Dianna-like touch, reminding me of her little (male, dammit) spider parked off to one side of her "Rug by Dianna." She *would* put a couple of bluebirds above the rainbow, where you would least expect to find them. And she knew if bluebirds could reach that magical place where "troubles melt like lemon drops," she could, too.

And so she has.

This song *is* Dianna… a poignant innocence, unflagging optimism, laced with whimsy, all marinated in her eternal faith in the mystery of life. Her unshakable quality of imagining life as it could be, no matter how disappointing it might be in the moment.

Was this song written for her?

Certainly for everyone like her. This special slice of being is thin—not many of us are designed this way. Certainly not me. I think way too much.

The Springville Church has a new pastor now, Pastor Marge. Pastor Melanie, with whom Dianna had bonded so tightly, has moved a few communities to the west. Dianna would have liked each one to play a role, so I ask Pastor Melanie to do the service in Mount Pleasant. She agrees. As it will turn out, she will play a Dianna-style concerto, a humor-filled and heartfelt eulogy. With her very being, Melanie brings Dianna into the room, laughing and crying with us.

David McNeil, the chaplain at St. Joe's, calls while I am putting on my brand new black suit with micro-thin blue pin stripes. Feels like a suit of armor, which, in some respects, I suppose it is.

"John, I hope I'm not bothering you at a time like this, but many of the doctors, nurses, and staff here at the hospital want to attend Dianna's funeral, but they can't all leave at the same time. We were wondering if you would consider allowing us to hold a service here at the hospital chapel, in her honor so everyone can pay their respects."

"Oh, Dianna would love that. As you must know, she created another whole family at St. Joe's. She would want to say goodbye, to hold them close once more."

I feel everything is going the way Dianna would like it to go. But as she knows only too well, a down side to *three* funerals—I'm skipping the part about being put through the emotional wringer three times—is I'll have to wear this damned suit three times.

She tilts her head at me right now, smiling. Stop your whining and get on with it. These words come to me silently inside my head, but I laugh out loud.

I write her eulogy the night before the first funeral in Adrian. It flows out of me like water. In the middle of the night, I wake up knowing there is something more to say, or say differently. I can feel Dianna at my shoulder as I write, and it is easy to tell when we are both satisfied with it. I type it up and go back to sleep.

Remembering Dianna

I never thought I would see this day; but then, Dianna always was full of surprises.

She is the light of my life. She is the love of my life.

I am supremely fortunate she chose to love me, to spend her life with me. I think it is worth knowing the same sparkling person you came to know was the same person I lived with every day. There were not many Diannas, but only one. She never played games. She played only the Game of Life, the same remarkable human being whether she was in a crowd of hundreds or alone with me. The conversation might be different, but the Spirit was always Dianna.

It was as if there was this fairy princess dancing through life, hurrying from here to there, reaching out with her magic wand, touching each person she met, whether for a brief moment in a grocery line or for long strings of moments with lifelong friends. She never tired of being Present to each person she was with.

The word that fits best when I see her in my mind's eye is Appreciation. She took nothing and no one for granted. To be in her presence was to feel loved, respected, and heard. She sprinkled her energy through life with a delightful and surprising sense of humor. She made us laugh, and she unselfconsciously laughed at herself.

So she changed me into someone better than who I was. She became my purpose in life—I would often kid her—she was the rocket, and my job was to be the rocket launcher. Not without some twisting and turning, I came to truly love being who she needed me to be, and finally learned it cost me nothing. To the contrary, I became more of who I needed to be.

In the beginning, since I was at least a hundred years older than Dianna, I thought I would be her teacher. As the years went by, I was gradually dissuaded from that stupid idea. I might have taught her a bit about the world as it is, but she taught me so much more about the world as it could be.

Even in her last days, she was still teaching. I used to feel she was breaking my heart a thousand times a day in these past few months; but really, she was simply still forging me into a more complete human being.

In the end, when I think of Dianna, I must fall back on an old saying. When struggling to understand what to do in life, I try to remember to ask myself the question, "What would love do?" Really, this is just another way of asking, "What would Dianna do?" I never saw there to be a difference.

Her life purpose, at least in part, is clear to me. She modeled for others how to be Love expressed in the most practical ways imaginable. No one I know better understood that our thoughts create our reality, so why not choose positive thoughts? Then do the work it takes to bring them to fruition…that love is for giving…that Attitude is everything. She lived it moment by moment by moment, effortlessly, naturally.

How could she be anything but a bright shining star in our universe and in our hearts?

She will be sorely missed and her legacy lives on in all of us, making each one of us so much better for having known her. There is no higher honor we could offer her than to emulate her model.

So now it is time to say, Goodbye, my love. You are now in better hands than mine.

My love always,
Your devoted husband
John

There is no way on earth I can read this out loud in front of everyone without falling apart, so I hand it off to my sister Elena. She does so well what I have no capacity for doing at all.

Consuelo sings heartbreakingly beautifully at both funerals. Though I know it's hard for her, she gives Dianna-like performances, completely from the heart, yet emotionally controlled, like the professional Consuelo has trained herself to be. Senna is so distraught she wants to leave, but doesn't. I'm mentally numb, but feeling everything.

At the funerals, some people comfort me with "At least the burden is gone…," and "It must have been so hard for you taking care of her…." And as their words float into my consciousness, I know they are just struggling to find the right ones—I have done the same thing. I can only reply with what is true for me, "Dianna was never a burden. She was—and still is—a gift in my life. I regret not one second of it…, I would give anything to have her here still…." then, give them a hug and move on, putting one foot in front of the other.

One lady approaches me and says simply, "I only met Dianna once, and I cannot explain how, but she changed my life. When I heard about her death, I had to come. I just wanted you to know this." Then she turns on her heel and evaporates into the crowd. I don't know who she is, and I never see her again.

Dr. Stella speaks movingly at the hospital service as do several of the nurses, and finally…the all of it is over, all the goodbyes spoken, all the hugs hugged, all the kisses kissed, and all our friends fly away.

Alone.

I take off my suit, slip into a pair of old sweats and a ragged sweater. The last time I wore these things, Dianna was alive, I am thinking, looking out the window into a gray somber light.

Now it's Chili and me… in a house I barely recognize, the energy is so radically different. A house is empty when the one you love is gone, and it is empty in a completely different way when they are gone and never coming back.

For a month, friends and family call, email often, and there are many cards and letters, sprinkled with suggestions, "Take some pills, get out more, good time for a vacation, visit friends, need to be with people right now, don't be alone, and…." until the attention finally dwindles away. People, as they must, move on.

I'm relieved. I just want to be alone.

I don't want any pills. I don't want any distractions. I want to experience all the pain, all the sadness, all the grief, and work through all of it in my own way. I cry every day, newly amazed she is gone every day, and miss her so much my body literally aches every day.

Chili and I are joined at the hip. Each day, we religiously walk the snowy woods and fields around home. He makes few suggestions beyond picking up my socks and boring a hole through me when it's past time to go.

It is one long, painful, valuable day after another, periods of numbness scrubbed raw with unheralded waves of crushing grief. I can't listen to the radio. I can't play music.

Still, I must listen to the two songs Consuelo recorded for me, "The Look of Love," which she sang at Dianna's 50th birthday party, and "Over the Rainbow." I have Hank Adkins fill up a couple of CDs with just those two songs playing over and over so I can listen to them at home or in the car.

I use them as tools to modulate the amount of grief I can handle in any given moment. They also keep me close to my feelings, to Dianna, to what we still are together in a way I do not yet comprehend.

When I listen to "The Look of Love," memories come alive, our first meeting, falling in love, her quirky mannerisms, Dianna on the beach relentlessly waving bread at seagulls, the million laughs, the practical jokes we played on each other, our love for each other. Ironically, that song ends with "...Don't ever go." ...and she did anyway. Apparently, she didn't listen all the way to the end.

When I play "Over the Rainbow," other images and feelings rush in, watching her struggle with the letting go of this life, imagining her delight at returning to spirit, leaving pain and suffering behind, and most of all, her childlike innocence, optimism, faith. I know she's home again. I just miss her being physically here with me, the sound of her voice, the scent of her body, her energy in the room.

How could this amazing being, this explosion of Light into every space she entered, into every life she touched, be gone? Disbelief is my daily companion.

Mornings are the worst, awakening to discover, once again, nothing has changed. The bed is still empty beside me, and I lie here immersed in a deafening silence. I'll not hear her voice this day, either.

Bedtime is better. Emotionally exhausted, I fall asleep quickly, often waking several times during the night to record vivid dreams, some with Dianna in them.

My neighbors complain they can never tell whether I'm home or not. The house always looks dark. Without Dianna around to flip on our seventy-four accent lights, the only light I have on is the single one I'm using.

In the darkness of winter, it is not hard for me to accept that her work here was done. When our work is done, when we have done all we can do, we leave. And we can always tell when our work is not done; we're still here. I believe this is always true, without exception, whether our lives end at four, forty, or 100, whether we can explain it or not. Truth is, we can't explain anything really important anyway. Death, like life, is a mystery, making it both exquisitely delicious, and sometimes exquisitely painful.

Winter dissolves into spring, my first without her in a lifetime.

Spring is a busy time on the lake—flights of too many species to count ducks and geese pass through Loch Erin this time of year on their way to nesting grounds in northern Canadian marshes between the border and Hudson Bay. Now they are trading back and forth across the water and into nearby cornfields. The day is perfect for them—windy, rainy, overcast—great duck hunting weather if I still did that.

I stand on the deck with Chili, listening, watching. Sand hill cranes shatter the cool spring air with their guttural calls, prehistoric echoes from long ago, and a lone blue heron is poised just offshore, a frozen statue—and this day, a bonus, a male bald eagle I can barely make out perched on the very top branch of a tall straggly oak on the far side of Goose Bay.

I wish Dianna was here to complain about the mallards mating each year outside our bedroom window. Now she is gone. Inexplicably, so are they. Maybe they know their audience is gone. Maybe they have died, too. One more fractional mystery of life.

When I sit down on a deck chair, a wave of emptiness overwhelms me. Almost instantly, Chili presses his paw hard into my knee, his claws digging deep, almost hurting. When I look to him, I'm startled by the intensity of his stare, his eyes achingly soft and liquid.

What does he understand that I don't?

Maybe everything.

Dianna's father has been in a nursing home for some time. When he is told Dianna has died, he immediately stops eating and dies on April 2.

I'm not thinking about dying. I'm hanging on by my fingernails, but I'm working hard, too. My mind is in a daze, but my heart is alive. I feel like there is something more for me to do.

80

The Ugly Chef

One day in April, I'm standing in the kitchen and glance over at those French chef prints Dianna loved...and I hated.

"Well, dammit, they're coming down now," I say out loud.

Chili, who is stretched out on the kitchen floor, lifts his head, tilting it toward me, striving to understand the sounds I'm making. He stares at me as I step over him, walk over to prints, and unceremoniously lift them off the wall.

I stand in the middle of the room, holding them, wondering what to do next.

At least I've done something.

81

Letting Go, Lightening Up, Creating Space

Once in action, I can't stop. Each day, though most of April and all of May, I'm up early and work late into the evening until I'm too tired to work anymore.

I've decided to go through the entire house, garage, attic, and let go of everything I don't need or want. The annual lake-wide yard sale in early June provides me with a target date for getting it done. I start with the most formidable room, a storage room so packed with stuff I cannot fully open the door, much less walk through it. I discover lots of hidden ideas Dianna had in her mind's eye, stashed away for some other day.

I decide to leave our two upstairs guest bedrooms completely untouched, the way Dianna last decorated them. They will be my "Dianna greeting our guests" rooms. I never go up there anyway. I also leave all the "female stuff" surrounding our Jacuzzi, the one she loved, and the one I have never used and, no doubt, never will. These feel like nice touches to me.

I make piles of things I want to disappear, gradually filling the open areas of the living room and family room almost head high. Not dawdling with sentimental things, I put loose photos, cards, and letters in bins labeled "sentimental" and keep on going. If I stop to look at them now, my momentum will evaporate. I'll return to them later.

Dianna had filled an entire second storage room with just Christmas things. I save a three-foot tree she created herself and one plastic bin of decorations—all the rest goes, including the tall, narrow tree she always placed in the living room.

In a certain sense, I enjoy these days—pain being released through sweat and action. My mind is clearing as *our* house is becoming a clearing. Though my heart is doused daily with unavoidable moments of crushing heartache that take my breath away when this photo or that letter drives another arrow into my heart, I just keep on going, one drawer, one closet, one memory at a time.

In late May, I invite Dianna's family to take everything they want from the piles I've created. Pat brings an entourage of females down, and they drive away with two carloads and a pickup truck full.

None of them want her clothes.

"Only Dianna could pull off the style she dressed in," one quips. I guess they're right. She always looked great but delighted in being "edgy," too.

Some want her watermelon outfit, though. *That* is not happening. Mine.

I keep her wedding gown, too. Dianna wanted it for Senna, for her own wedding one day, if she wants to wear it. I donate everything else to Goodwill, the Salvation Army, and the local women's shelter.

I count twenty-two wigs and donate all of them. Some she wore frequently and some I barely remember. Good riddance to the blonde mushroom. I give away all but one of twenty-four "chemo caps," knit stocking caps for those no-hair days when she didn't feel like wearing a wig. I keep the white one she was wearing when she died. I bury my face in it until I am swimming in her scent. Stopped cold, I have to take Chili for a walk.

This project ends with a yard sale, aided by Marji and Cris.

Finally, the house no longer has dishes or baskets on the walls, and no fake flowers, either. And while Dianna had a decorative "theme" for every season and holiday, I have arrived at a single theme, which I entitle "my decade" theme. This is about as frequently as I can imagine changing it.

Some things, though, are sacred.

Dianna's delightfully painted furniture, her decoupage work on the walls and ceilings, her painted rug on the deck, the words she painted over the front entrance and…an eighteen-inch-tall, quirky, red-haired doll she had stood up against one corner of the dining room. When did she put that there? Just too much her to let it go.

It's still there, right where she last placed it.

One day in summer, I emerge out of my cloud long enough to realize others are suffering, too. Principally, our granddaughter Senna, now nine years old. Dianna's continuing active influence in her life has ended, leaving a mammoth vacuum. I can no longer lounge in the background and watch. Because Dianna's light was so bright, I had always hovered in the shadows, so my gut feeling says Senna is not completely sure about me.

I break out of my monastic life long enough to take her out to lunch. We go to Big Boys. She likes French fries and an equally evil concoction, chicken tenders.

Senna is sweet, as always, and happy to see me. A beautiful, bright, straight-A student and astute beyond her years, there's no point beating around the bush talking about the weather.

"So, how are you feeling these days, Senna? About Grandma, I mean."

She doesn't answer, bowing her head, her gaze dropping to the table. She feels like a delicate flower drifting to the ground. I reach over and take her hand.

"I feel real bad, too, Senna. It's okay. It's the right time to feel this way. We will get through this by remembering how much we love her and how much she loves us."

She still has her head down, but she's not crying.

"We can keep her in our prayers and use how she lived as a guide for our own lives. This is what I'm doing."

She's listening.

"She would probably order chicken tenders and French fries, too," I say. She probably would. Senna knows *I* believe she should be ordering broccoli and peas.

A little laugh escapes from her, and she perks up. The food comes and she starts eating right away.

"You know, Grandma is not really gone. She's still around you, watching over you. She will always love you. She's just in Spirit now."

Senna stops eating. She looks at me with eyes dry and wide open.

"I know," she says softly in a tone suggesting I have just told her two plus two equals four. She tosses me a small smile.

Well, I think to myself, so much for bestowing my infinite wisdom on this one. I might as well pass on my esoteric knowledge to someone else.

She has a second helping of fries.

When we get up to leave, I realize this is the beginning of something new for us. We're both rookies.

Well, I am, anyway.

Later on, Senna will give me a poem for Christmas:

Grandma Dianna

She was our friend. She stayed with us till the end.
We loved her more than she will ever know
And she loved us the same in a circular flow.

When she died, everyone was sad
For us
But she was also glad.

She was happy because she was in no pain.
She knew we would discover the reason
Even if it meant we had to go through the same thing.

So we will always remember her.
She will always know that,
And our hopes for her and her new life
Will never fall flat.

It is not until after I have emptied the house in June that I actually see, for the first time really, the home Dianna created.

Once all the extra stuff has been stripped away, I'm struck by what a talented artist she was—and if her greatest work of art was the life she created, then this house is certainly another vibrant and complementary expression of it. I finally understand why it hurt her so much when I emptied out the living room that day, a lifetime ago. What if I had taken a knife and slashed one of Jon's favorite paintings?

How could I have done that?

Like every other hurt she experienced in life, though, Dianna went through it, forgave it, and let it go. She had the emotional freedom to choose *not* to give time and energy to resentment or anger. Consequently, my savaging her room became just one more story we could have fun with for years.

It's July Fourth weekend, with cars packing into driveways and lining both sides of the street, boisterous parties pumping loud music, kids yelling, people laughing, and the lake buzzing with mechanical floating things. People having fun.

Not me.

Chili is lying by my side. I often describe him to others as a gentle, loving dog with no sense of humor. No wonder. It suddenly dawns on me while looking at him, dogs are like sponges, stuck with absorbing whatever energy is around them. They have no defense for it.

Chili has only me, and I have offered no other energy but sadness and grief.

He let go of Dianna at the nursing home, when he sensed she was dying and on her way to somewhere else. He accepted this and did not try to hang onto her. Like dogs do, he lives in the present for the most part. But now he's stuck with a present that is me, my present.

Poor guy. He's doing the best he can.

But so am I.

He hangs around, sniffing here and there, barking at passersby or stretching out on the cool garage cement floor while I spend the entire three-day holiday, smoking, writing, and rewriting a five-page letter to Dianna, detailing all my sins, regrets, betrayals, ineptitudes, insults, deficiencies. Through an avalanche of tears, I beg her forgiveness, even as I know I already have it. But it's the path I must take to reach self-forgiveness. It takes me three days, but I mostly get there. In the final analysis, I understand I did what we all do, the best we can, given who we are in that particular moment.

As the clouds of lake visitors trail away, one by one, and the neighborhood falls silent, the only gnawing regret I'm still struggling with after all the others have been released is a disarmingly simple one.

I so wish I would have lain in bed by her side much more than I did during those last days, when her world was shrinking down to just her and me. I wish I would have watched *Regis and Kelly* with her more, laughed with her more, rubbed her legs more, brought her little surprise things to eat or drink more, instead of bailing out, too often, to do other things.

I was given a finite number of minutes to be with her. *They could be counted, for God's sake.* It was my choice to make them count the way I did.

What makes this regret even harder to swallow is Dianna was always infinitely grateful for the minutes I did give, never complaining about the ones I didn't. Maybe she understood she was dealing with an emotional child.

I hope so.

She probably also realized there is always more we could have done, no matter how much we did. Regret, shame, guilt are simply an unavoidable part of this grieving process. I can either let it distort my being, becoming less, or release it, freeing myself to become more.

So I have cleared out my physical house and, now, my emotional one as well. Almost.

Happy Independence Day.

82

Going Vertical

In July, I begin expressing myself in this house Dianna created. I combine Dianna's art with works by my son Jon, my friend Giovanni Sanitate, and Brian Andreas, evolving a blend of quintessential Dianna and an emerging me. I can't help desperately hanging photos of Dianna all over the house. Maybe if I just put up enough of them....

One day, I'm staring at a portrait of Dianna done by Jon in 1990, the year she was first diagnosed with cancer. Jon did it in a somewhat stylized way—a faithful reproduction of what she looked like, but a kind of austere gestalt. Dianna liked it from the beginning, and I never liked it. I thought it portrayed her as being too hard, too severe. *Not* the Dianna I knew.

Suddenly, as I am staring at the portrait, *I get it.* What Jon painted was what I was only dimly aware of, the fierce determination and rock-solid resolve beneath Dianna's joyfulness, optimism, and delight we all loved so much. It was not just a sunny attitude that got her through seventeen years of cancer—it was this powerful quality showing up in Jon's painting! Why didn't I see this before? What a gift, I realize, tears streaming down my face.

So, I get a lesson in art appreciation. If the artist is good, trust him to summon what is crying to show up, then be open enough to let the art teach me.

This lesson is not lost on me with regard to Dianna, either. Her life was the canvas she used to create her finest work of art. I have an opportunity now to allow *her* art to teach me, too.

While she was alive, she was like the air around me. I breathed her in without noticing who she was unless the wind shifted a little—that is, unless something changed, about her, about us. But now that she is gone, I have some distance and a rapidly changing perspective. This truly amazing being is coming into sharper focus even as I feel her presence. She is gone...and she isn't.

What is she teaching me now, I wonder.

I'm not interested in the horizontal dimensions of growth—more travel, more activities or, right now, even more people. I want to explore the vertical dimension—reaching down as deeply within myself as I can, peeling all the onions I find there, and stretching as high toward Spirit as I can. I seek a more complete integration of self with Self.

I make a pilgrimage to the tombstone place, about two hours north. Walking through the door, it takes me less than one minute to pick out a large black granite stone shaped like an arch standing tall against a far wall, almost beckoning to me.

Kathy shows up shortly thereafter, giving me instructions about what needs to be on it. "John, she wanted you somehow included on the gravestone even though she knew only she would be buried there."

Okay.

She never told me *that*.

I'd already decided to have her photograph laser-etched into the top part of the stone (the same photo Jon used as a model to create the 1990 portrait as well as the drawing he did for the dedication page of this book). Below her photograph will be "The brightest Star in our sky" and "born June 10, 1957, and "reborn February 20, 2008." There's still plenty of room, so I add an etching of two entwined rings with a photo of us together etched below it, along with our wedding date.

"She will like that," Kathy says, smiling, content now.

I write thank you letters to Dr. Stella, the nurses in both the oncology clinic and the 11th floor oncology unit. *Dianna wants me to do this* and I do, too. I call them earth angels, while thanking them for all they've done for us.

Earlier in life, I meditated twice a day for fifteen years and, growing up Catholic, I knew about prayer, too. For me, praying is speaking to Spirit, and meditating is listening. I start doing both as a daily practice.

I create my own prayers for meditation, meals, walking, bedtime, and even one for writing. I develop a genuine appreciation for the Muslim practice of interrupting the flow of mundane life by praying five times each day. What a powerful way to stay focused on the spiritual meaning of life. I become increasingly fascinated by the meal prayer I have created. Each day it immerses me in Gratitude, in the realization that everyone and everything has brought this meal to me. It becomes my "five times a day" prayer.

Out of these meditations, it is easy to see the source of all suffering is, indeed, unconsciousness. Each of us is trapped in our own tiny bubble of separateness, so it looks like what happens to others happens to others, not to ourselves. It requires a huge shift in consciousness to fully appreciate that everything happening to each one of us is happening to all of us. I'm kind of there intellectually, but I surely cannot say I own it in consciousness; that is, that I *be* in that space, day in, day out.

However, I do finally appreciate what Abraham Joshua Heschel meant when he said, *"Some are guilty but all are responsible."*

While listening to a Deepak Chopra lecture, I stumble across a beautiful poem he shares, written by an ancient, unknown Egyptian writer, and begin to include it in my daily meditation:

Journey into Healing

You split me and tore my heart open
And filled me with love
You poured your Spirit into mine
I know You as I know myself
My eyes are radiant with your Light
My ears delight in your Music
My nostrils are filled with your Fragrance
And my face is covered with your Dew
You have made me see all things shining
You have made me see all things new
You have granted me perfect ease
And I have become like paradise
And having become like paradise
My Soul is healed.

While reciting it one day, I realize this is *exactly* what Dianna did. She split me and tore my heart open with her living…and with her dying, too. For someone as mental as I'm inclined to be, it took everything she had to get my attention.

From this moment on, I'm speaking directly to Dianna *and* directly to Spirit as I recite this poem each day. In my heart, this is becoming a distinction without a difference.

I continue modulating my pace for processing grief with the two songs recorded by Consuelo. Otherwise, for the next two years, I will listen to no music at all, avoiding random pain I'm not ready to process. Weeks pass without turning on TV. When I do peek in to catch the news, I instantly notice nearly all of it is a complete waste of time—all heat, no light, and precious little real substance, either. Noise. Life feels incredibly more valuable without it. I will never again give time and attention to this source of pointless, sometimes even harmful, contamination of my spirit.

Gradually, I cease to experience silence as the absence of anything—or everything. Rather, it begins to take on a rich, ineffable texture of its own. Being in silence is simply being in the presence of No Thing, the All That Is, listening to the music of the gods.

As I record my dreams, filling several notebooks, Dianna continues showing up in them. I am sensing ever more clearly we *are* still communicating, still working together, only in a different way.

Whether I remember my dreams or not, I'm resolving problems in the dream state. As insights flood in, I record them in my morning journal, striving to better integrate the multiple realities I'm trafficking in. It's clear to me that waking reality is only one of them, and it, too, is only a dream.

What is reality? I don't know. I suspect there are many.

I maintain a meditation journal, recording insights as they show up. Always a "busy" meditator, I rarely go into the deep states some people do. Still, I'm experiencing a tranquility and lucidity new to me. I feel my perspective broadening, my fix on what I believe to be true, loosening.

I sense guides around me, and one suggestion during meditation is that it would be useful to relate to Dianna as a quality of energy rather than her form. This is difficult, but I begin practicing; and I do notice my grief diffusing and losing intensity.

As I muddle along on this inner journey, I notice I grieve letting go of grieving. Grief feels like the most tangible link I have left with Dianna, the most accessible emotional connection I can get my arms around. It's also a struggle to let go of hundreds of images in my mind during those last months of her life, those nuanced stages of dying that ripped me apart, piece by piece. My guides—or Self—or Dianna—I'm not sure, suggest I let go of this attachment to grief. I begin practicing, reluctantly. There is a perverse comfort in grief.

Gradually I discern that grief is simply a form of emotional energy. So, my goal need not be to disappear grief, but rather, to transform it into a more useful energy: love, then express love through action, helping to create a life I want to live.

One morning, I wake up with the clear realization: *this is what Dianna did each day of her life.*

If there was ever anyone who expressed love in the most mundane interactions and activities of daily life, it was Dianna. Confronted with energy routinely showing up for her as chronic pain, crushing disappointment, nagging fear and worry, she just as routinely, and almost instantly, transformed it into giving, supporting, loving others with her optimism, humor, and kindness. She was practicing a form of Karma yoga, connecting to Spirit through daily Service, releasing selfishness, egoism, attachment. She was saying without ever saying it, "Don't feel sorry for me because I don't feel sorry for me. Let's play!"

My process is different. I treat grief and suffering like everything else in my life, as grist for the mill, another way to understand things better, akin to Jnana yoga, the mental path to higher consciousness.

None of this is either/or. Organized religions appeal to some while others choose agnosticism, atheism, materialism, or don't give a thought to any ism. Doesn't matter. The All That Is embraces all that is.

That being said, I increasingly welcome what I am beginning to discern as Dianna's "way," a teaching path for me, with Dianna as my teacher. Expressing Love through daily action is not my strong suit.

While the mental/emotional part of my work includes writing, meditating, prayer, and dreamwork, I also take advantage of psychics, who offer some pointed insights that are surprising yet confirming.

I visit a well-regarded psychic in late fall, 2008. I tell her nothing other than Dianna is in spirit, and does Dianna have anything to say to me?

The woman goes through her little routine then, suddenly, bolts upright in her chair, like someone stuck a metal pole up her spine. I muse to myself she is sitting up straight, like someone else I know.

"Wow, she has a lot of…enthusiasm, …doesn't she?" She's quiet for a long moment, then smiles. "She has a good sense of humor, too." She is not asking me these things, just commenting on the energy she is tapping into somehow.

I smile.

"She is saying she will stay close with you awhile longer, consoling you. Sometimes she spoons with you while you're sleeping. But soon it will be time to move on. Emotionally, that is. To stop feeling sorry for yourself... she is patient, but you need to get on with it, too, buster."

The lady says this with the same sort of lilt I recognize as a quality about Dianna...even the word "buster," which she used occasionally when she wanted to admonish me on a happy note. She goes on to say Dianna will never leave me, but my focus needs to shift. The psychic says Dianna is playing with me, but serious, too.

Some things never change.

In the winter of 2008–09, I hire Maria Shaw, a professional astrologer, to interpret Dianna's birth chart. She insists I give her only Dianna's birthplace and date. I do tell her Dianna is in spirit.

"I'll do a better job if I don't know anything else," she says. Having done charts for others in the past myself, I understand what she means. It's easier to practice this science/art when uninfluenced by opinions.

She gives me the results over the phone. With her permission, I tape it. She speaks and I listen without confirming or elaborating.

She nails Dianna's personality to a tee: total honesty, thirst for knowledge, sense of humor, appreciation of simple things, likes stuff but doesn't need it, willing to hide little things from me (I have already discovered this while cleaning out the house!), could be blunt, tells it like it is but in a gentle way, and a lot more. But of course, I'm not interested in all this. I already know astrology works, and I already know Dianna's personality. "I'm interested in her spiritual orientation and purpose, Maria."

"I know. I'm coming to that. Dianna's life lesson was to be of service to others. Her destiny was to help others," Maria says.

I'm thinking, well, isn't this true for everyone? then quickly realize, well, no it isn't. Look around.

"Her karmic lesson was to learn how to develop authentic friendships, apparently, a quality or skill she felt needed to be improved. She would be driven to do this, probably unconsciously. In order to do this, she had to learn to trust."

Well, I'm thinking, she certainly got the friendship part down pat—she devoted most of her energy to it—but I still say nothing.

"Her Soul lesson, the central opportunity of her life, was to transform not only herself, but to assist in transforming others," she says.

"Transform?" I ask. "I look at transformation as a shorthand for shifting to a higher level of consciousness, a deeper understanding of what life is about, a deeper connection with Spirit. How do *you* mean it?"

"Dianna was dealing with trust and being of service. For her, transformation would be a shift from not trusting to trusting, from being self-focused to being other-focused. Like that," Maria explains.

"Okay. But I don't get the part about trust. She always seemed trusting to me."

Maria hesitates, then asks for my own birth information and does some quick calculations to compare our charts.

"Oh, I see now. She learned to trust by trusting you. Your role in her life was to be a safe space for her. She, in some ways, was like a little girl inside, and you surrounded her with a sense of security. From this place of safety, she could reach out to the world, pour all her energy into her work without worrying about the home front, you know?"

"I knew it. She married me for my health insurance."

Maria laughs.

"John, you provided a lot more than health insurance.... Well, maybe *life insurance* in the broadest sense, actually. You two were a good team. You helped each other. A lot."

It's hard for me to let in my own contribution. Probably why I'd rather joke about it.

Later, on my own, I put together a composite astrological chart for Dianna and myself. I am completely in sync with the symbol translation for the focal point of the entire astrological pattern:

"Two lovebirds sitting on a fence. Nature's Delight."

Later, thinking about it, I feel trust has never been an issue for *me*.... Well, nice story, my man, but, unfortunately, as I would learn soon enough, fictional.

What *is* true is I have always known there is a God, that I am loved, protected, that the universe is a safe place. I feel I was born this way; and without a doubt, my parents did nothing to dispel these feelings, so I was/ am blessed. When people violate my trust, as we all do from time to time, my response is to shrug, forgive them, and move on. Their problem, not mine.

But what about my deep conditioning of what it means to be a man: "I'm self-sufficient and need no one?" And I sense, there is something even more beyond *that*. What? Hmmmmm.

Throughout 2009 I continue a long-time practice of blending mind/heart work with body work for a balance that has always worked for me and works now.

My body work is daily aerobics and weight training, using home equipment...and diet. I eat healthy foods, whole grains, grow my own garden, eat local eggs and chickens, avoid factory farm meat...without turning it all into a religion.

And, of course, I go to church with Chili each day.

Leaves drift down out of the trees like rain as our walking places turn into a kaleidoscope of color..., and too soon, inexorably, fall disappears into winter.

It's November 2009 when the first real snow of the year shows up, huge ragged half dollars spinning in the wind and sticking to everything. Chili and I hurry over to Hidden Lake Gardens, almost at dark, going in the back way over a fence and into the wild part. We trace a well-worn deer trail and up ahead; a buck and two does spot us, melt into the pines and disappear, silent ghosts. The trees are fluffed white on their top sides and, just as I was hoping, whiting the woods in winter light. We, too, are silent, our steps into the wet earth inaudible. No words spoken.

On our way out an hour later, the Big Dipper pops out into a black clearing sky, pointing the way home.

Home.

Where would that be now?

In midwinter, a light powdery snow slams in sideways, pushed by a fierce wind for a third day in a row. This is the second Alberta Clipper we've had in the past two weeks, very cold, dry air racing across the plains from the lee side of the Rockies within hours—why they call it a clipper, I guess—and picking up moisture over Lake Michigan. It is near zero outside with a wind chill way below that. Chili and I look at each other. He sits down, staring intently into my eyes, riveting his whole attention on me, almost vibrating. Are we going now?

Yes.

While he watches me patiently, I put on heavy socks, boots, ice cleats, winter coat, balaclava, gloves, wool cap, and out we go to see what this day is about. How does *he* do it? He sits comfortably inside this warm house, then bursts out through the doorway with no preparation *I can detect*, immediately rolls into a snowbank near the garage to ruffle up his coat before he casually sniffs about exactly as he would on any bright warm summer day. Same coat, no boots, just a body that understands how to do things my body has long since forgotten how to do.

Life is amazing.

The more I know, the less I know I know. In the end, I know only what my heart tells me…and, in this particular moment, what Chili teaches me.

In the spring of 2010 I return to the Landmark work (Forum) and participate in their Communication Workshops (CWS) I and II. I do the first one in April and the second in December. Two important breakthroughs occur for me, opening the way for acquiring a deeper listening to what Dianna has been trying to tell me.

The first relates to vulnerability or, I should say, my unwillingness to be vulnerable.

Trust.

During Landmark work done years ago, I had already brought to consciousness a childhood memory of being abandoned by my father (he didn't really—but my nine-year-old brain said he did). Since I absolutely idolized him and he was my world in many ways, I determined I would *never* allow *that* to happen to me again.

What shows up now is my unwillingness to be vulnerable intensified during the last years Dianna and I were together. We both knew, deep inside, she was dying. We just didn't know when. So in 2001–02, when I fell apart at work, I touched into that truth directly, like poking a stick into an open wound. How I handled it was to back away emotionally when it hurt too much. My heart knew she *was* going to abandon me sooner or later.

Looking back, I can see we fell into a pattern of tiptoeing around each other when it came to the prospect of her dying. Maybe she chose not to share her darkest fears, or those moments when she wondered if she could go on, because she did not want me to feel worse than I already did. I *do* know I chose not to share my fear of her dying or how much I was hurting, thinking she had enough to worry about already. I didn't have the courage for that discussion. Of course, we both worried about each other…separately and alone.

Dianna was wise enough to understand all this, at least intuitively, accepting whatever I had the courage to offer. She didn't push it. In fact, she surrounded me with a loving okay-ness, no matter how she was feeling.

So our level of intimacy could be a bit ragged at times. Fortunately, much of our communication happened without words, with touching, with doing the daily things love does, and we shared a fully alive sense of humor that never abandoned either of us. And beneath all the surface noise of life, neither of us ever doubted we could count on each other, no matter what.

I finally fully comprehend that my unwillingness to be vulnerable was what prevented me from letting go of my last regret on July 4, 2008. Why didn't I spend more time with her in those last days? Because it hurt too much. So I "chickened out" and went off to do… something… anything. And what did this cost? It cost us some of the intimacy, texture, richness, and depth our relationship had to offer, perhaps including my capacity to have a sexual relationship with her as well.

I feel as if I've just washed some dirty laundry, and now it's hanging out to dry. At last, I can forgive myself. In the end, it's simple. It was the best I could do then; I promise myself I will do better now.

The second insight begins to surface at the end of CWS I. We have a great session leader who moves us repeatedly with her profound authenticity. She and I joust throughout the workshop in a constructive, friendly way.

At the end of the workshop, I walk up and we give each other a big hug. She steps back, both her hands on my shoulders, and says, "John, you are a powerful person, and I love you for it…, and you have an issue with the rules."

"What do you mean?"

"Just think about it."

We say goodbye, but it nags at me throughout 2010.

Since Dianna's death, and Bernie's soon after, Pat has been focused on being strong for her family. I can see it coming. Probably we all can. As those around her begin to knit their lives back together, hers comes apart. Her work is done. She dies on July 5, 2010.

I feel a familiar harbinger in late August as the air subtly shifts from a balmy Florida roundness to a Canadian texture with sharp edges. The temperatures are still "summery," but the air has gone crisp. Summer is over. We just haven't declared it yet.

83

The Rules Revisited - Dianna's Secret

The rules

In the thirty months after Dianna's death, I gather in four traffic violations—and probably deserve three times that many, mostly for speeding—and manage to get into three accidents, all minor, but still, couldn't stop hitting things with many near misses, too. My insurance company wisely drops me, costing me thousands when I'm banished to the high-risk pool with all the other idiots.

Dianna often hounded me about driving too fast and her protégé, Senna, has taken up the cause right where she left off. Obviously, I'm not listening. So while my lifelong driving record has always been peppered with irresponsibility, 2008–10 are banner years.

In the summer of 2010 I'm stopped again while cruising over the limit on M-50. The policeman is walking up to my car when a little light bulb goes off. Finally, I've had enough. I decide, right then and there, I'm going to embrace this ticket as a gift.

I'm *not* going to do *this* anymore.

As he reaches my car and before he can open his mouth, I lean out the window and say, "I know I was speeding and, what's worse, I have no idea how fast I was going."

He just looks at me for a moment, then asks for the usual. He's an older man with a round stomach and kind face. While he's looking over my paperwork, I say, "I want to thank you for stopping me. This is a wake-up call for me." I actually mean this from the bottom of my heart.

He steps back. I imagine he's used to attitude, but not exactly this one. After a bit of back and forth, he chooses to let me off with a warning. I thank him for that, too.

As I slowly drive away, I smile and wave. I can't tell if he's smiling, but he does wave back.

I feel pretty good. I think he does, too. I've made his day just a little bit nicer. He, on the other hand, has provided me with exactly what I needed, exactly when I needed it. This is my practical introduction to consciously living life by the rules.

Truth is, I've never paid much attention to the rules. Of course, I mostly followed them in an unthinking way—as long as they didn't conflict with what I wanted to do.

It's not until I'm participating in CWS II in December 2010 that "the rules" receive my full attention, one of the benefits of being immersed in an environment where the phones don't ring and tons of energy in the room is guided effectively.

I use this intense environment to explore what I want my life to be, going forward. Well, I want what we all want, a life with a positive strategic flow (even a wise strategic path is sprinkled with occasional tactical mistakes) characterized by love, joy, satisfaction, kindness, making a difference, contributing to the whole, personal growth, doing no harm, creating win-win outcomes.

How might the rules contribute to this vision, I wonder?

I think back to the incident with the policeman on M-50. Being the slow learner I am, it occurs to me we have many mundane societal rules, all the way from stopping at red lights to making contracts—from buying a house to getting married. All of these rules are based on a collective sense of fairness, a desire to minimize friction and promote general workability. All of these rules are also fundamentally based on giving our word and keeping it. So, bottom line, they work if we practice life with some level of integrity, and we trust others to do the same. We sail through a green light because we trust others will stop at a red light.

I can also see keeping our word would reduce the frequency of tortured dramas characteristic of a life not working, sapping our energy. It's not even about right/wrong, good/bad, but simply about what works and what doesn't.

It suddenly hits me. *Dianna already owned and expressed this level of integrity from the very beginning.*

When she was only two years old, she put her candy back into the jar. Nothing ever changed after that for her. She handled the candy jars of life in the same consistent way, day in day out, to the very end.

Without realizing what I was looking at, I watched her naturally, apparently without effort, bypass all the drama associated with rule breaking, preserving her energy for exploring the more valuable opportunities life had to offer. One reason, I believe, in spite of absorbing huge quantities of lethal drugs on an almost continuous basis, she had such extraordinary energy to remain so remarkably On Purpose.

Simply put, she did not waste her energy on self-created bullshit resulting from poor choices, or avoiding responsibility for the choices she did make, or dragging around the myriad could-have-beens and should-have-beens we all can point to in our lives—the ones we rarely even notice, much less let go of… *ever*. Hanging onto them gives us the excuse we are looking for to explain why our lives did not turn out.

She even had the grace not to lecture me. She honored—even protected—my space to screw up, smoke, drive too fast, or whatever else I was up to that didn't work. She might occasionally point toward my foibles in her gentle, often humorous, way, but I never felt judged. She let me be. As far as I can tell, she let everyone be.

Can I learn to do this, too?

Sometime during the workshop, I make a commitment to follow these simple rules of life to the best of my ability. This will become another daily practice for me.

I wake up the morning after the workshop and feel Dianna smiling… *Is her hand lying gently on my right cheek as I look out the window?* More tears. Overwhelmed with appreciation…of the beauty of her energy, of the thin winter sun backlighting faint purple clouds low on the horizon, of the shimmering light across Goose Bay, of…everything.

The Rules

After the workshop and throughout the winter of 2010–2011 I notice I have been giving short shrift to the Rules, too—the ones I think of as Natural Law. These are not man-made rules but, some might say, God-given rules, or Universal Law.

So what are they? I wonder. Well, Amy Brilliant once said, quite brilliantly, "Life is the only game where the object of the game is to learn the Rules." So learning them is a process of unfoldment, paying attention, refining, redefining.

Of course, I will never know them all. Life will always be a delicious mystery. Still, it's part of my DNA to explore…and perhaps better understand how Dianna managed to sparkle so brilliantly in the life she lived.

As the winter days and nights fold over on each other, I continue meditating, recording dreams, and writing in my morning journal.

A fog is quietly, gently evaporating. Dianna's energy is all around me, sometimes very intensely, sometimes hardly at all. It is startling to realize our current relationship, in this way, parallels the one we had when she was in body. Sometimes together, sometimes not, but always connected.

Winter ends with a whimper.

One fine spring day in 2011 I walk out on the deck with a cup of coffee and lay out a dog pillow for Chili so he will be comfortable.

The air is still, clear, cool, but warm enough. Mesmerized by light playing on the water and a hundred tree swallows dipping and diving, skimming the water's surface, I drift into an inner mental journey—not into what I know—I don't *know* anything—but into my tentative, evolving perception of "reality."

I notice—or create—what may or may not be a useful distinction between the Context for life in this reality and the Rules for operating within it. The Context could be considered the ballpark this game of life is played within. The Rules are simply the Rules of the game, the way the game works.

After nosing around the entire deck, checking for interlopers, Chili finally lays down on the pillow next to my chair. I reach down and stroke his silky neck and back. He feels so good to me. With a sigh, he flops over on his side, taking up the full length of the pillow, his legs stretched all the way out, paws neatly folded over each other at the ankles. Dogs really know how to relax.

I wonder about the Context.

My sense is, no matter what it *looks* like, we are all One, even Chili, even the chair I am sitting on, all part of the All That Is.

Secondly, as Pierre Teilhard de Chardin noticed, we are not human beings on a spiritual journey, but spiritual beings on a human journey.

This much seems obvious to me.

So this would suggest, while still in spirit, we choose to take on a physical body (birth), like putting on a uniform. And when we have completed whatever we were up to, we leave (death), letting go of our uniform and returning to spirit. Game over.

This, then, suggests there are two I's we may identify with while playing the game. The I-John, who takes out the garbage, and the spirit-I who provides the context for I-John. Some might call this "contextual I" the soul or higher Self in various systems of thought.

This not-so-thick line between life and death feels deeply true to me and consistent with my inner experience. Dianna and I have communicated often since she died. And I have had similar experiences with others, too, all as real to me as Chili lying here, soaking up the sun.

So far, so good.

As to birth, I find it intriguing that scripture alludes to the original sin ("original" meaning the first one, and "sin," a term used in archery, indicating the shot was "off the mark"). I see immediately these are a perfect choice of words to describe how we enter this reality, accepting the *illusion*, the *mental* construct, that permits us to forget who we really are (spirit), so born believing we are, instead, physical matter encapsulated in form. This *is* our original sin. As a consequence, we believe we are separate and alone—and so is everyone and everything else. It sure looks that way.

Fear is born.

So is materialism, selfishness, competition, and the belief, "there is not enough." Not enough food, money, love, not enough of whatever it is we need and want. So, life within the *illusion* looks like a zero sum game based on a struggle for survival.

Still, the game seems fair to me because we are given the tools we need to dissolve the *illusion*—Love and Light, ways of experiencing God even while immersed in this reality.

As I think about this, it occurs to me it would be impossible to be with Dianna and experience life as a zero sum game. She demonstrated the more we love, the more loved we are; the more we live, the more alive we are; the more we give to others, the more we have to give. Her way of being exploded the myths of this reality.

So, expressing Love connects us with "other" through our hearts, bypassing the *illusion*, which, again, is essentially a *mental* construct. In this way, Love may dissolve fear.

Light (right brain, gut brain, intuition, maybe left brain, too, maybe even cellular intelligence) is the tool we may use to dissolve unconsciousness, our amnesia, our forgetting of who we really are. That is, recognizing both the Context and Rules of the game for what they are pierces the *illusion*, which may dissolve fear, depending on the clarity of our perception …and whether we "take it to heart."

I get up and walk over to the railing. The swallows are thinning out now, breakfast almost over. I am starting to get hungry myself and wonder if we should go in, but Chili is dozing. He looks so content I decide to let this sleeping dog lie awhile longer. As I study him, love flooding my heart, I slide back into my thoughts.

Why must we enter the game, apparently limited by form, suffering from amnesia and immersed in fear? Easy one, I realize. If we remembered who we *really* are, we wouldn't play the game as if our very survival is at stake, as if it all *matters.*

This game is ingeniously designed: we have a body always demanding food and water, so we have to play pretty intensively just to insure "survival." A powerful sex drive insures a steady supply of players to keep the game going while providing a sub-game to remind us we are here to create in this reality. To avoid becoming totally disoriented while in body (we are spirits after all), we are given the dream state (psychological/spiritual regeneration) and sleep (physical regeneration) to continually reconnect with Spirit, get things sorted out, heal some bruises, get a few pats on the back, so we can get back into the game upon waking. We would not last long without relief from our waking "reality,"—it takes all the energy we have to play this game (maintain the mental agreements) even for a single day.

As I lean over the deck railing, ideas keep bubbling up. Chili looks lost to the cool spring air, serenaded by a cacophony of chirping birds—sparrows, wrens, robins, finches—flitting back and forth through the trees, welcome music after the long silence of winter past.

So much life.

Clearly our experience of space is also a mental construct, part of the *illusion,* and shaped by form. We are in-formed (made aware of) by every *thing* around us. Are not all "forms of knowledge" satisfying pathways for re-membering (to think again in a new way) our true nature (spirit)? Is not the beauty we see in form but God calling us toward the Truth?

Conversely, if I am interested in accessing other realities (experiencing no form), through these tenuously thin mental constructs, to some degree, I can. Those who communicate with "the dead" (those in spirit) offer a simple example of this. Again, we are mostly too busy with the game to spend energy this way. Not crucial that we do or we don't.

And is not time another mental construct peculiar to this reality? Our sensory experience of time (movement, sequence) must be part of the *illusion*, consistent with physical reality simply because our physical senses, as designed, cannot process everything all at once—or so we *think*, anyway.

Time is handy though. It allows us to parse out the distinctions between actions and consequences, aiding us in gaining consciousness, critical to not only skillfully playing the game but eventually dissolving the *illusion*. Still, if I am spirit with everything happening now, there must be a fluidity laced into living in this reality. To whatever degree I'm open to it, it may be possible to access a probable future—or one, or more, of the "multiple nows" happening all at once—so I might occasionally slip through the mental constructs of time, as some psychics do. Probably we could all do this if we *believed* we could, thereby altering our perception and the way we *think*.

Of course, I don't need to be psychic to re-member the past. This practice has been highly valuable for me, for a "later I" to re-view my past from a new (more enlightened) perspective, facilitating the process of self-forgiveness and self-love by releasing guilt, shame, blame, and judgment, a valuable contribution to healing (self integration).

However, by inference, form and time are *mental* distinctions that do not exist in spirit. In spirit, there is only now—here, the Present.

The All That Is must be, in every moment, all that is.

If these insights are even approximately true, I can also see, from God's point of view, the game has a benign design, organized to be win-win, no matter how badly we play it. There is really no way to lose. However, immersed in the *illusion* (original sin), we, of course, often experience life as win-lose or lose-lose, so life can be painful, and always, our body's survival is at stake. Fear usually rules.

Chili is awake now and looking at me in puzzlement. Kind of like, well, I'm ready. What about you? Let's go. When I smile, his ears lift up and he tilts his head. Do I actually get it for once? he seems to be asking.

Okay.

But first, I want to follow my last thoughts through to the end here.

Clearly, we are born with free will, but how does this work?

What if God is akin to electricity (energy), always on, always available, supplied to any lamp (each of us) who wants to plug in and turn on (play the game)? What if this Source Energy, itself, is completely unconcerned with why, how, what, or when the energy is used? Then, what we do with it is up to us.

Free will.

So the Source Energy—and the focus we provide it—combine to co-create specific results in this reality.

If God isn't voting on how energy is used but simply supplying it, wouldn't this explain why all things "good" and "bad" happen in our reality? It is simply how we have chosen to use the energy available to us to create, either consciously or unconsciously, whether individually or collectively, the world we experience. So we can stop blaming God. God didn't do it. We can also stop expecting God to "handle it" without we, ourselves, doing our part. We can also stop worrying about a judgmental God, which is simply a projection of our own fear, distorting the all-encompassing, all-inclusive All That Is.

This seems consistent with how I experience life.

Not bad.

Try creating a 3D video game better than this!

As to the Rules of the game, I don't know too many of them other than to note, broadly speaking, we co-create our own reality with our thoughts, words, and deeds. Our creations result in consequences, and in this soup of experience, the goal of the game is to have fun (re-creation) while dissolving the *illusion* using Light and Love, the tools available to us in this reality.

Chili gets up and starts pushing his nose against my leg. He's anxious to go now.

Okay.

I grab a banana and we jump into the FJ Cruiser. I decide to try the Onsted Game Area for a change. High ground, less muddy in this spring season, and Chili can explore in peace. Unlikely anyone will be there this time of year, this time of day.

When we get there, the area is deserted.

After walking a narrow trail circling the swamp, I reach a cluster of green and decide to break, stretching out on my side into the pungent odor of pine needles. Feels good here, cool, dry, washed in a dappled light under a canopy of tall, skinny red pines, and overlooking a gentle slope that slides down into Grass Lake. I pick up my train of thought while Chili noses around in the cattails below, enjoying the coal-black mud that is now up to his chest. Oh well.

I think most of us play the game while immersed in the *illusion*, often motivated by fear, unconsciously bumping into the rules and the Rules, careening into dramas we, without exception, create but are seldom willing to own. As long as we believe we are our bodies, separate from all other, there isn't any other way to play.

What is tougher to appreciate is that none of this is right or wrong, good or bad. It's simply one way to play, and it works the way it works.

A few of us do play the game quite differently though. I was married to one of them, which is why this investigation won't leave me alone.

Chili saunters up, nudging me to pet him. I don't think so. He's dripping wet and sharply two-toned now—gold and black. I scratch the top of his head lightly, then pointedly ignore him. He gives up on me and trots off, heading up the hill, disappearing into a cluster of low evergreens. A light offshore breeze drifts down toward the lake, and I zip up my coat as the afternoon sun arcs into the tree line.

I lay back into the cool earth and, with Dianna in mind, conclude there are only two fundamental motivations within the game of life: fear and Love. Clearly, all other motivations are simply derivatives of these. Having Dianna in my life made this easy to notice. She was so radically different from most of us with the clarity, consistency, and simplicity of her motivation.

I laugh out loud as I stretch out on soft, slippery pine needles, thinking about these things, staring up through the pine boughs. I can't help but notice what a pretty day it is. Chili trots up to me, looking satisfied. He looks considerably cleaner. Wind dried and brushed by evergreens and grass, most of the mud has disappeared.

In a way, the whole thing, life that is, seems silly sometimes. I mean, it all turns out in the end anyway. All choices, all paths, lead to the same place, a return to Spirit—though, certainly some paths may appear to be shorter, more fun, less painful, than others.

We get back home toward evening. I go out on the deck. The lake looks like a sheet of glass, and the light is melting gold. Being in this light is like taking a warm bath while listening to soft ethereal music. I feel like I am drifting into the faint, blurred edges of this reality and bumping into a parallel, gentler one.

Heaven on earth.

Which gets me to thinking again.

My sense is heaven and hell are real but certainly not in the way conventional wisdom suggests. Clearly, heaven is simply being one with spirit, consciously reuniting with the All That Is. We may even touch heaven in *this* reality when we are one with the present moment. Hell, on the other hand, almost by definition, can only be a state of being where one feels totally isolated and alone, separated from the All That Is, suffocating with fear—either in this reality—or when in spirit.

But a permanent state of hell—permanent separation—is clearly incongruent with the All That Is that *must*, when all is said and done, *include* all that is. Period. The only God possible is an all-encompassing God. So no matter how one has played the game, whether Hitler, Osama bin Laden, or Jesus Christ, every apparently distinct being, when the *illusion* is dispelled, reunites with God, Allah, or pick a name.

As an aside, what about terminology? All That Is is the most accurate term, even if it is, well, clumsy. I do like the English word, God, as a shorthand, mostly because any word that spells dog backwards—no accident—can't be far wrong. So although religions have perversely and copiously cloaked their descriptions of God in the language of the *illusion*, too often selling an angry, wrathful, judgmental God they construct by looking in the mirror of their own images, "God" is still too handy to throw away. So I use it interchangeably with Spirit, the All That Is or Source Energy.

Lastly, I wonder about a personal versus an impersonal God. Have played with this all my life in one way or another.

A robin plunks itself down on a skinny branch a few feet away, then twists its body to stare at me. Am I okay? It stays, fidgeting. Maybe I'm okay.

Suddenly smiling inside, I realize the All That Is includes all the ways we choose to relate to God. Feel free to choose from the huge buffet we, ourselves, have created.

Immersed in the *illusion*, it is hard for us to avoid compressing the formless, infinite, pure Spirit into some *thing* separate from ourselves, with boundaries, with form. Then we can love God as we would love any *other separate being, any other thing.* And we can count on this separate being, more powerful than ourselves, to "take care of it" for us, a nifty way to avoid responsibility—and even assign blame if things don't work out.

The robin, maybe nervous about my presence, launches into flight.

I see I am done with all this—that there really *is* no *other*, that we are all One, dissolving the entire question of personal versus impersonal. It is hard to be less impersonal than this.

Many years ago, while still working at Dow, in a burst of intuition, I printed stationary notes that carried the salutation, "From John Catenacci, i.e. God." partly as a way to make people smile and partly as a wake-up call. Created lots of fun and discussion, giving me a chance to declare we are all (part of) God. So there!

I relax, leaning against the deck railing. I don't know why, but I have always felt at peace, embraced, protected, loved, and why Catholicism never really "took" with me. I am good with a formless God. Feels...complete.

Can we still relate to the All That Is as a personal God?

Go for it. Why not? It's included on the buffet.

I call Chili over to me and catch his collar, then start hosing him down. He doesn't like it, but he's stoic. He even mechanically lifts each leg when I am squirting him underneath, where he needs it most. I love this dog. Right now, he is serenely tolerating me and the inexplicable demands I make on our relationship.

The instant I finish washing him down and straighten up, he races off the deck to roll in the grass and begin drying himself.

Life in this reality can be a really fun game. We experiment by creating, then receive direct feedback (consequences) on how close we came to creating what we intended. We are mini-gods, stumbling masters of our own little universes. But we are also interwoven with each other's creations in ways far too complex to call life anything other than a mystery.

So why would God want to create such a game? That part is no mystery to me. It seems totally consistent with the infinite nature of God. In the space of limitlessness, there can be no limit to creation, to the kinds of games being played, ours being only one. It's like, well, why not? We could just as well say, God loves to play.

I wrap up the hose and toss it into a corner of the deck just as Chili saunters back, looking like his normal self, if a little damp, with a few blades of grass still sticking to his coat. We are equally satisfied with each other now.

Some will certainly say my particular perception of reality is bullshit. Could be. Okay with me. It's my own bullshit and how I enjoy playing the game.

As Shakyamuni Buddha said, "...Don't believe anything you see, read, or hear from others, whether of authority, religious teachers or texts.

Don't rely on logic alone, nor speculation. Don't infer or be deceived by appearances.... Find out for yourself what is true, what is real."

Others will surely say there is no science to support any of this, and this may be true. Though in many respects it appears high physics is beginning to point in a similar direction, science does not address the meaning of life, that is, the context of this reality...at least, not yet. I feel no imperative to hold my breath until it does.

In any case, whatever way others choose to play is absolutely fine with me.

I do wonder, though, does any of this mental exploration actually matter? In the world of matter (the game) it does, but not otherwise. There is abundant evidence to support the idea that what we believe shapes our perception of reality. And in an endless feedback loop, what we perceive to be real reinforces our beliefs. So within this loop, what we believe to be true deeply affects how we play the game.

However, my sense is what we believe or think has no bearing on the ultimate outcome. In spite of our myriad, tortured pathways of perception, we all eventually end up in the same place anyway, Home, one with Spirit. As Dianna demonstrated on a daily basis, it helps to have a sense of humor about it all. I am reminded, once again, whatever else there is to do, lighten up. It's a game, for God's sake!

On the other hand, as long as I am here in this game, I might as well learn to play better. Treat it as a challenge. So, during these days, my drill becomes to act, observe what happens as a consequence of my actions, then make suitable adjustments as needed—that is, treat living as a sort of science project, sniffing out the data as I go. Otherwise, all this mental masturbation and five dollars will get me a cup of coffee at Starbucks. Or is it ten dollars now? Been so long.

My interim report—it will always be an interim report—is that practicing life with this overall perspective works for me. Less stress, fewer regrets, and more fun.

Possibly I might even be behaving a bit more like Dianna!

Something still nags at me, though. Something more about becoming a better player, I guess.

I realize my mind is inside a bubble of my own perception, and this bubble is encapsulated within a still larger bubble forming this particular reality (the *illusion*); so apprehending Truth (God) directly via the mind alone is a difficult path, indeed—why H. P. Blavatsky noted, "The mind is the great slayer of the Real."

So why even try? First, it's fun. Secondly, I'm thrown to do it. It just seems to be the way I'm designed. But, while having a mental grasp of the game may be genuinely helpful, it's not the expressway to God.

The heart is.

Which brings me back to Dianna.

The Cardinal Rule

Blaise Pascal once said, *"The heart has reasons that reason does not know."*

I never bothered Dianna with my mental explorations, nor did she concern herself with them. She didn't have to. In her own way, she already knew all this stuff, and more, perhaps in some better way, at some intuitive level and, I suspect, from the very beginning.

By the time I met her, Dianna seemed to have living in the *Present* down pat. Or maybe she was born with this Talent, like Mozart was born to write music.

At first, this quality threw me off, as it did many others when they first met her. Many wondered if this sparkling, cheerful explosion of being was simply a version of Pollyanna or maybe a "people pleaser." But, soon enough, it became clear she was, indeed, keenly aware of—and intimately familiar with—the dark side of life. She simply, routinely, effortlessly it seemed, chose the Light. Nor did she focus on whether people liked her or not—she was serenely content being herself, motivated by something *inside* rather than by anything or anyone *outside*.

Not long after Dianna died, I began tapping into her way of being by consciously asking myself, when faced with any situation, "What would Dianna do now?" which naturally morphed into, "What would Love do now?"

That first summer in 2008, still immersed in grief, I had raced down to Hobby Lobby to have this framed:

What would love do now?
(In the middle of the frame)

Did you do it?
(at the bottom of the frame)

I hung it in the kitchen over my coffeepot so I would see it every morning and throughout the day. Thus began a practice discipline.

If uncertain about the abstraction, "What would Love do now?" I take it back to the more concrete again by asking myself, well, dummy, if you still don't get it, then, what would Dianna have done in this situation? Engineers are attracted to concrete examples, I guess.

In the days, months, and seasons that have passed since I first hung that little reminder, I can see, "Doing what Love does" is becoming my most fundamental Rule of all, the Cardinal Rule, the one that contextualizes all the other rules within a more holistic, integrated framework, clarifying my priorities, pointing to where and when to focus my energy.

Gradually, I begin to notice I cannot do what love does without thinking what love thinks and feeling what love feels. It's all one gestalt. Me.

In the past, too often, I *mentally* apprehended how this reality works while being out of touch with my own feelings. This is neither right nor wrong, but simply unbalanced and dis-integrated. When guided by mind alone, I sometimes fail to notice which side of my mental sword is the cutting edge—a brilliant insight or the other side, the one that cuts, hurts, damages.

Unsurprisingly, I've created a ton of unnoticed, unintended, and unappreciated (by me) consequences, the proverbial bull in the china shop. Born as a man, conditioned as a man in a man's world, trained in science and working as an engineer, I suppose none of this is particularly shocking.

It took Dianna breaking me open so I could touch my own heart, to begin connecting words and actions to consequences at the feeling level, not simply at the mental and physical levels.

Being aware of one's feelings is one thing, but having the skill or emotional freedom to *choose* which feelings to embody—and express—is quite another level of mastery. In this, I am still a rookie.

Did Dianna understand the practical consequences of choosing which thoughts to invest her attention (energy) into? She could have chosen to make her reality about cancer, pain, and suffering. All I know is, she didn't. Instead, day in day out, she *transformed* her suffering into love so routinely, the rest of us barely noticed, usually taking it for granted…, and, most blessed of all, she filled our lives with laughter while doing it, making it all look easy.

Was she really unwilling to allow malice, revenge, envy, or hate to influence how she shaped her life, seeing them as a waste of time and energy? All I can report is: I never observed the slightest hint of such feelings, in word or action. When less negative feelings like disappointment, anger, or fear did show up, I could almost watch her shaking them off like a duck shakes water out of its feathers, letting them go.

And when they were gone, they were gone. No residual.

Amazing.

Nor did I ever see her struggling over the multitude of daily choices we all face between serving self and serving other. Was this a duality that did not exist for her? Is this what *being* the context, we are All One, actually looks like?

I might have some consciousness *about* the game, but she *played* the game at a level that not only respected the rules and the Rules, but she did so wholeheartedly, with unabashed enthusiasm and delight. She "lived life out loud," to quote Emile Zola. She exited this life satisfied, with nothing left undone. Hope I will be able to say that too when my time comes, I think to myself.

I see her as a light being, a teacher patrolling the earth in the most mundane suit of clothes, driven to show us we can all be this way—not in her way exactly—but in our own way…exactly.

At her funeral services, everyone consoled me also, and at the same time colored their sorrow with the same brushstroke, "She inspired me to *be*…."

She was a space for people to be who they *really* are… a space we could relax into being our best selves. No acts needed or expected.

So as I see her, Dianna followed the path of the heart, but she did so in the Light, that is, with an innate awareness of who she really is, how the game is designed, and how to have the most fun playing it, regardless of the circumstances.

Considering the entire spectrum of her behavior, she looked to me to be consistently motivated by Love rather than fear. So I conclude, within my own lexicon, she *was*, in her own way, aware of the *illusion*—yet *not* determined by it.

Dianna's secret.

Is my window into reality—and into the how and why of Dianna—smudged, flawed here and there? I don't know. Probably.

All I know for sure is: I want to play more like she played. So I'm paying attention to what she is *still* teaching me, and deeply grateful she chose to show up in my life…at the very least, to laugh with me…, and I know damned well, to laugh *at* me, too. Everyone, even Dianna, needs a little entertainment.

Always the gentle, patient teacher, the only question would always be, am I a willing student? While painfully slow coming to the party, I'm awakening now. Even if I wasn't born with her Talent, I am committed to embodying it through practice as best I can.

Armed with her guidance, I begin to shape a dream, a journey, deeper into the magic and mystery of life.

84

Daybreak

In late April 2011, I awaken to the wind howling in the darkness outside my window, the house creaking, and a single thought in my head. Dianna has been in one of my teaching dreams. Leaving the light off, I begin scribbling furiously in my notebook.

Dianna is not the only one, I write.

There are others, light beings, living life consistently motivated by Love rather than fear, so in my lexicon, not deceived by the *illusion*.

They are sprinkled among us, modeling this behavior with their daily practice. They offer us the healthiest food on the planet. We can peruse this buffet and choose to emulate whichever entrees best suit our own way of being.

I flop back into my pillow in the predawn darkness, glancing at the clock. The red digital display blinks to 6:05. More thoughts show up. I begin writing again.

Light beings, as well as the rest of us fumbling around still mentally immersed in the *illusion*, are all part of the same All That Is. So whatever it may look like in any given moment, we are all on the same team, playing the same game, each in our own way.

We may not have mastered the entire game, but we are mastering our own roles. Each of us can still practice letting go of judgment, of the black/white, right/wrong language of the *illusion*, observing, instead, what causes pain and what causes joy, what feels like win-win and what doesn't, paying attention to what our heart tells us works and what doesn't.

Pay attention, she says suddenly.

I sit up straighter. Something more personal here.

When Dianna died, my instinct was to escape into my familiar John version of being male, my "I don't need anyone" decision to be alone. Even though Dianna gently suggested, with a humorous lilt, I did not have to be

332

alone, I had little emotional freedom in the matter.

Just as well, she says.

Being physically isolated and alone has provided me an opportunity to open my own doors of perception, to see beyond the apparently solid boundaries shaping the *illusion.* The possibility that we are never alone was an idea I had known only intellectually. But with Chili nudging here and Dianna nudging there, in fits and starts, I am gaining the capacity to experience oneness with my whole being.

Now I see why I was gently guided and encouraged to let go of relating to Dianna in form. While mentally entranced by form, I remain experientially separate—she is gone, "dead," and I am still John, here in this reality, caught up in the *illusion.*

Once I began relating to the quality of her energy instead of her form, we could continue our relationship in the context it now thrives in, a parallel reality that allows our energies to comingle and remain connected across the apparent boundaries of the *illusion.*

Energized, I throw back the covers. Chili jumps off the bed, and we greet the new day together.

I do love this game.

I realize I do love form, too, as I say hello to him with my hands, kneeling in front of him, lavishly caressing his thin muscled body.

I think he loves form, too. He loves being touched, anyway.

Don't we all?

It's so much more fun with him than it would be without him, I'm thinking, as I kiss him firmly on his forehead.

Light is exploding over the eastern horizon.

More form.

How can we not be enchanted?

Still... nice to be enchanted *and* awake, too.

85

Piercing the Veil

I wake up swimming in a dream. Women I don't recognize are exchanging a key with one another. The key is sacred. Their exchange is soft, mellow, gliding—my male analogy for it is akin to the smooth shifting of gears by a flawless transmission while increasing speed. No noticeable bumps, no grinding. And there is something about hats, too.

What is *this* about?

Why is the key, and the transferring of the key, sacred? That is, an act somehow related to God and outside the ordinary mundane flow of life.

A few minutes later, as I begin to write in my morning journal (a habit gifted to me by Julia Cameron in her book, *The Artist's Way*), Dianna gives me another nudge—*more must be said about the importance of her relationships with her friends*, she says without words.

Okay.

Now I write with great trepidation. Not being a woman, I don't know what I'm talking about here. I must simply do the best I can to follow instructions, probably Dianna's instructions, like a child in grade school.

I remember the astrologer's interpretation of Dianna's karmic purpose—her passion to develop meaningful relationships with friends, mostly women.

As to hats, I suddenly remember a photo of Dianna's Mount Pleasant group. I dig through my photo albums and there it is. Kathy Preston, Chris Fowler, Allie Langlois, D'Anna Degen, and others gathered together, all wearing hats. When I call them, Kathy and Chris tell me they did such "hat events" for no reason they were conscious of other than "it was fun." I am certain God deeply believes in fun, I think to myself. I notice there were no men in the group.

Other memories flood in—Dianna getting together with her Midland group, Marji Noesen, Linda Muller, and Carrie Kram, for "tea ceremonies," while wearing an assortment of edgy, even outlandish, hats. When I ask Marji, she can only tell me *they generally don't wear hats in the routine mundane flow of their lives,* so this was one way of making their gathering *special.* Such gatherings were always women only.

I wonder, *is "special" a shadowy version of sacred?* Is there something she knows but can't tell me because she doesn't have a language for it—or, instinctively knows we don't speak the same language?

Marji goes on to remind me of one Christmas when the Midland women descended on our home with the express purpose of enveloping Dianna in a healing circle. Another meaning of healing is integration. Well, I do know what this is—bringing body, mind, and spirit into harmony with God, the most complete integration of Self.

This *is* sacred.

During Dianna's last days at St. Joe's, these same women came again, bringing hats and tea (still hot somehow), creating another healing circle in her hospital room (I should have known I didn't belong there, and they were too polite to kick me in the ass and send me down the hall). It was their gentle way of saying we love you, Dianna, and without saying it, saying goodbye. For surely all of them, including Dianna, knew they would not see each other again in this life. For this male, it felt sad, touching, funny (only because my energy toyed with theirs—if I had been actually *awake,* I might have, instead, fallen to my knees in appreciation and gratitude) and achingly beautiful all at the same time.

This event was sacred, too.

So my sense is, for reasons I may never understand, "tea ceremonies with hats" offer these women a delightful way to amplify female energy for *connecting.* Though immersed in form, they simply follow their feminine instincts to pierce the veil of *illusion,* the one that insists each of us believe we are separate and alone. In their *hearts,* they appreciate, instead, what is True.

I call Sandy Johnson. She tells me more about the Monday night groups Dianna participated in for years and their annual weekend retreats. They named themselves the Gaia group with each woman choosing a "Gaia name" for themselves (Dianna picked Goddess of the Moon). This group put energy into consciously creating a sacred space for their meetings, using ritual and intention. Men were not generally included in this group, either.

Sacred. They openly declared it to be so.

My dream metaphor describing women passing the sacred key to one another suddenly comes clear—their Key to piercing the veil of *illusion* is Love, the path of the heart.

This is not a mental theory for them, but a *practice*. The path of the heart does not need to "explain" itself whether I want it explained or not. These women could not explain what they are doing, because it would go over my head. I would never get it with my brain; but perhaps, one day, I might comprehend it in my heart.

Do these women consciously notice what they are doing is holy, or is it all too much like breathing the air they breathe—so natural to who they are, it fails to draw attention to itself? I have no idea.

No wonder they perform these activities best without male energy around to "clog up the gears," disrupting the flow (as I did in the hospital that day).

I sense other dimensions to female reality beyond my own understanding, but I simply do not swim in those waters. Will I ever? I don't know.

Still, a gathering of men may pierce the veil, too, though in their own unique way.

This happens best for me when I lean on Nature, Herself, an inherently connecting, integrative, feminine energy.

When I am alone in the silence, immersed in the music of trees and grass, with only my *dog* assisting, I, too, pierce the veil. More days than not.

My brother, my sons, and I sometimes escape the *illusion* with deer hunting trips into the isolated spaces of the far northern Michigan woods, flattening yellow grass in the right place, where, at most, only our own camp has been before, spending the before-dawn-to-after-dark days, one tumbling after another, hunting alone in a deepening silence, widening our separation from the noise of life with each passing day, then coming together around a campfire each night and, once the day's events are quietly dispensed with, falling into silence saturated only with crackling fire, sparks spiraling into a black sky, wind humming though naked aspen, sheltering cedars, prickly firs, and gentle hemlocks, blurring the edges of our everyday reality, until some sort of peripheral, if ephemeral, vision takes over.

As a by the way, in *this* space, hunting, the act of taking the life of another being, naturally comes home into what it is—a profoundly sacred ritual—and never *sport*, which is the language of the *illusion* and from a perspective totally out of touch with our First nature.

We allow no women in this sacred space, save Nature, Herself. Why this is so would be another book.

Enough to say, we need *Her*, the calming, softening, connecting tissue for our male blending into the All That Is.

While living in this reality, any of us can individually pierce the veil in various ways...during the sexual act, meditation, creating art, music, dance, even woodworking or bricklaying or...in any moment when we become "lost in the moment," when time stands still (disappears), when we are Present, unencumbered with past or future, when the "I" we hang out with during any "normal" day, disappears. What is left in such moments is pure being. We touch our "First Nature," the Now Here, the All That Is. We are in heaven.

In *those* moments, despite the overwhelming evidence to the contrary saturating our daily lives, immersed in the game, we all know who we really are. We are enlightened, if only for a moment.

While immersed in the *illusion* we call reality, we are the only variable.

The All That Is is constant, ever Present, ever waiting.

86

Cancer as a Tool

We're crossing a huge open meadow under a diffuse pale-blue sky in early May 2011. Chili is casting back and forth ahead of me, nose to the ground, pushing through knee-high grass flashing in the wind. A single huge red oak, its still-tender pale-green leaves partnered with long strands of beaded chartreuse catkins, marks the center of the meadow up ahead on a gentle rise. I decide to break there. Soon after slumping down against its rough serrated bark, Chili circles back and drops down beside me, temporarily content to pick up on the wind, nose twitching. We share a long view of the low rolling hills rippling out in front of us to the east.

I start thinking about how Dianna appeared to be, in most ways of the world, an ordinary human being, but, like each of us, with extraordinary Talents.

Those who knew her marveled at how she routinely flipped the negative energy coming at her into the positive energy she expressed in her life with a stunningly simple grace. Her song was bright and consistent, "Look at me! If I can do this, so can you."

Chili nudges me hard with his nose. "Pay attention to me." While gently passing my hand through his silky hair, I muse about how cancer turned out to be a tool she used for achieving her Purpose. Many more people would pay attention to how she handled life if she had cancer than if she didn't, finding her behavior all the more remarkable. My intuition is she understood this, and it was all part of a game plan she created before birth.

Having cancer benefited *her,* too, keeping her keenly aware her days *were certainly* numbered, motivating her to make the most of every single one— which has nothing to do with working, not working, traveling, not traveling, having things, not having things, or even having love, not having love—but simply being *Present* to whatever is in our lives *now,* in each moment. She somehow understood, this is the only space where joy lives. So as I see it, her having cancer not only enhanced her capacity for being the transformative teacher she was in her life, but also for transforming herself.

Neither could I miss that an important focus of her attention was toward *me*. Always the gentle teacher, short on words, long on action, she used her way of being—and her cancer—as a way to draw me into what *I* most needed to learn, to touch my own heart, to practice living the path of the heart, providing me with endless opportunities for expressing it in very practical, "down to earth" ways, whether it was noticing the need for a tiramisu moment, helping her get on and off a portable potty, cleaning her gently with soft wipes, fetching coffee, changing diapers, or the million laughs we shared while extraditing ourselves from the endless predicaments we found ourselves in.

I'm not suggesting Dianna consciously "wanted cancer." Nobody wants cancer. Only that, in the living out of her Life Purpose, it *would* be useful. Others, wanting to stick with the reality they are comfortable with, may say if anyone could turn lemons into lemonade, it was Dianna. Or, she simply played the cards she drew. We each prefer whatever meaning confirms our own beliefs. All are internally consistent anyway.

Neither would I say her attitude helped stave off cancer. This may or may not be true. Certainly, her way of being is not the only way to live with cancer—or do one's life, for that matter.

Chili gets up, impatient to move as the sun slides off its zenith.

Okay.

I start walking again, imbued with the single thought that, whatever else may be so, Dianna understood the game at a very deep level and played that way.

87

Surrender

The meditation prayer I created, a lifetime ago it seems, points to a central issue I struggle with in my life…and one Dianna barely needed to give a thought to, I am certain.

> Meditation Prayer
>
> I surrender to Spirit.
> I am with you in appreciation for All That Is, gratitude for All That Is, love for All That Is. I am open to guidance and grateful for all opportunities to contribute and receive in abundance, to feel what Love feels, to think what Love thinks, to say what Love says and do what Love does.

I spent the first half of my life committed to "being right." Though I still stumble now and then, I've mostly let this go. Any idiot can learn *something*.

Still, there is at least one more layer to this onion, too.

While I may have let go of being right, I still have not relinquished ego control. The "I" who says "I do not need anyone" is still too often unwilling to be guided by an unseen higher Self when "I" (the John who pays the bills, gets breakfast) can't see how it is going to turn out.

All my life, I've resisted surrender, surrender to the I that is my higher Self, much less to the All That Is. It's too frightening.

Dianna, on the other hand, simply went with the flow, saying yes to every opportunity, totally giving herself away to whatever the need of the moment happened to be without a trace of fear, resentment, or reservation. She did not follow a plan, she followed her heart. If sometimes things didn't turn out, she shrugged and moved on, her optimism and trust undiminished, whether it involved people or seagulls.

There were no pity parties with her because she did not see herself as a victim, as someone to be pitied, and would not entertain it from others.

She did not need it, or want it, or miss it. It was not part of her personal way of being.

Her faith was unshaken throughout all the hardships she endured and even as death beckoned her.

Where does *this* quality of being come from?

Late afternoon.

A feathery, almost invisible rain is barely reaching the ground, and I go out on the deck to see how it feels.

Cold.

Still, I linger, not wanting to go in, leaning on the railing, looking out across Goose Bay. Chili is pacing back and forth, nose twitching, living in a world I cannot dream. I'm dressed warm, and he dressed in his usual. We watch the light dying, houselights flipping on across the lake, one by one, sending long thin shimmering silver streaks across a placid bay. A Canada goose barks once, receives no answer. Silence. Finally, I go back inside, left with the same lingering question.

I wake up the next morning with my answer. Dianna was with me once again. Or still.

This quality comes from surrender.

In the space of surrender, Dianna accessed the infinite creativity, appreciation, gratitude, and Love available to any of us in any moment we are open to it. She was always plugged in, turned on, and focused. I feel like I've just poked my head into a different reality.

Within *this* tenuous space she danced in most moments of her life, I can actually *feel* how the game of Life is designed. It *is* a win-win game. Life *is* inherently Good. There *is* nothing to fear.

So, surrender is a choice I can make in any moment. And I can continue choosing it, even when I fall down—and as Dianna did over and over again—especially when I fall down, until it becomes "second nature."

Really, our First Nature.

The hard part for me, the proverbial head guy, is the quality of surrender is such that it cannot be an act of will but must be an act of faith. It comes not from my mind but only from my heart, not from understanding but only from trusting.

Trust.

I was with Dianna up close for more than twenty years. I never noticed her wondering how to be. She was beyond struggling with an act. She had no act. She expressed her being as effortlessly as a flower opening to the morning sun, dripping with dew. A flower does not need to think about whether to bloom or not. It just does.

When I am in touch with my First Nature, it's what I do, too. When I am out of touch, it's not what I do, and I cannot will myself to do it. The paradox is either it is easy to surrender…or impossible.

Dianna did not know everything, but she knew these things.

She taught me—and so many others who met her in life, however briefly—such things, without preaching, without judgment, without comment, but simply by *being*.

Changing the world, one simple, unnoticed act at a time.

In this space, Dianna could see people as they are without losing sight of who they could be. So, I'll say she saw something in me I did not see in myself.

When immersed in this parallel reality—in the space of surrender—we have no internal resistance to life, to living, to others, to simply being.

I am guessing, surrender was Dianna's everyday reality.

Dianna's way.

In so far as I understand it now.

88

Light

Winter.

I turn off all the lights in the house and sit in my office, looking out over the lake at twilight, my elbows on the desk, hands cupping my chin, just watching this *happening*.

Snow white everywhere under a solid shapeless dove-gray sky. And where sky meets earth, a ragged tree line across the lake stands silent, blurred by a faint blue haze.

So slender soft, so delicate, this Light.

I watch this movie until it dissolves into blackness.

Early the next morning, I come back down to my office. Glancing out the window, I'm stunned. Waiting for me is last night's movie—it has returned! *Exactly!*

The Light waits for me, finds me.

Thank God.

Epilogue

I've always liked beginnings better than endings. However, in this particular reality, we have both. Losing Dianna brought me to my knees. And yet, every now and then, spirit wraps me in the ethereal sense of a never ending, where I can feel the smooth skin of her arm, her wicked smile, her exploding sense of humor…and the joy of watching her hugging life tight…sitting up pertly in bed, wiggling in delight as I carry in a cup of coffee with cocoa and whipped cream on top, her eyes sparkling, her energy lighting up the room with a "Thank you *so* much, honey!"

No, honey. Thank you so much…for everything.

When Dianna and I married, the photographer captured us standing, arms around each other, looking out into Dow Gardens, looking out into the world, completely unconscious of our purpose together. For us, it was not to be children after all. It was to be something else.

For her, as I see it now, she was modeling for others—and for me—a way of being, a daily practice for transformation, transforming herself in the process.

For me, it was an opportunity to learn how to live with an open heart, trusting my Self, surrendering, and finally, putting this way of being into action.

When I met Dianna, I was a pretty smart guy, focused on the mental pathway to enlightenment. Nothing wrong with that. But I'm reminded of an old proverb I often used in my own team-building work:

"No one cares what you know until they know you care."

A lifetime later, at her fiftieth birthday party, and only a few short months before she died, another photographer, Giovanni Sanitate, captured us on film as we stood together, arms around each other, looking outward to the world, as we had on our wedding day. I decided to use that photograph for the cover of this book. We had stumbled here and there, but we were no less filled with wonder, resolve, optimism, and courage. In that moment, without saying it, we knew we had done our business well, and we had done it together.

Chili dies on June 23, 2011.

We are at the Michigan State University Veterinary Hospital. Chili is lying on an operating table, terror in his eyes as he looks at me sideways, unable to lift his head. What's wrong, what's going on? he asks. I lean down and press my face firmly against his, whispering softly, stroking him gently. I feel him calming, his breathing sliding into an even in and out as he relaxes.

He trusts me.

He is counting on me, too.

I rise up for a moment, glancing around. The lights are too bright. There are tubes sticking into him everywhere with a half-dozen female veterinary students milling around and a senior one standing next to me. She is silent, looking down at the floor.

Not the way I wanted it to be. Not the way I imagined it would be.

Wonder how it is for all these women, watching a grown man coming undone, watching his heart breaking.

I keep my hands on Chili's neck, still stroking him slowly, then turn to the vet and say, without hesitation, "We are *not* going to do *this* to him."

Without a word, she quickly prepares the injection, and I bend into him, pressing my head tight against his once again, whispering, tears tumbling in a torrential rain into his hair. Then…just like that, in a single instant…he doesn't hear me anymore, and he doesn't need to hear me anymore. He is free.

A sacred bond—but, in this reality only—is broken.

So deeply do I miss his gentle teaching spirit. I always will. Did I serve him as well as he served me? Impossible. Still, I loved touching him, and he loved touching me. Some days I walked him, and some days he walked me. Whatever else, we walked together, immersed in One Nature.

Now I know what it feels like to feel empty.

The spectrum of knowledge a dog has is not congruent with our own, so we deem them less intelligent. Fundamentally, I absolutely know this is not true. Truth is, we have barely a clue about what they know.

I do know, while Dianna lived in the Present almost all of the time, and I am an occasional visitor, it was Chili's default way of being in every moment. This creates a wisdom we simply do not understand, do not even realize we do not understand, and certainly have no way to language. It is wisdom living in the language of the unspeakable.

I loved being Present to them both, even when the Present is the pure searing brilliance of pain. They pulled me into *being*, where passion lives, through the only doorway out of this *illusion* I live in way too much of the time.

When in the presence of one fully alive—not without flaws or weaknesses, not perfect in any way except perfectly alive, we are drawn *into* them. And here, in this sacred space, they reintroduce us to our own *being*.

It is a warm still summer night, black in the new moon. I lean over the deck rail, watching countless, silent blinking lights here, there, then over here again. I wish I could feel my arm around Dianna once more, watching these fireflies in their mating dance, listening to her delight, completely amazed as a child might be, but unlike a child, without the slightest desire to capture them in a jar. She, like I, know where they belong, and they are already there. When we come back around to where we began, we are not who we were.

These fireflies are different for me in another way, too. I am alone now…and never alone now…and this changes everything.

Standing here in the warm, blessed by these tiny flashing lights, I am reminded of a Franz Kafka insight,

> You do not need to leave your room. Remain sitting at your table and listen. Do not even listen. Simply wait. Do not even wait. Be quiet, still and solitary. The world will freely offer itself to you… unmasked. It has no choice. It will roll in ecstasy at your feet.

There may be times when it seems the Light has gone out. Even then, even in the darkness, I need only open my eyes and my heart. I need only surrender.

The Light is always present.

Now. Here.

Acknowledgments

My thanks to:

Dianna, most of all, for being the gentle teacher she still is for me. Certainly, there are other lives for us to live together.

Dianna's family: Pat, Bernie, Julian, Tricia, and David, as well as their families, all of whom gave Dianna the love and space she needed to be and to become. They were "all in" all the time. They have done no less for me.

Dianna's "other families": our dear friends, Kathy Preston, Chris Fowler, Consuelo Campbell, Marji Noesen, Najla Bathish, Allie Langlois, Robin Phelps, Linda Salvador, Zena Biocca, Sandy Johnson, Suzy Mushcab, Pam Pfau, Jana Parkes—this list could go on and on, literally, for pages—a list of special women—and some men, too—who indefatigably stood by her—and me—when we most needed them in our darkest moments and invariably made them brighter, without being asked, with amazing timing.

My own siblings, Elena and Ed; and friends, Steve Kridelbaugh, Alex Vogel, Mark and Rhonda Schlereth, Dave Nutting, who stood by me even when I have been at my most ignoble, most clumsy, most clueless. I have been blessed to have better parents, siblings, wives, and friends than I could have ever imagined or deserved.

Doctor Phillip Stella, Dianna's principle oncologist, and the oncology nurses at Ann Arbor Oncology, earth angels who missed the bus and ended up on earth—and to all we met at St. Joseph Mercy Hospital in Ypsilanti, Michigan, dedicated beyond our imagination. Dianna loved, and is still loved and remembered by them, one and all.

Jon Catenacci, my eldest son, a talented and accomplished artist, for providing Dianna's portraits and my Spiritdogtalking logo; and Giovanni Sanitate, dear friend and fine artist/photographer, who prepared the photographs for this book.

Helga Schierloh, Consuelo Campbell, and Stephen Kridelbaugh, for their hugely helpful editing.

Marly Cornell, who helped make this book so much more than I could have imagined it to be. Marly is an accomplished artist, editor, and author of the amazing book, *The Able Life of Cody Jane*.

Julia Cameron, author of *The Artist's Way* and many other creative successes. Her book helped me get off square one when my feet were hopelessly stuck in concrete.

If I have learned nothing else in life, I have learned we accomplish *absolutely nothing* alone.

About the Author

John Catenacci, 2012

All his life, John has felt fortunate to be doing work he felt passionate about, supported by amazing family, friends, and coworkers.

While doing cement construction work at a tender age under his father's watchful eye, he was tossed into a bundle of Italian immigrants and black laborers who shared their way of living with him—homemade wine, genuine Italian-bread-roasted-pepper sandwiches, fried chicken and drenched-in-oil-right-out-of-the-can sardines, garnished with a simple wisdom bathed in a luminosity that shaped his life.

Discovering molecules and atoms in high school, he was instantly drawn into chemical engineering. After twenty-five years of an immensely satisfying camaraderie only engineers can understand, the white collar/blue collar divide caught his attention, stimulating a curiosity about group dynamics, leading to a twenty-year, team-building career that took him across the US, Canada, Europe, and Saudi Arabia.

A common thread throughout has been a passion for writing, with a sprinkling of published short stories and articles in small magazines along the way, including a couple of *Chicken Soup for the Soul* stories. *Dianna's Way* is his first book.

To contact the author:
jcatenacci@comcast.net
Blog: www.spiritdogtalking.com
7773 Wexford Court, Onsted, Michigan 49265